ACCIDENT OF F

LIFE WRITING SERIES

In the **Life Writing Series**, Wilfrid Laurier University Press publishes life writing and new life-writing criticism and theory in order to promote autobiographical accounts, diaries, letters, and testimonials written and/or told by women and men whose political, literary, or philosophical purposes are central to their lives. The Series features accounts written in English, or translated into English from French or the languages of the First Nations, or any of the languages of immigration to Canada.

From its inception, **Life Writing** has aimed to foreground the stories of those who may never have imagined themselves as writers or as people with lives worthy of being (re)told. Its readership has expanded to include scholars, youth, and avid general readers both in Canada and abroad. The Series hopes to continue its work as a leading publisher of life writing of all kinds, as an imprint that aims for both broad representation and scholarly excellence, and as a tool for both historical and autobiographical research.

As its mandate stipulates, the Series privileges those individuals and communities whose stories may not, under normal circumstances, find a welcoming home with a publisher. **Life Writing** also publishes original theoretical investigations about life writing, as long as they are not limited to one author or text.

Series Editor
Marlene Kadar
Humanities Division, York University

Manuscripts to be sent to:
Lisa Quinn, Acquisitions Editor
Wilfrid Laurier University Press
75 University Avenue West
Waterloo, Ontario N2L 3C5, Canada

IMRE ROCHLITZ

WITH JOSEPH ROCHLITZ

ACCIDENT OF FATE

A Personal Account | 1938–1945

WILFRID LAURIER
UNIVERSITY PRESS

Wilfrid Laurier University Press acknowledges the financial support of the Government of Canada through the Canada Book Fund for our publishing activities.

Library and Archives Canada Cataloguing in Publication

Rochlitz, Imre, 1925–
    Accident of fate : a personal account, 1938–1945 / Imre Rochlitz with Joseph Rochlitz.

(Life writing)
Includes bibliographical references and index.
Also issued in electronic format.
ISBN 978-1-55458-267-9

    1. Rochlitz, Imre, 1925–. 2. World War, 1939–1945—Personal narratives, Jewish. 3. World War, 1939–1945—Personal narratives, Hungarian. 4. World War, 1939–1945—Underground movements—Yugoslavia—Biography. 5. Jews—Yugoslavia—Biography. 6. World War, 1939–1945—Prisoners and prisons, Italian. 7. Holocaust, Jewish (1939–1945). I. Rochlitz, Joseph, 1956– II. Title. III. Series: Life writing series

DS135.H93R63 2011   940.53'18092   C2010-907866-7

Electronic formats.
ISBN 978-1-55458-317-1 (PDF), ISBN 978-1-55458-355-2 (EPUB)

    1. Rochlitz, Imre, 1925–. 2. World War, 1939–1945—Personal narratives, Jewish. 3. World War, 1939–1945—Personal narratives, Hungarian. 4. World War, 1939–1945—Underground movements—Yugoslavia—Biography. 5. Jews—Yugoslavia—Biography. 6. World War, 1939–1945—Prisoners and prisons, Italian. 7. Holocaust, Jewish (1939–1945). I. Rochlitz, Joseph, 1956– II. Title. III. Series: Life writing series (Online)

DS135.H93R63 2011B   940.53'18092   C2010-907867-5

BOOK DESIGN, COVER DESIGN & MAPS: Ornan Rotem. COVER IMAGE: Order from headquarters of Partisan 4th Corps, dated 27 August 1944, dispatching "expert" Comrade Mirko Rohlić (Partisan alias of Imre Rochlitz) to the Turopolje region of Croatia, where an equine scabies epidemic had broken out (see page 137).

This book is printed on FSC recycled paper and is certified Ecologo. It is made from 100% postconsumer fibre, processed chlorine free, and manufactured using biogas energy.

Printed in Canada

Published by Wilfrid Laurier University Press
Waterloo, Ontario, Canada
www.wlupress.wlu.ca

RECYCLED
Paper made from recycled material
FSC FSC® C103567

To Tamara, Naomi, and Matan

... it is even less defensible to refrain from writing
than to go on with it, however senseless it may seem.

W. G. Sebald
Against the Irreversible: On Jean Améry

CONTENTS

LIST OF ILLUSTRATIONS

PREFACE

BY THE TIME I TURNED TWENTY in January 1945, my father was long dead of tuberculosis, my mother had been murdered in Auschwitz, and my aunt Camilla and uncles Ferdinand and Oskar had been shot by the SS. I had been on the run for almost seven years, dug mass graves as a prisoner in the Jasenovac death camp, escaped deportation to Auschwitz thanks to the protection of the army of Fascist Italy, and was now a second lieutenant in Tito's Communist Partisans.

Over the years, people of all kinds had tried to kill me: Austrian and German Nazis, Croatian and Bosnian Fascists, and even a Royalist Chetnik mole planted among the Yugoslav Partisans. During those same years, people of all kinds had done what they could to save or at least to help me: our Catholic Croatian peasant maid in Zagreb, a Jewish shopkeeper in a border town in Hungary, an anonymous Croatian waiter in a train station restaurant, soldiers of the army of Fascist Italy, the Communist political commissar of my Partisan unit—and even, incredibly, a Nazi general.

Overall, my story is one of persecution, suffering, betrayal, and death. It is also, however, one in which flashes of elementary respect for human life appear at times and in places in which they might least be expected. Repeatedly during those terrible years, I witnessed the immense power of the random individual to tip the balance of fate from death to life. More often than not, no courage or particular conviction was required; the basic propensity to behave decently was enough.

Overwhelmingly, however, my personal survival is due to pure chance. Those who tried to kill me or, conversely, to help me, behaved similarly towards many others. There was nothing special about me, and there is no reason or justification for the fact that I survived while so many others with probably much more—and certainly not less—

innocence, will to live, strength of mind and body, courage and cunning did not. I witnessed crude manifestations of the blindness of fate over and over again.

Knowing that my personal stamina or resourcefulness played an insignificant role in my survival, and that religious belief played no role at all, I am deeply disturbed by the occasional suggestion that those who survived somehow did so thanks to their courage, their resilience, or their faith. The implication that those who perished could also have survived if only they had shown the same qualities is profoundly disparaging of their memory. It is, in fact, nothing but mindless nonsense that flies in the face of the stark evidence. We who survived owe our lives to chance; in no way were we more worthy, wise, or strong than those who were gassed, hanged, shot, or slaughtered.

If I have lived to write these words, then, it has been nothing but an accident of fate. And I must seize the opportunity.

Imre Rochlitz

1938: CENTRAL EUROPE BEFORE THE ANSCHLUSS

ESTONIA

SWEDEN

LATVIA

DENMARK

LITHUANIA

BALTIC SEA

NORTH SEA

EAST PRUSSIA

NETHERLANDS

BELGIUM

GERMANY

⊙ BERLIN

WARSAW ⊙

POLAND

PARIS

⊙ PRAGUE

⊙ CRACOW

CZECHOSLOVAKIA

FRANCE

MUNICH ⊙

VIENNA ⊙

⊙ BUDAPEST

SWITZERLAND

AUSTRIA

HUNGARY

ROMANIA

MILAN ⊙

TRIESTE

⊙ ZAGREB

ITALY

YUGOSLAVIA

MARSEILLE

BELGRADE ⊙

ADRIATIC SEA

SPLIT

⊙ SARAJEVO

BULGARIA

SOFIA ⊙

ROME

BARI

ALBANIA

GREECE

ATHENS

PALERMO

PROLOGUE: VIENNA

ONE DAY IN EARLY NOVEMBER 1927, my mother took my brother Max and me to visit our father. He was in a ward for the terminally ill in the Hoffmann sanatorium in Kierling, a suburb of Vienna. He had fallen sick a year earlier with tuberculosis and was now also suffering from pneumonia.

Today, over three-quarters of a century later, the only clear image I retain of my father is from that visit: a very thin, pale man lying in a narrow bed by a window, through which a few rays of sunlight shine weakly. According to Max, he propped himself up on one elbow when we came in, and laughed.

He died a few days after our visit. Most Jews were buried in the *Zentralfriedhof*, the Central Cemetery of Vienna, but probably because our mother could not afford the expense, our father was buried near the sanatorium, in a small Jewish cemetery in the village of Klosterneuburg. Two months later, on 23 January 1928, I turned three, on the same day that he would have been forty; Max turned six two days later.

Our lives changed suddenly and drastically. My father's small currency-brokering business at the Vienna Stock Exchange was liquidated, but turned out to be worth practically nothing. This was in part because he had been ill and unable to work, but was also a consequence of the acute economic recession gripping Austria. At the age of twenty-nine, my mother abruptly found herself widowed and almost penniless. She was forced to give up our spacious apartment at Zelinkagasse 5, in the fashionable First District of Vienna, and to move in with her mother. For the next two years, we lived with our grandmother in Pötzleinsdorf, on the outskirts of Vienna. Then, as economic conditions continued to worsen, we moved back into the city, eventually into a small apartment at Grünentorgasse 26, in the middle-class Ninth District. We were joined

◄ *My father Josef,
mother Irene, and
brother Max in
the late summer of
1924. My mother
was several months
pregnant with me.*

by an aunt and two uncles (my mother's unmarried sister and brothers), who moved into the same apartment with my mother, grandmother, brother, and me. Following my father's death, we were in effect absorbed into my mother's large family and only rarely saw his relatives, most of whom lived in Hungary and Romania.

During our childhood, our mother devoted herself entirely to caring for Max and me, sacrificing everything for us in an attempt to ensure that we did not feel deprived in the company of our more fortunate schoolmates. But as nearly all my friends had both parents and were much better off, a feeling of insecurity and penury never left me. Although all my uncles were very kind, and always treated Max and me like sons, I felt the lack of a father as an all-pervasive and deeply painful deprivation, an incompleteness impossible to overcome and impossible to forget, even for an instant. And because my family was incomplete, I felt that I too was inadequate. For a long time, I secretly refused to accept that my father was dead. On the anniversary of his death, my mother would take Max and me to visit his grave in the little cemetery in Klosterneuburg. She would always break into tears and speak of him with great affection and sorrow, and although no one else at home ever seemed to mention his name, we heard from older cousins how much she had loved him. I never gave up hoping that his death and burial were all a mistake, fantasizing that the man in the grave was not him at all, that he would reappear one day and that we would live together forever after as a happy family.

Left to right: my mother, Max, and me, in about 1935 ▸

I am not sure why my mother's relatives refrained from mentioning my father, but it may have been to avoid reopening old wounds. I heard stories, many years later, that my parents' marriage had not been trouble-free. They had been married in Vienna in 1921, where my brother Max (Maximilian) was born in 1922. Then, according to unverifiable family gossip, they separated, and my father, who was a Hungarian citizen, returned to Budapest. According to the same gossip, a reconciliation took place between them in 1924, of which I am the product. They supposedly then decided to start a new life in Budapest, where I was born in January 1925. The fact that they named me Imre, as typically Hungarian a name as can be imagined, indicates that they planned on staying in Budapest; no one in their right mind would otherwise have dreamed of so naming their son. Yet for some unknown reason, they moved back to Vienna when I was only six months old. My father fell ill a year later and spent the final months of his life in tuberculosis sanatoriums.

> *Only in 2000 did I learn the exact year of my father's death—*
> *1927—and that it had occurred in the Hoffmann sanatorium,*
> *outside Vienna, where Franz Kafka had died three years earlier*
> *at nearly the same age (Kafka was forty, my father thirty-nine) of*
> *the same disease.*

After my father's death, my mother stayed on in Vienna to remain close to her immediate relatives. The seemingly odd family unit I grew up in, composed of bachelor uncles, a spinster aunt, widows, and small children, was not unusual in Vienna between the world wars; it was a city where the out-of-the-ordinary came to be ordinary. I can remember an overriding sensation of truncation, not only of the Austro-Hungarian Empire, which had met its violent end only a few years earlier, but also of most people's personal lives. There seemed to be no permanency, no clearly laid out goals to achieve, no ideals to attain. The adults in my family looked back with nostalgia to the days of Emperor Franz Josef, whose figure had provided a sense of protection and security to the Jews of the Empire. In the politically, economically, and socially unstable climate that now prevailed, that protection was palpably gone. My mother often expressed the hope that my brother would become a lawyer and I a doctor (I then preferred dentistry, because of its non-confrontational nature and apparently assured livelihood). But to me, even this never seemed realistic. There were so many contradictions in our situation as Hungarian Jews of German mother tongue living in Vienna, so many conflicting tendencies and loyalties, so many questions of identity and identification, that almost any scenario could be imagined, except one resulting in a happy and useful life.

The living example of this sense of truncation was Uncle Ferdinand, my mother's eldest brother. A man in his early forties, he was a graduate of the University of Vienna, with a degree in mechanical engineering. He had immigrated to the United States in 1908, and embarked on a successful career in Detroit in the design and construction of bridges, when in 1912 he received word that his father (my maternal grandfather) had suffered a heart attack. He caught the first ship back to Europe, but by the time he reached Vienna, his father was dead. On his mother's request, he agreed to remain in Vienna until she and his teenage brothers and sisters had reordered their lives. For unknown reasons, his stay stretched to over two

*Uncle Ferdinand
Dénes, in about
1908, when he left
Vienna for the
United States* ▸

years. In 1914, just as he was about to return to the United States, the First World War broke out. Ferdinand was drafted into the Austro-Hungarian Army and dispatched to the Russian Front. This most mild-mannered and self-effacing of men proved to be an astonishingly brave combatant, storming and capturing a Russian machine gun nest practically single-handed. For this feat he was awarded the highest Austro-Hungarian decoration for valour on the battlefield, the *Goldene Tapferkeitsmedaille*. When the war was over, however, he felt that he could no longer go back to America. After fighting for an adversary of the United States, he was unable to envisage returning and resuming his engineering career as though nothing had happened. Thus, Uncle Ferdinand remained in Vienna and from the age of thirty became a man who lived in the past, practically retiring from active life. He whiled away his time writing a meticulously detailed history of the Russian Front during the war, and spent afternoons tinkering in his mechanical workshop; occasionally he accepted the invitations of social clubs to give lectures on the United States. Even as a child, I was struck and unsettled by the patent waste of such a talented and resourceful man's life. But it was Uncle Ferdinand's

5

unreserved enthusiasm for the United States where, he said, success depended only on your ambitions and abilities, that made Max and me begin to dream of living there one day.

Uncle Ferdinand's mechanical workshop did give rise to one of the more exciting episodes of my childhood. In the early 1930s, he received a commission to construct a model train for King Michael of Romania, then still a boy. Over several months, he constructed a reduced-scale steam locomotive, about one metre long, that was fully functional. He also made several passenger carriages and a length of railway track. By the time the gift was ready, however, the mysterious commissioner had disappeared. The amazing train set was never paid for and sat for years gathering dust in the recesses of the workshop. Naturally, Max and I coveted it intensely, hoping against hope, every time we visited the workshop, that our uncle might allow us to take it home. He never did—but even if he had, we would never have been able to assemble it in our cramped and overcrowded apartment, as the train had been designed for a boy with the run of a royal palace. Nevertheless, for a long time I dreamed that one day it might be mine.

Although Uncle Ferdinand did occasionally derive some income from his workshop, it was Uncle Robert who bore the main burden of supporting the seven of us who lived together. Robert, who was two years younger than Ferdinand, owned a small necktie business. He imported fine silks and other fabrics from Italy, had them fashioned into neckties and scarves in Vienna, and then distributed them to his clients' shops throughout the city.

The other uncle living with us, Uncle Julius, was very cultured and erudite but never held a job. I once heard someone define him as "a good friend of many people," which, in a way, summed up his primary occupation. It was Uncle Julius who usually took Max and me to soccer matches on weekends; the rest of the time, he could generally be found conversing, smoking, or reading the newspaper at his customary table in his favourite coffee house. My mother's younger sister, Aunt Camilla, who was in her thirties, assisted my mother and grandmother in running the household.

Like his brother Ferdinand, Uncle Robert had served in the Austro-Hungarian Army during the war; he had been stationed on the Italian Front and returned home unscathed and unbemedalled.

Another brother, named Hugo (my mother had five brothers and three sisters), had also been dispatched to the Russian Front. But he had not

Uncle Robert on the Italian front near Rovereto during WW I ▸

returned, and his body had never been found. Although it was almost certain that he had been killed, there were some reports that he might have been taken prisoner by the Russians; my grandmother never abandoned hope that one day he would reappear. Every time our doorbell rang she would turn around and glance anxiously at the door, hoping it would be Hugo.

Officially, my grandmother had a fourth unmarried son, my uncle Alfred, who supposedly lived by himself in a small bachelor's studio. In his early thirties and the youngest of my mother's brothers, he was lucky to hold a good job as a customs broker, with such perks as an office car and a personal driver. He was, however, no bachelor: Alfred was married and lived with his wife, a lovely young Viennese lady by the name of Paula. The "trouble with Paula" was that she was not Jewish. Uncle Alfred was convinced that this would cause his mother such profound distress that he was never able to confess his marriage to her. Everyone else in the family, however, knew perfectly well, though they had agreed to remain silent. Thus, for a time, I believed that I was privy to a sensational and carefully

On the eve of World War I, standing (left to right): my mother aged 16, and Uncle Hugo. Fourth and fifth from the left are Uncles Robert and Julius, last on the right is Aunt Camilla. Seated, second from left, is Uncle Ferdinand.

guarded secret—until I discovered that things were not quite as they seemed. From the age of about ten, I sometimes spent the weekend with Alfred and Paula in their pretty little cottage in the suburbs, with its small swimming pool and garden full of fruit trees. My mother had cautioned me not to speak of Paula in my grandmother's presence, but I was only a child and could not help myself. One summer evening I came home carrying a basket brimming over with peaches and strawberries, which Paula had helped me pick, and in my excitement I blurted out her name. My initial alarm at my slip-up turned to astonishment when I noticed that my grandmother, who was clearly within earshot, was obviously pretending not to have heard. When this happened more than once—without my grandmother ever questioning me on the subject— it dawned on me that she knew and that Alfred knew that she knew. Moreover, I realized that she knew that Alfred knew that she knew. But nothing changed: Alfred continued to pretend he was a bachelor, coming home nearly every evening to have dinner with us, before returning to his "bachelor's pad" for the night. Neither his marriage nor his subsequent divorce from Paula in 1938 was ever mentioned in front of my grandmother.

All of my bachelor uncles were, at one time or another, engaged to be married, but their marriages never materialized—primarily, I believe, for economic reasons. It was so difficult to make a living in Vienna, let alone to marry and start new families, that they preferred not to take on the responsibility. But all my uncles, as well as my aunt Camilla, always did their best to make Max and me feel loved and wanted. I was not offended when I overheard one of the uncles observe, in implied criticism of my mother and of her eldest sister Gisella, who had five children, that "it was irresponsible to bring children into the world in times like these." Times were indeed very difficult. Although I personally enjoyed the hubbub and confusion generated by seven people confined in a small space, the adults enjoyed it somewhat less, and occasionally squabbled. We had no hot water, central heating, telephone, radio, or icebox, and although these amenities were relatively recent novelties in Vienna, our lack of money did not even permit us to aspire to them. To take a hot bath, we had to walk over to the home of Aunt Gisella, who lived on Praterstrasse with her husband Heinrich Grünhut and their five children. Their apartment had a gas stove in the bathroom with which they could heat water. My mother visited her sister about once a week, usually taking advantage of the occasion to ensure Max and me had a good wash; but if for some reason we didn't visit the Grünhuts, she would take us to the nearest public bathhouse, where, for a few *groschen*, we could take a hot bath.

The struggle to make ends meet never ceased. Our ponderous wooden furniture—a vestige of the days when my father was alive and my parents quite wealthy—was impounded more than once by a court bailiff. We were also served with several eviction notices, which we ignored and later somehow managed to have rescinded. Whenever the situation became desperate, the very few objects of any value that we did possess—such as some jewellery and silverware—were pawned by my mother at the *Dorotheum*, the Government pawn office.

Despite the hardships, I identified profoundly with Austria, and became enthralled with the language and culture from a very young age. Although Max and I were formally Hungarian citizens (because of our father), we strove with all our might for acceptance and integration. I came to pride myself in my mastery of the German language, and almost made a point of never learning a word of Hungarian. My nationalistic fervour was such that I even adopted the Austrian attitude of disdain and condescension towards the culture of our German neighbours, which we looked down upon as far less refined and sophisticated than our own. Our Austrian pride was such that Max and I once got into a fierce fistfight with a cousin in Budapest, during a summer vacation visit to our father's relatives. He had had the audacity to boast that a certain building in Budapest was taller than any building in Vienna, a notion that neither Max nor I could tolerate. (A few years later, that cousin was murdered by the Arrow Cross, the Hungarian Fascists, and the Austrian Nazis tried their best to do away with us.) But although we so proudly identified with Austria, we knew that our Hungarian passports and our Jewish religion made us completely unacceptable to the Austrians themselves.

Our attitude towards Judaism was ambivalent. In our anxiety to be accepted by Gentile society, we did our best to conceal any exterior signs of being Jewish. It was out of the question to grow side curls or wear a skullcap, and we took special pains to speak only the most correct German, avoiding Yiddish and even Yiddish expressions. But at the same time, at home, we scrupulously observed Jewish traditions. My mother kept a kosher home, and our family observed the Jewish holidays, fasting on Yom Kippur and celebrating the Seder at Passover. When I attended school on Saturdays, I never took notes, in accordance with the Jewish law prohibiting all forms of work, including writing, on the Sabbath.

We considered ourselves to be good Jews, although I never sensed that we were believing Jews. The nearest synagogue was around the corner from our home, on Müllnergasse, where I attended services every Friday evening. But neither the prayers nor the sermons meant much to me. The only part I did enjoy was the cantor's singing, but only as music, not as an expression of worship. Even the Jewish holidays held no real significance for me and gave me no true joy. I dreaded the hours spent in synagogue, particularly on the High Holidays, mouthing interminable prayers in Hebrew, a language I did not understand. The translations into archaic German that were usually printed beside the Hebrew did not make much sense to me either. I particularly disliked the Kappara ceremony on Yom Kippur, the Day of Atonement, during which worshippers transferred their sins to an innocent cock or hen (depending on the penitent's own gender) by swirling it around their heads while chanting the appropriate prayers. The hapless fowl were then taken to our local kosher butcher, slaughtered, and festively consumed for dinner.

*Max and me
in 1933, on the
banks of the
Danube Canal,
near our home* ▸

The month of December was noteworthy not so much because of the Jewish festival of Hannuka, but because of Christmas—which we awaited with apprehension. Christmas was still very much imbued with religious significance, in that it commemorated the birth of Christ the Saviour who had been murdered by the Jews. It was anything but a joyous occasion for us, accentuating as it did the gulf that separated Jews from the Gentile majority and providing the occasion for Gentile boys to beat us up.

Christmas in Vienna was heralded not by Santa Claus but by St. Nikolaus, a staff-bearing bishop who appeared on 5 December. He was preceded by Krampus, a red, club-footed devil who haunted the city's neighbourhoods. Men would dress up as Krampus and cavort about the streets, spanking any children they could catch. Soon after, St. Nikolaus would appear, chase away Krampus and distribute candy to the children. As Christmas was a strictly Christian affair, *Krist Kindl* (the Christ Child) brought gifts only to Christian children, and it was unthinkable, even for the most assimilated of Jews, to erect a Christmas tree or to exchange gifts.

The only holidays I genuinely enjoyed were Purim, the Jewish carnival, when we dressed up in costumes and exchanged gifts, and Passover, when a big family dinner was held to which we invited relatives whom we rarely saw during the rest of the year. My personal favourite was high-spirited and loquacious Aunt Hannah, a retired schoolteacher in her seventies. A rather distant relative herself, she would entertain us with the latest gossip about Hedy Kiesler, an even more distant relative, who later moved to Hollywood and changed her name to Hedy Lamarr. Hedy Kiesler was already then widely renowned for her great beauty; as a budding actress, she had created an international sensation by appearing nude in the film *Ecstasy* (1933), apparently the first such scene in the history of cinema. According to Aunt Hannah, however, she had been the protagonist of a good number of saucy stories even before. To my regret, I was usually sent off to bed before all the facts were told, but I still remember the tingle of excitement at the mere mention of Hedy Kiesler's name.

I had just turned eight when, in 1933, Hitler took power in Germany, and it was around then that I began to grow aware of anti-Semitism. Because of the tensions arising from questions of national identity and religious faith, many Jewish families had already by then begun to take drastic steps towards assimilation. Some stopped having their sons circumcised— as no Gentile at that time was ever circumcised, this constituted incontrovertible proof that one was Jewish. I can remember feeling uneasy myself at being circumcised, forever marked as a Jew. Others sought to mask their Jewishness by bureaucratic means. As practically all official documents (identity cards, passports, school certificates, etc.) indicated the religion of the bearer, some Jews converted outright to Christianity, at least outwardly. Others adopted a new term, to be utilized in official documents: *konfessionslos*, "without religion." The use of this term was also encouraged by the Socialist Party, which was actively trying to reduce the importance of religious identity in Austrian society. But whatever the circumstances of its usage, everyone knew that *konfessionslos* generally meant "Jewish but does not want to say so." As far as I know, no non-Jew or atheist ever defined himself as such. There were quite a few *konfessionslos* Jewish boys in the high school I attended, whom I came to view with some envy: as religious instruction was compulsory only for avowed Christians and Jews (who, of course, took the class separately), those who described themselves as *konfessionslos* were permitted to take the time off.

Paradoxically, some of the increasingly virulent Nazi propaganda began to rub off on us too; anti-Semitic prejudice penetrated not only the consciousness of the general public, but also seeped into our own. Feelings of animosity towards the unassimilated Jewish masses of Eastern Europe became "acceptable" even to us. We disdained typically Jewish features and mannerisms; to tell a Jew that he didn't look Jewish and that one would never have guessed that he was a Jew, was considered the highest of compliments. We were also extremely proud to be native German speakers, looking down upon and even ridiculing the Jews from Poland and Russia who spoke German with Yiddish or other eastern accents. We did not, however, similarly scorn Jews who spoke with Hungarian, Czech, or Yugoslav accents. The Yiddish language itself was anathema to all assimilated Jews; when I came home one day and blurted out a juicy Yiddish expression that I had picked up on the street, my mother reacted sharply with a rapid smack over the back of my head. Our family, like many others, was determined to distance itself as much as possible from its eastern European roots.

My mother had been born in the Slovakian village of Dubodiel, where her father owned a distillery that produced *Borovička*, a brandy made from juniper berries. At the end of the nineteenth century, the family had changed its name from the distinctly Jewish-sounding "Deutelbaum" to the Hungarian-sounding "Dénes" and moved to Vienna. In our home in Vienna, it became strictly taboo for anyone to even mention that "Dénes" had once been "Deutelbaum." My father's family was from another part of the Austro-Hungarian Empire, the town of Máramarossziget, a major Jewish centre in Hungarian Transylvania (today known as Sighetu Marmatiei and part of Romania). As "Rochlitz" is not an exclusively Jewish name, they evidently felt no need to change it when they moved to Budapest in the early 1900s.

When I started going to school, I generally used the name Emmerich, the German equivalent of Imre, thus completing my outward assimilation into Austrian society. Max and I also had Hebrew names (his was Meir, mine Moshe), but we used them only in synagogue.

The elementary school I attended was the *Schubertschule*, just down the road from where we lived. It was named after Franz Schubert, who had taught there briefly and unhappily in 1818, while his father was headmaster. As a child, I was told that Schubert was considered one of the world's great composers, but as there were no opportunities for me to hear his music, I could not judge for myself. We had no radio or gramophone at home and could not afford tickets to concerts, so it was years before I managed to hear Schubert's music. When I finally did, he became one of my favourites.

In 1935, at the age of ten, I entered the *Wasa Gymnasium*, a state high school for boys. It was only a few minutes' walk beyond the *Schubertschule*. About one-third to one-half of the students there were Jewish (or *konfessionslos*).

My class photograph, 1936. In the centre is Prof. Nicetas Draxler, our class teacher who also taught us Latin and Greek (I always wondered how his parents could have been so prescient as to name him Nicetas, a classical Greek name). I am standing in the row behind him, fifth from the left. Prof. Draxler was very strict and unforgiving, sometimes to the point of cruelty, but he was always fair and treated Jewish and Gentile boys equally. When I returned to Vienna in the early 1960s, for the first time since the war, I decided to look him up. We met for coffee at the Hotel Sacher. A bachelor in his forties when he had taught me, he was now in his seventies, married, with a 20-year-old son. He remembered my brother and me well and had brought along his class ledgers from the 1930s which showed the subjects I had studied and my grades. We had a very pleasant conversation and before parting I said to him, "You know Professor Draxler, you are the only person in

Vienna from before the war that I am looking up because you never gave me the feeling you were a Nazi." He was silent for a moment, and then responded, "Herr Rochlitz, ich war auch eine Nazi" (Mr. Rochlitz, I too was a Nazi). He admitted that he had secretly been a member of the Nazi party even before it took power in Austria, when the party was still illegal. He continued, somewhat apologetically, "I just did not imagine that things would deteriorate the way they did." I was deeply troubled by his words but could not help appreciating his candour.

Between 1935 and 1938, on my way every day to and from school, I unknowingly walked by Berggasse 19, the home and consulting room of Sigmund Freud (I only learned his address decades later, when I read his biography). I can remember the name Sigmund Freud being mentioned a few times at home, in a rather disapproving tone. My family—and, I presume, other somewhat conservative Jewish families like ours—considered him a borderline lunatic, at best a shameless charlatan peddling an array of rather indecent theories. Just as they debated whether the latest political development was going to prove "good or bad for the Jews," my uncles often discussed whether this or that eminent Jew was someone the Jewish people could be proud of. Sigmund Freud, in their view, was not.

Conversation was always animated and lively at home, even though our cultural interests were very restricted. Reading was mostly limited to the popular novels, no one played a musical instrument (although it was said that my father had been a good violinist), and it was very rare that anyone attended a concert. For most of my childhood we had no radio, although for a short time we did have a small crystal set on which we managed to pick up news broadcasts and soccer games, but not music. The only music my brother and I heard during those years were marches, excerpts from operettas, and *Schlagers* (popular songs) played by military or spa bands in the public gardens. On one occasion we attended an outdoor production of Verdi's *Aida,* but the famous composers such as Mozart, Schubert, Beethoven, and Brahms, all of whom had lived in Vienna, were only names to me.

Most of our entertainment was provided by the movies, my meagre pocket money permitting me to go about once a week. I was a fan of Laurel and Hardy, of their French counterparts Pat and Patachou, of American film stars such as Tom Mix, and of Westerns. One of my absolute favourites was Charlie Chaplin, whose films, I assumed, were strictly for children. I was therefore astounded when Uncle Ferdinand, whose seriousness and erudition were respected by all, one day pronounced Chaplin to be the greatest actor alive. I also saw German films, some of which were very Teutonic and already tinged with Nazi ideology.

A major event was the release of *Der Blaue Engel* (The Blue Angel), a film for which I was much too young but which my mother and Aunt Gisella eagerly went to see. Both of them had been great fans of Marlene Dietrich, who was already a star, but by the time they returned home, their opinion had altered drastically: they were shocked by the way she had treated the fine and respected actor Emil Jannings. In the movie, Dietrich plays a nightclub entertainer who forces an elderly professor enamoured of her, played by Jannings, to humiliate himself by crowing like a rooster. Although my mother and her sister knew full well that Dietrich and Jannings were only acting, they were scandalized by her conduct, unable (and unwilling) to distinguish between the movie star and the fictional character. When I saw *The Blue Angel* years later, it felt as though my mother and aunt were watching it beside me, and I could sense anew their disappointment with Dietrich.

I had two older cousins, Blanka and Lizzie Grünhut (daughters of Aunt Gisella), who were devoted fans of the theatre. As they cheerfully admitted to me, they were not particularly interested in the dramatic arts as such, but rather in the excitement and sense of occasion engendered by a glamorous night out. They eagerly looked forward to seeing, and perhaps even meeting, the popular stars of the day, such as Paul Hartmann, the Hörbiger brothers, and Raoul Aslan. Generally, they did not have enough money to pay for tickets and were obliged to elaborate sophisticated schemes in order to gain entry; I was always fascinated by their descriptions of how they did it. One of their most successful capers involved telling the theatre doorman that the person with their tickets had already entered the hall. Leaving their watches behind as guarantees, they were usually permitted to enter the theatre and "search" for the holder of their tickets. The girls would then exit through another door, obtaining a slip that permitted re-entry. They would return to the original doorman and retrieve their watches, saying that unfortunately they had been unable to find the person with their tickets. Then, using their re-entry slips, they would access the theatre through another door and make their way to the standing-room sections, from which they could enjoy the performance undisturbed.

My mother also sometimes went to the theatre and opera—I am fairly certain with bona fide tickets. My brother and I would eagerly look forward to the following morning, when she would recount the plot to us in great detail. I was also quite fortunate to see several plays myself, mostly German classics such as Schiller's *Maria Stuart* and *Die Räuber*, and Grillparzer's *Der Traum ein Leben*, at the state theatre, the *Burgtheater*. I usually went with tickets I had been awarded for obtaining good grades at school (I was often chosen to recite poems at *Akademies*—school literary evenings) or had won by sending in correct solutions to puzzles in children's newspapers.

The only member of Vienna's legendary intelligentsia whom I ever saw was the writer Arthur Schnitzler. It was while we were living with my grandmother in her small villa in the Viennese suburb of Pötzleinsdorf, probably in 1930, when I was five and my brother eight. Max, who was far more gregarious and outgoing than I, loved to sit on the gatepost in front of our house and strike up conversations with passersby. I was rather timid and more withdrawn but greatly enjoyed standing beside him and listening in. One day, a venerable, old, bearded gentleman, whom I knew well by sight because *Herr Professor*, as he was respectfully called by all, lived only a few streets away from us, strolled by and stopped for a moment to chat with Max. He informed my brother that he intended to sell his house and asked whether Max would help him by spreading the news. Max was only too delighted and from then on stopped practically everyone who walked by our gate to tell them that *Herr Professor's* villa was on the market. At home, this became a topic of great hilarity: "Maxie is only eight but he's already a real estate agent and his first client is Arthur Schnitzler!" The great writer died a year later, and I never learned whether he had succeeded in selling his house. For his part, decades later, Max became a successful real estate agent in Seattle, Washington.

On my way home from school, I often made a short detour to the *Stammkaffee* of my Uncle Julius. The *Stammkaffee*, or "habitual café," was something of a Viennese institution; it was the coffee house one usually went to, every day at more or less the same time. One sat at one's usual table, the *Stammtisch*, and was attended by one's usual waiter, the *Stammkellner*, who already knew exactly how one liked one's coffee (strong or weak, with or without cream) and whether one wanted a slice of cake or not. Uncle Julius's *Stammkellner* also knew exactly what newspapers my uncle liked to read and would fetch them as soon as he walked in. As we had no telephone at home, friends and acquaintances who were not necessarily patrons of the same *Stammkaffee* could leave messages for Uncle Julius with his *Stammkellner*. Uncle Ferdinand, on the other hand, did not enjoy the coffee house atmosphere and rarely set foot in one. But he had purchased a "sub-subscription" to the copy of *The Times* of London that arrived every day at Uncle Julius's *Stammkaffee*. The newspaper would arrive by train several days after publication, be kept for one day in the café for the benefit of customers, and then be passed on to Uncle Ferdinand. I regularly stopped by to pick it up for him on my way home from school.

My greatest interest was soccer. I loved to play, although it was very difficult to find the space to do so. The physical education hour at school was usually devoted to drills and marching in formation, and all public parks and quays were strictly off limits for ball games. But we played there just the same, often getting caught by policemen, told off, and sent home. The only way to play without being harassed was to rent a playing field. Together with a few friends, we would pool our pocket money and rent a field about an hour's walk from our neighbourhood. We would spend the afternoon playing soccer or ground hockey, invariably returning home late to find our mothers agitated and worried. Naturally, I was an ardent soccer fan, in particular of the Austrian national side, which was so successful that for a time it was called the *Wunderteam*. We were strong supporters of the First Division team Austria Vienna—not of the Jewish club *Hakoah* (the Hebrew word for strength), although it had been Austrian champion several times in the mid-1920s. Admittedly, we were proud of its accomplishments, but supporting a team that was not specifically Jewish was another way for us to express our aspiration to become full-fledged members of Austrian society. Moreover, my idol, the great Mathias Sindelar, played for Austria Vienna.

Uncle Julius was the biggest soccer fan in the family; he would often go to matches on weekends, taking along my brother Max. I was very annoyed that everyone in the family seemed to feel I was still too young to join them. I was particularly incensed when, one day, Uncle Julius and

Max invoked a highly unlikely pretext for going out together, obviously seeking to conceal their real purpose from me. I decided that I would no longer accept this injustice. I raced out of the house, reached the nearest tram stop before they did, and waited for them defiantly. Kind-hearted Uncle Julius graciously acknowledged defeat, and from then on I was usually allowed to go to matches with them. After the games were over, the three of us would often continue on to a square in the centre of town, where football fans congregated to comment on the day's games. The discussions were always very heated and animated, sometimes degenerating into shouting and shoving matches. The matches that aroused the most enthusiasm and nationalistic fervour were the international ones, especially those which pitted Austria against Italy, Czechoslovakia, or Hungary. Despite our Hungarian passports, Max and I passionately supported Austria.

All the while, anti-Semitism lurked in the background. But it seemed to us—or at least that was what we wanted to believe—that it was an unavoidable evil one could find a way to live with. Although we knew that Austrian society was imbued with anti-Jewish prejudice, we comforted ourselves with the notion that it was far more sophisticated and worldly-wise than its brutish German counterpart. Grave excesses against the Jews would never be permitted here, we reassured one another, often quoting the received wisdom that the Austrian national temperament was fundamentally *gemütlich*, or good-natured. No one could have guessed that only a few years later such a high proportion of Nazis implementing extermination policies would be Austrians.

It never crossed our minds that our physical survival might be at stake; even the occasional warning signal did not fully register in our consciousness. A case in point is the episode involving one of my schoolteachers, Anton Hirschenauer. It took place in 1935, two years after Hitler came to power in Germany and three years before the *Anschluss*, when the Nazis annexed Austria. Hirschenauer, who was not Jewish, was my class teacher at my elementary school, the *Schubertschule*. He was a leading member of the *Heimwehr*, an Austrian nationalist movement that opposed the Nazis (then still an illegal movement). Because of his political activities, he was absent from school fairly often; as I was his favourite student, he would place me in charge of the class until he returned. One day, he summoned my mother to see him. When she returned home, she was extremely upset, and for a moment I feared that Hirschenauer had complained to her about some misdeed of mine. But the truth turned out to be quite different. He had advised my mother that we should leave the country as soon as possible, that the Nazis would eventually take over in Austria too, and that when they did, the consequences for the Jews would be disastrous. My mother took his warning seriously and was profoundly shaken by his words. But it was immensely problematical for us to just pack up and leave our home; we had very little money and nowhere to go.

A major family debate ensued. Why should they persecute us? The various accusations of the Nazis did not seem to fit us: we were not rich, we did not exploit Gentiles, we certainly were not international conspirators, financiers, or Zionists, our culture was Germanic, we spoke *Hochdeutsch* (High German) without an accent, and we did not even have big noses. They could not possibly mean *us;* surely their hostility was directed against Jews of other cultures and nationalities, some of whom—we secretly thought—might even deserve a small dose of discipline.

Looking back, I sometimes wonder what would have happened had Nazi ideology allowed a distinction between assimilated Jews of German culture, like ourselves, and the unassimilated, Yiddish-speaking Eastern Jews. Given the opportunity, I believe that some of the assimilated Jews would have joined the Nazi Party and taken part in the repression—if not the violent persecution—of their unassimilated brethren.

We reassured ourselves that nothing really serious was likely to happen to us, and remained in Vienna. When part of our family did decide to emigrate, it was mainly in order to alleviate the overcrowding in our apartment and because of our economic difficulties—not because of the political situation. Thus, in the mid-1930s, Uncle Robert and Aunt Camilla moved to Yugoslavia, taking along Grandmother Fanny (Franzisca). They settled in the city of Zagreb, where Uncle Robert set up a necktie-manufacturing business similar to the one he had run in Vienna. During my summer vacations, I enjoyed going to visit them in their large apartment in central Zagreb.

In January 1938, I turned thirteen and celebrated my Bar Mitzva in the Müllnergasse synagogue, near our home (Max's, three years earlier, had been held in the Central Synagogue on Seitenstettengasse and had been a much grander affair). The best memory I have of the event is the gift I received from Uncle Alfred, who paid for me to join my class on a one-week ski trip to Innsbruck. The *Anschluss* was still three months away and the Nazis were still an illegal movement, but they had become increasingly powerful and times were changing fast. The supervisor of the trip was our gymnastics instructor, Professor Franz Stefan. Although he was very strict and unpopular, it must be said that he took great pains to be equally unpleasant to all, showing no particular hostility towards Jewish students. He was, however, an active supporter of the clandestine Nazi Party, and although outward manifestations of sympathy with Nazism were still prohibited by law, he forced all of us, including the Jewish boys, to sing the *Horst Wessel Lied*, the Nazi Party's anthem. It included lines such as: "The streets are clear for the Stormtroopers / Millions already look to the swastika full of hope / All of us stand prepared for the fight / Hitler's flags will soon flutter over the barricades." None of the other teachers present, let alone any of the students, dared to report him.

The story of my brief acting career illustrates, in its way, how the *Anschluss* of March 1938 put an end to my world. The previous winter, my school had staged a farce by the playwright Johann Nepomuk Nestroy (1801–1862), titled *Die Schlimmen Buben in der Schule* (The Naughty Boys in School), in which I had a supporting role. This play was often produced by schools. We were very excited when one of the leading film and stage actresses of the day, Paula Wessely, attended a performance one evening. She evidently enjoyed our production and thought it deserved a wider audience, because she personally recommended it to the famous Viennese stage director Rudolf Beer (the successor to Max Reinhardt at the Deutsches Theater in Berlin). Beer agreed to see the play, and a special performance was organized for him in an open-air theatre in the Prater, the Viennese fairgrounds. He seemed to enjoy it, but felt that it was too short for a commercial production, suggesting that we quickly learn an additional short comedy to complete the bill. We were thrilled at this prospect and immediately began to study a new play, the name of which escapes me, although I do remember that I was to play the Bishop. We rehearsed eagerly, looking forward to our run of public performances, which were scheduled for the early summer of 1938.

On 12 March, however, our lives came to a brutal halt. The German army invaded Austria, welcomed with open arms by most of the population. The Austrian Republic ceased to exist, its territory incorporated into the Nazi Reich as the province of Ostmark. With all the other Jewish boys in

◄ *Rudolf Beer*
(1878 – 1938)

my school (*konfessionslos* or not), I was segregated from my non-Jewish classmates and notified that I would be expelled from the state school system in June, at the end of the school year. Rudolf Beer, who was Jewish, was attacked and viciously beaten by a gang of Nazis; less than two months after the *Anschluss,* he killed himself.

Paula Wessely's career continued to flourish; she went on to star in the racist Nazi propaganda film *Heimkehr* ("Homecoming," 1941). After a brief period of postwar "disgrace," she was fully rehabilitated, recovering her position as *grande dame* of the Austrian stage. She died in 2000, aged ninety-three.

1 ANSCHLUSS

WALKING TO SCHOOL on Hitler's birthday, five weeks after the *Anschluss*, I got a grim visual reminder that times had changed. Until only recently, the Nazis had been a clandestine, illegal movement, but now practically every shop window along my route displayed Hitler's portrait, decorated with wreaths and ribbons. Austria's favourite son had come home.

I was only thirteen and did not yet know much about politics, but I could sense how dangerous it had become just to walk the streets; for the first time in my life, I was afraid. One day, Max told me that a gang of bullies had cornered him on his way home from school, taunting him for being Jewish. They were about to beat him up, but let him go when he convinced them he was not Jewish but Hungarian. Everyone now wore an insignia in their lapel that defined their identity: most Austrians wore a swastika and foreign citizens displayed the colours of their own country. The only segment of the population not entitled to wear any insignia at all were the Austrian Jews, which made them stand out as glaringly as if they had been wearing the yellow star. This was a curious reversal from the pre-*Anschluss* days, when the great majority wore no special sign of identity, while the Nazis wore knee-high white stockings as a means of mutual recognition and an expression of defiance of the authorities. Although our claim to Hungarian nationality was tenuous, my mother, brother, and I wore little Hungarian flags in our lapels. We knew this could at best provide only temporary and uncertain protection; it might have dissuaded Nazis on the street, but the Hungarian authorities would certainly not have intervened on our behalf had we been attacked or arrested.

Few of the nearly 200,000 Jews living in Vienna had tried to emigrate before 1938; and apart from Uncle Robert, Aunt Camilla, and Grandmother Fanny, who had moved to Zagreb for economic reasons, none of our other relatives or close friends had done so. Now that it had become clear that we had to leave—and the sooner the better—a host of practical questions arose: where could we go, and how? Like many other Jewish families with limited means, we had practically no options. Most countries, even those in the West with no official anti-Semitic policies, severely restricted the admission of Jews from German-controlled areas. Our first choice would have been to immigrate to the United States. Unfortunately we had no relatives there, and the quota system then in force would have meant waiting for several years at the very least before obtaining visas. The Americans allocated a fixed annual immigration quota to every country, which in the case of most central European countries was very small and vastly oversubscribed. Complicating matters for us, this quota system was based on the applicant's country of birth, not of residence or nationality. This would have placed my mother, brother, and me on three separate waiting lists: she had been born in Slovakia, which was now part of Czechoslovakia; Max had been born in Austria and I in Hungary. Moreover, we would have required an affidavit of support from a well-to-do resident of the United States, a document we had no way of obtaining. Had Uncle Ferdinand overcome his qualms and returned to the United States after the last war, he could have sponsored our immigration and saved us (and himself) from the horrors awaiting us. But with no one in America, there was no sense in even attempting this route.

Great Britain was also a very desirable destination, but it was practically impossible for people like us, with no relations or connections there, to obtain a visa. However, our local vinegar peddler, who was Jewish, one day astonished the entire neighbourhood. I knew him as the shabbily dressed man who pushed his cart down our street, making a meagre living by ladling vinegar out of foul-smelling bottles. A short time after the *Anschluss,* it emerged that by some quirk of fate he had been born in London. He told us that he had taken his birth certificate to the British Consulate, where his claim to become a subject of His Majesty King George V had been recognized. He was issued a British passport, and within a few weeks he and his family emigrated to England—and safety.

Another possible destination was Palestine, then under British mandate. But there were severe restrictions on Jewish immigration, and we had no relatives there either. Even if this option had been more accessible, it would have been among our very last choices. In our minds,

Zionism and Palestine were for others, perhaps for the Polish and Russian Jews who spoke Yiddish or Hebrew and who didn't mind living in ghettos. We had strived for so long to "get out of the ghetto" that the prospect of returning to one was not appealing. Nonetheless, my mother had been eligible to vote in Zionist elections before the *Anschluss*. I can remember the visit to our home of representatives of one of the Socialist Zionist parties, canvassing for my mother's support and trying to influence her vote by promising Max and me electric trains, Meccano sets, and other expensive toys. I do not know if my mother actually voted—and if she did, for whom—but I do know that we never received the promised toys, and the disappointment still smarts.

The only feasible destination for us was Zagreb, in Yugoslavia, where Uncle Robert lived with my grandmother and aunt in a spacious apartment. As his necktie business was doing quite well by now, he would be able to support us; above all, Yugoslavia was still an independent country, free of anti-Semitic legislation. Our objective was to enter the country legally and then, somehow, remain there—illegally, if necessary.

We needed valid passports in order to travel, but those were not easy to obtain. Nine months before the *Anschluss,* in the summer of 1937, my mother and brother and I had applied for Hungarian passports in order to visit our Zagreb relatives. When the Hungarian consul in Vienna discovered that neither Max nor I could speak a word of Hungarian, he refused to issue them, demanding that we first return to our homeland and learn our "native" tongue. My mother was not dissuaded and insisted on seeing his superior, the Consul General. A meeting was granted, to which she took along both Max and me. In contrast to his overzealous subordinate, the Consul General was a distinguished gentleman of the old school, obviously sensitive to the entreaties of a young widow with two boys. He overruled the consul and ordered him to grant us passports—with the proviso that they were to be valid for only two months, just long enough for us to visit our grandmother during the summer vacation. As Max still had exams to complete, only I applied immediately. Perhaps still in shock for having been overruled, the consul mistakenly issued me a passport that was valid for an entire year. By the time Max and my mother submitted their applications, he had recovered his senses, and he issued them passports valid only from July to September 1937. No one could have foreseen the consequences of this bureaucratic slip, but when the *Anschluss* took place nine months later, only my passport was still valid (albeit not for much longer). Although my mother tried to persuade the Hungarian consulate to renew her and my brother's passports, she was repeatedly turned down. As a last resort, she decided to send me ahead on my own, with the intention of somehow joining me later with Max.

There were other obstacles to be surmounted. It was not enough to have a valid passport; one also required a Yugoslav entry visa. Although there was no official anti-Semitism in Yugoslavia, the authorities there were less than eager to allow in Jews fleeing Nazi persecution. Thus, when I submitted my Hungarian passport—which clearly indicated that I was Jewish—to the Yugoslav consulate in Vienna, I was turned down. Undeterred, my mother tried again at the Yugoslav consulate in Budapest. As there was no official anti-Semitism in Hungary either, she hoped that the Yugoslav consul there would be less wary of the motives of a thirteen-year-old Jewish Hungarian applying for a tourist visa to Yugoslavia; there would be less reason to suspect that I was in fact fleeing anti-Semitism and intending to remain in Yugoslavia indefinitely.

My mother sent my Hungarian passport to one of my father's relatives, a lawyer in Budapest. He submitted it to the Yugoslav consulate and succeeded in obtaining a visa for me, valid for a stay of just one week. Evidently, the Yugoslav consul there either did not notice—or willfully ignored—that my passport was valid for only another few weeks, that I was a resident of Vienna, and that I was Jewish.

Time was running out fast. Although my passport was due to expire on 15 July 1938, my mother insisted that I undergo an operation for the removal of my tonsils and some polyps in my nose, which had been giving me trouble. The operation took place on 1 July. It was quite painful and for several days my throat ached so severely that I was unable to speak. Yet I remember that surgeon with great fondness, as the post-operative treatment he prescribed for me was "as much ice cream as the boy can eat."

On the morning of 8 July 1938, my mother accompanied me to the train station. We had reasoned that if I travelled to Yugoslavia directly from Austria, the Yugoslav authorities might suspect that I was a Jewish refugee fleeing the Nazis and turn me back at the border. In order to make it appear that I was coming from Hungary, my mother put me on a train to Budapest with instructions to get off in the town of Győr and there catch a southbound connection for Yugoslavia.

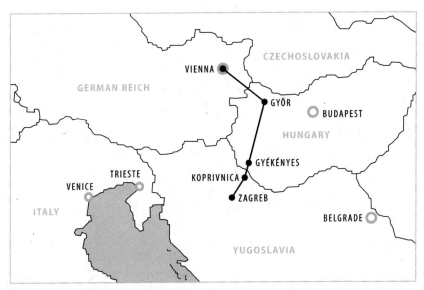

The route of my escape from Vienna in July 1938

I said goodbye to my mother and Max, hoping they would soon join me in Zagreb, and set out on a seven-year journey, at the end of which she would be dead and the world as I knew it would lie in ruins.

This was the first time I had ever crossed a border on my own, yet I remember feeling confident and unafraid. I changed trains in Hungary as planned and later that afternoon reached the border town of Gyékényes, the last stop before the Yugoslav border.

As was routine, a Yugoslav policeman boarded the train in Gyékényes and collected the passports of all the passengers. He took them away for verification in his compartment while the train slowly crossed the border. Just as we were entering the little town of Koprivnica, the first stop in Yugoslavia, the policeman returned to my compartment and gestured for me to follow him. I could not speak a word of Hungarian or Serbo-Croatian, but gathered from his pidgin German that I was being refused entry and being expelled back into Hungary. No explanation was offered but there was no point in arguing. I let the policeman lead me off the train and onto another one standing nearby. He then sat beside me as we rumbled back into Hungary.

The return trip to Gyékényes took no more than twenty minutes, but during that time a ticket collector came by and asked for my ticket.

I replied that I had none because my destination was Zagreb and it had never been my intention at all to return to Gyékényes. He was not impressed and insisted that I pay my fare, whereupon I retorted that I would do no such thing: I was making this return voyage against my free will, I said, and if anyone should pay for my ticket it was the Yugoslav policeman who was escorting me. The policeman himself burst out laughing when he understood my reply, and the ticket collector, who did not find the situation funny at all, eventually gave up and moved on to the next compartment. I was so proud that I had stood up to the ticket collector that for a moment I forgot how much trouble I was in.

My mother had envisaged the possibility that I might be refused entry into Yugoslavia. In such an event, she told me, I was not to return to Vienna but to make my way to Budapest and contact our cousins. However, I was now so tantalizingly close to the border that I decided to make another attempt to cross it.

I stepped down from the train in Gyékényes, a small, sleepy town with a single main street lined with one-storey houses. It was now evening, and although I was not frightened, I was beginning to feel tired. I slowly walked down the main street lugging my suitcase, which by now felt very heavy. I made an attempt to decipher some of the storefront signs, but soon gave up. As Hungarian has practically no common vocabulary with German, I could not even remotely guess what they meant. I assumed that some of the passersby, particularly the older ones, probably knew some German (from the time of the Austro-Hungarian Empire), but I was hesitant to start up a conversation with just anyone, in view of my precarious situation.

It occurred to me that my best bet was to find a local Jew, ask him for advice, and hope to obtain assistance. I slowly continued down the street until finally I came to a small grocery store with the name "Schwarz" painted above the doorway. Growing up in Vienna, one became very conscious of what constituted a Jewish-sounding name and what didn't, so I was well aware that "Schwarz" was by no means exclusively Jewish. But I was exhausted by now, could think of no alternative, and resolved to risk it. I walked into the shop and into a dream come true.

Mr. Schwarz turned out to be very kind, German-speaking, middle-aged, and Jewish. I explained how I had ended up in Gyékényes and that I wanted to reach my relatives in Zagreb. He immediately ushered me into the back of his shop and introduced me to Mrs. Schwarz, who, when she heard that I had not eaten for hours, served up great quantities of hot chicken soup and other delicacies. Mr. Schwarz told me that he was on friendly terms with a local Hungarian border guard, who might be able to provide advice on the best way to get me into Yugoslavia. After closing shop, Mr. Schwarz went off to speak to his friend while I stayed behind with his wife, feasting on hot cocoa and chocolate cake. He returned a short time later with the good news that the guard had provided the desired information: at about midnight, a train would stop in Gyékényes, on its way to the Adriatic coast of Yugoslavia. As this was a special holiday train, carrying Hungarian workers to a seaside resort, it was unlikely that the Yugoslav border police would be on the lookout for Jewish refugees; controls would probably be more lax and I stood a good chance of getting through.

Later that evening I bade farewell to Mrs. Schwarz, and her husband accompanied me to the railway station. He helped me onto the holiday train and waited until it departed. I left Gyékényes with my heart full of gratitude, but never saw or heard from Mr. or Mrs. Schwarz again, and dare not imagine what eventually became of them.

The border guard's prediction proved entirely correct, and although I waited with trepidation while my passport was being checked, it was returned to me without question, properly validated for a one-week stay in Yugoslavia. When the train made its first stop after crossing the border, I alighted—very conscious of the fact that I was the only passenger to do so. But no one took any notice of me, and later that morning I was able to catch a connecting train to Zagreb, where I eventually arrived nearly a day behind schedule.

Meanwhile, an exchange of frantic cables had been going on between my grandmother in Zagreb, my mother in Vienna, and my relatives in Budapest, none of whom had a telephone. Naturally, everyone had been duly worried. The welcome I received when I finally rang the doorbell of Uncle Robert's Zagreb apartment was overwhelming.

2 ZAGREB

UNCLE ROBERT LIVED IN A FIVE-ROOM apartment at Radišina ulica 1, in the centre of Zagreb. As he was the most pragmatic and hard working of my three bachelor uncles, when he moved from Vienna to Zagreb in the mid-1930s, it had been considered logical for his mother and his unmarried sister Camilla to make the move with him. They lived together, Grandmother Fanny supervising the household and Aunt Camilla lending a hand with the neckwear business, which had meanwhile expanded and was doing quite well.

◄ *Uncle Robert and Aunt Camilla (I have no photograph of my grandmother).*

As he had done previously in Vienna, Uncle Robert imported silks from northern Italy, employed local seamstresses to manufacture neckties and bowties, and distributed his wares to his clients' shops. He ran the business entirely from the apartment, where one room was devoted to the storage of inventory and another to bookkeeping and to the wrapping of packages for shipping.

I had no intention of complying with Yugoslav police regulations to register within twenty-four hours of my arrival because I knew full well that as soon as my visa and passport expired, I would be deported back to

Hungary or, worse, to Nazi Vienna. Although the Kingdom of Yugoslavia was still a free and comparatively liberal country when I arrived in July 1938—at least as far as the small Jewish community was concerned—this tolerance by no means extended to unwanted Jewish refugees from Nazism entering Yugoslavia illegally. Thus, within a week of my arrival, I had become a thirteen-year-old illegal alien. Failure to report to the authorities was considered a serious criminal offence, not only for the alien but also for anyone providing shelter or assistance, and my relatives were therefore taking great risks with their own legal status by harbouring me. But there was no alternative, and they took me in willingly.

I was warned to be as unobtrusive as possible, and for the next two years lived a rather strange and unnatural life for a boy of my age—although it was not necessarily always unpleasant. I was unhappy at not being able to go to school and missed socializing with other young people, but I was fully aware of my predicament and decided to make the best of it.

As it was dangerous for me to go out—the police were on the lookout for people like me and often made random identity checks—I initially spent most of my time in the apartment, reading. My favourites were the German translations of great American novels, such as *Vom Winde Verweht* (*Gone With the Wind*), *Die Fruchte des Zorns* (*The Grapes of Wrath*), and *Martin Eden*. I began to daydream that someday, somehow, I would make my way to America. In between my daydreams, I sometimes helped my uncle fill his orders for neckties, typing invoices for him. He taught me how to wrap boxes with brown paper into neat, snug packages ready for shipping, a skill I retain to this day.

Uncle Robert was a very kind, gentle, and industrious man who, like many of my other unmarried and childless relatives, treated me like the son he never had. He was in his late forties, rather short, balding, soft-spoken, and, it seemed to me, extremely wise and knowledgeable about the world (although I never once saw him open a book). He did have his quirks, though. He was extremely fastidious about his physical appearance, devoting hours to grooming himself—even if it was only to go out for a walk—endlessly polishing his shoes, ironing his trousers, and trimming his hair. He was also exceedingly shy, almost to the point of being unsociable. In his dealings with clients he could be very charming and talkative, but in his private life he had no personal friends, let alone romantic interests.

One day in 1939, the doorbell rang. It was a pair of unannounced visitors, who had come to see Aunt Camilla. Uncle Robert was quite flustered. He felt physically unprepared (perhaps he was unshaven or his shirt was wrinkled), and he simply could not face the idea of an unforeseen encounter with strangers. As he sometimes did in such circumstances, he just disappeared. No one gave much thought to his whereabouts, and Aunt Camilla let the visitors in. She chatted with them for a short time and then for some mysterious reason led them to the large cupboard that stood in the corner of our living room. I was sitting on the sofa, watching her and absent-mindedly listening to the conversation. When she suddenly opened the cupboard door, everyone let out a gasp of astonishment: huddled inside the cupboard was Uncle Robert! There was a long moment of stunned silence, during which he turned beet red, smiled sheepishly, stepped gingerly out of the cupboard, and disappeared into his office. I do not remember what ensued, only that there was a general sense of extreme embarrassment. To this day, when I think back on the incident I cannot help but feel sorry for him.

My grandmother Fanny was already seventy-five years old when I arrived in Zagreb in 1938. She died a year later, of natural causes— although the tension and worry for the fate of her children who were still in Nazi Vienna undoubtedly hastened her death.

While my grandmother was alive—and even more so after her death— Uncle Robert found it intolerable that Fanny, our full-time, live-in maid, should bear the same name as his mother. He therefore made up a variety of nicknames for her, which he insisted that we use. I chose the simplest, Fanika, and developed a very special friendship with her. She was a peasant girl from a Croatian village outside Zagreb, about twenty-five years old, an exceptionally bright and cheerful person and the most extraordinary housekeeper I have ever seen. I would watch her with fascination as she cleaned and polished with what seemed to me admirable virtuosity. To top it all, she was also an excellent cook. Cooped up in the apartment as I was, I spent a great deal of time in her company, and it was from her that I learned to speak Serbo-Croatian. The fact that she was completely illiterate did not constitute a serious obstacle, as Serbo-Croatian is an entirely phonetic language. Very soon I could write it too.

I was deeply impressed with how very much in love Fanika was— not with one man, but with two. She often confided to me that deep in her heart she really couldn't decide whom she loved more. When she eventually gave birth to a baby boy, however, there could not be much doubt as to who the father was: it had to be the handsome gendarme with the impressive, well-waxed moustache, who often came by our apartment to visit her. The other love of her life lived in Hollywood and went by the name of Nelson Eddy, the baritone who starred with Jeannette MacDonald in several films that were then all the rage in Zagreb. At first, however, the gendarme refused to admit paternity. Fanika had to sue him for child support, and although he did not go as far as to claim that Nelson Eddy could be the father, he did make the following statement under oath: "Who is this woman? I have never seen her before in my life." The court was not impressed, decreed that he was indeed the father, and ordered him to pay child support. Suddenly, he recovered his memory and took up again with Fanika. The practical result of their renewed relationship was that instead of receiving child support, she found herself spending most of her salary on him. He did write her long love letters, though, which she could neither read nor reply to. This was where my new-found expertise proved useful: I would read out his letters and then take dictation for her replies, often making my own comments or suggestions as to what to write back, an activity I enjoyed immensely.

After a few months, I simply could no longer bear to remain shut up in the apartment all day. I was eventually allowed to go out, on condition that I went straight to the movies and then directly home after the showing. Thus began my own intense love affair with American films. I went to the movies very frequently, often to two different movie theatres on the same day. For the most part, I saw American films subtitled in Serbo-Croatian or, occasionally, dubbed into German. They nourished my growing desire to escape the oppression and persecution that I was experiencing in Europe. In 1939 and 1940, Yugoslavia was still independent, trying to resist Nazi and Fascist influence, and American films were permitted as well as extremely popular. Like Fanika, I too fell in love with a movie star—the teen heartthrob Deanna Durbin. I wrote her a long and passionate letter and mailed it off to her, c/o Universal Studios in Hollywood. But I never received a reply.

The image I formed of the United States, based on the films I saw, was perfect in every respect but one. I was not physically strong and in school in Vienna had always relied on my older brother Max, who was muscular and athletic, to protect me from bullying. According to American movies, however, if you wanted to "get the girl"—and I did—you had to engage in a number of violent fistfights against much bigger and stronger opponents, taking a great deal of punishment before (so one hoped) prevailing. This was the only fly in the ointment, and I often wondered how I would deal with it, even toying with the idea of taking boxing lessons.

I continued to go to American movies and saw so many of them that I became intimately familiar with the stars and with entire casts of supporting actors. When the opening or end credits did not specify which roles the various actors had played, I would carefully study the film posters, memorize the actors' names, and then by association and exclusion match them with the faces I had seen. Thus I became a fan and admirer not only of the world-famous stars but also of the lesser-known actors such as Slim Summerville, Andy Devine, Donald Crisp, Donald Meek, Arthur Treacher, Alan Mowbray, Henry Davenport, Edward J. Bromberg, Lionel Atwill, Nigel Bruce, and Gale Sondergaard. In the unreal, twilight existence I was leading they became familiar characters and almost friends to me. I carried on lengthy imaginary conversations with them about life in the United States, where I desperately hoped to live one day. Their presence kept me company, even though I still knew no English and they no German or Serbo-Croatian.

One evening in 1939, I was hurrying home after the movies. Dusk had already fallen and I was walking briskly in order to reduce the chance of a random identity check. About one block before our apartment, a form suddenly stepped out of a doorway and called out my name. I was taken aback at first but then recognized Yovanka, Fanika's younger sister, who sometimes also worked for us. Yovanka warned me that two policemen were sitting in our living room, waiting to arrest me. She said that my uncle's instructions were to spend the night at the home of a relative, a lawyer by the name of Dr. Šik. I did as I was told, and the next day, after receiving a message that the coast was clear, went home and learned what had happened. In the early afternoon of the previous day, two plainclothes detectives had called at our apartment looking specifically for a young boy. Someone (probably our concierge, despite the frequent tips she accepted from Uncle Robert) had reported that an unregistered person was living in our apartment. Fortunately, I was not home and everyone strenuously denied any knowledge of my existence. The detectives were not dissuaded, forbade anyone to leave, and settled down to wait for me. As evening drew near, Yovanka began to insist that she had to leave to catch the last train back to her village, claiming (truthfully) that she came into Zagreb early every morning with milk, butter, and cheese to be delivered to us and other regular customers—including a prominent Croatian personality who would be very displeased with the police if they denied him his fresh country produce. Something of an argument ensued, until finally, evidently not wanting to get into trouble, the policemen let her leave just in time to catch her train. Instead of going to the station, Yovanka had waited for me in a nearby doorway to warn me away. The same sequence of events occurred twice, in an identical fashion, over a period of a few weeks, and on both occasions it was Yovanka's resourcefulness and loyalty that thwarted my arrest.

> *I believe that the important personality to whom Yovanka delivered her dairy products was Colonel Slavko Kvaternik, later named Minister of the Army of the Ustashe (Croatian Fascist) "Independent State of Croatia." Kvaternik's wife was of Jewish descent. Their son, Eugen "Dido" Kvaternik, became one of the Ustashe regime's worst criminals. It is alleged that Mrs. Kvaternik committed suicide in 1942, appalled by the atrocities perpetrated by her son.*

One of the few places where I felt completely safe was in the home of Dr. Lavoslav Šik, a prominent Zagreb lawyer and distant relative of ours at whose home I had hidden when the police came looking for me. He was a corpulent, jovial man with a booming voice and a mischievous sense of humour. He was in his fifties and married, but had no children, and he too came to treat me as the son he never had. At first, I would go to his home only about once a week, to help organize and catalogue his huge and chaotic library, which consisted primarily of Judaica.

> *I was amazed to learn that Dr. Šik's Judaica library, which was confiscated by the Ustashe when he was arrested and murdered in 1942, survived the war. It was returned to the Jewish community of Zagreb, together with his personal papers, in 1989.*

As time wore on and I became more proficient in Serbo-Croatian, Dr. Šik began to give me some typing and translations to do for his very successful legal practice. His sense of humour and self-confidence were such that when he had business to attend to in neighbouring towns, he often took me—an illegal refugee—along for the ride. I would climb into his elegant, chauffeur-driven black car and together we would drive off to meetings with clients or appearances in court. Naturally, I was very uneasy every time a policeman drew near, but Dr. Šik assured me that everyone knew who he was and that no policeman in his right mind would ever dare to ask an assistant of his for papers. One day, however, he pushed his reasoning to the extreme. He was defending a Jewish illegal immigrant who had been arrested and who was about to be expelled from Yugoslavia. Although there was no way to avoid the expulsion, he hoped to convince the Chief of Police to deport the refugee to a country other than Germany, where his life might be in immediate danger. Dr. Šik prepared a file on the case and set an appointment with the Chief of Police at central headquarters. At the very last minute, however, Dr. Šik informed me that he was unable to go. Instead, he said with a chuckle, he proposed to send me—an illegal Jewish refugee in my own right. I was taken aback by his proposition but did not argue, trusting his judgment blindly. Nevertheless, I remember feeling extremely tense as I entered the police building. I was ushered into the office of the Chief of Police, who received me in person. He leafed through the file I had brought and replied that I could inform Dr. Šik that his request to deport the refugee to a country other than Germany had been granted. I then walked out of the headquarters undisturbed; it had not even occurred to the Chief of Police to inquire into the status of the personal emissary of the esteemed Dr. Šik.

During 1939 and 1940, other members of my family succeeded in fleeing Vienna. In August 1939, only a few days before the Second World War broke out, my mother managed to send my brother Max to safety in England, as part of a Zionist agricultural youth training program. She herself crossed illegally into Yugoslavia in February 1940, hiring a mountain guide to lead her across the mountains between southern Austria and Slovenia. When she joined us in Zagreb, I was elated; I had been separated from her for over a year and a half. I was much less happy to meet the gentleman accompanying her, whom she had meanwhile married. He was a cultivated, well-groomed, and handsome man by the name of Friedrich Löbl, to whom I took an instant dislike. He was about fifty, had never been married before, and was as self-centred as he was attached to his aged mother, whom he had brought along. I should have been more tolerant, as he always behaved correctly towards me, and more understanding of my mother, who was then forty-two and had been a widow for eleven years. But I found it difficult to conceal my instinctive hostility, which stemmed from elementary childish jealousy. There were some moments of unpleasantness, but we eventually worked out a modus vivendi (which consisted primarily in our politely ignoring each other).

> *Just over a year later, in the spring of 1941, I would be cooped up with my mother, her husband, and his mother in a little village in Bosnia. The Nazis had just overrun Yugoslavia, and we were living in precarious conditions in a tiny rented house. My resentment towards my stepfather began to surface more frequently—although I usually found a way to take it out on my mother. I disapproved, for example, of the fact that she had gone along with her new husband in no longer respecting Kashruth (Jewish dietary law). I refused to touch the food they ate, obliging her to make the extra effort—in living conditions that were already difficult—of cooking and serving my meals separately. I did not fully realize it at the time, but my stubborn insistence on Kosher food was really a means for me to compete for her attention and to "punish" her for remarrying (a year later, I abandoned Kashruth myself). I should have known better, as I was already sixteen, but I was unable to restrain my feelings. Needless to say, remorse for my misbehaviour has not left me—especially since, as it turned out, the few months I spent with my mother in that little Bosnian village in the spring and summer of 1941 were our last together.*

During the early part of 1940, my uncles Ferdinand and Julius, as well as my cousin Blanka, also crossed into Yugoslavia illegally and joined us in Zagreb, with the result that by mid-year there were nine of us living in the apartment. To obtain legal residence papers, Blanka and Aunt Camilla contracted fictitious marriages with local men (a thriving commerce), divorcing shortly afterwards. But then Aunt Camilla remarried, this time in earnest. Her new husband was a Viennese refugee by the name of Oskar Stern. He too moved in with us, increasing the population of our apartment to ten. In order to cope, one room was designated the "men's bedroom," another the "women's," with the overflow camped out in the living room. It was cramped, and there were occasional squabbles, but we managed to live together fairly civilly. Despite my irritation with my mother's new husband, I was very happy to be reunited with her and relieved to know that Max was safe in the Free World.

Although my cousin Blanka was fourteen years my senior, we belonged more or less to the same generation and got along very well. We would often wait until the family had gone to bed and then, at about 10:30 p.m., when we were sure everyone had fallen asleep, dress quietly and slip out of the apartment. Sometimes we would just go for a walk, but more often we would go to a wrestling match or to a nightclub. Blanka enjoyed dancing but would of course never have dared enter a nightclub alone. I was still only fifteen, and too young to dance, but my presence as chaperone enabled her to accept invitations to dance from other young men. We would silently return home in the early hours of dawn, creep into our beds, and sleep late into the morning. The adults never suspected anything; on the contrary, they were delighted that we were getting such a good night's sleep.

My twilight existence in Yugoslavia reached a turning point in mid-1940. The ruler of Yugoslavia, the Prince Regent Paul, returned from a state visit to Great Britain and declared an amnesty for illegal immigrants (most of whom, like us, were Jews fleeing Nazi persecution). Everyone in my family assumed that the amnesty had been granted at the request of the British government, but like most Jewish refugees at the time, we tended to idealize the British, attributing to them more concern for our well-being than they actually harboured.

The new decree stipulated that illegal immigrants who reported to the police within a few days would no longer face expulsion from Yugoslavia. They would, however, be evacuated from the larger towns to villages in the countryside, where they would be obliged to report periodically to local authorities. Refugees would not be permitted to work, but local Jewish communities would provide assistance to those without funds. Naturally, we eagerly took advantage of this decree, which legitimized the status of my mother, my stepfather, his mother, my uncles Ferdinand and Julius, and me. Its practical implementation, however, resulted in our family being split up: Uncles Ferdinand and Julius were assigned by the police to the village of Samobor, just outside Zagreb, while my mother and her husband and mother-in-law were sent to Derventa, a small town in Bosnia over 150 kilometres away.

At fifteen, and still a minor, I would normally have been sent away with my mother. But I had lost two full school years owing to my forced clandestinity, and now that I had regained my legal status I was desperate to resume my studies. Thanks to Dr. Šik, who intervened and pulled his weight (which was considerable, both figuratively and literally) with the authorities, I obtained a special police permit to remain in Zagreb to attend high school. Thus, in the early summer of 1940, I was again separated from my mother. She went to live in Derventa while I stayed on in the apartment in Zagreb with Uncles Robert and Oskar and Aunt Camilla. I was unhappy to see my mother go but thrilled at the prospect of returning to a normal life and being able to socialize again with people my own age.

One of the very first things I did was join Maccabi Zagreb, the city's Jewish sports club. Perhaps the activity I had most sorely missed during my two years "underground" had been playing soccer. I had been a fullback on my school team in Vienna, and I loved the game. As long as my status in Zagreb was illegal, it had been unthinkable for me to play soccer at all. Now I yearned to join the Maccabi boys' soccer team. I was told that the position of fullback was already taken but that the team could use a goalkeeper. I accepted with delight and even came to enjoy playing that position.

The star of the Maccabi club was without question the boxing coach. Although I was not at all attracted by the sport, this particular coach exerted a powerful hold over me: he was the first American I had ever seen. Most of the young people in the club, including me, were starry-eyed about the United States. We often used the word "Amerika" to describe anything wonderful or unique. A beautiful girl, a delicious cake, or fine new shoes could qualify for the superlative "Amerika." We were therefore all immensely proud of our coach, whose name was Jimmy Lyggett, probably the only black American then living in Zagreb. He was something of a celebrity around town, a status he seemed to enjoy. I never actually screwed up the courage to speak to him, but I often loitered in his vicinity, watching him coach (in fluent Serbo-Croatian) and generally basking in his "Americanism."

In G. W. Pabst's silent masterpiece Abwege (Crisis), filmed in Berlin in 1928, there is a small role played by a black boxer (this frame is taken from the film). His name appears in the end credits as Jimmy Lygelt, but this is in fact our coach Jimmy Lyggett, who had been a well-known boxer in Germany in the 1920s. During his career, he fought twice against the legendary Max Schmeling, losing once and drawing once. I do not know the circumstances of his move from Berlin to Zagreb, where he had been hired by the Jewish sports club, although it may have been to escape racial discrimination. The publication Who's Who in the Independent State of Croatia (Minerva, 1997) claims that Lyggett had a Croatian wife and that he stayed on in Zagreb for the duration of the war, even becoming the trainer of the boxing team of the Ustashe state. A native of Philadelphia, he reportedly returned to the United States in 1945 and died in 1955.

When I met Lyggett in 1940, the notion of racial discrimination against blacks was quite foreign to me; five years later, however, it reared its head unexpectedly. It was 1945, and I was in Allied-liberated southern Italy, working for the United Nations Relief and Rehabilitation Administration (UNRRA). I was stationed in the small town of Santo Spirito, a few kilometres north of Bari. As there was not much to do in Santo Spirito in *the evening, I usually went into the city after work. The Allies provided all kinds of entertainment for the troops in Bari, such as movies, shows, dances, and concerts. As an employee of* UNRRA, *I could wear a US uniform, which entitled me to enter Allied entertainment facilities and also to hitch rides on military vehicles (this was never a problem—there were hundreds of them on the roads, many of them joyriding).*

Late one evening, after going to the movies in Bari, I hitched a ride back to Santo Spirito. An Allied army truck stopped, and two of us climbed aboard, a black American soldier and myself. We found two British soldiers already sitting in the back of the truck, both of them quite drunk. When they noticed that both I and the black soldier were wearing US uniforms, they turned on me and began to assail me with insults, cursing all white Americans for the way they mistreated their black citizens. I tried to explain that despite my uniform, I was not an American citizen (albeit much to my chagrin) and that in any case I harboured no prejudices of any kind against blacks. But the two were far too drunk to pay attention, and their behaviour became increasingly violent. Spewing obscenities, they began to approach me threateningly, clearly intent on roughing me up. At that moment, the black soldier intervened; he shouted at them to calm down and positioned himself to stop them from getting any closer. Still mumbling curses, the drunkards withdrew.

Naturally, I was extremely grateful. When the American soldier confided to me that he was returning to base after curfew and risked being punished, I gladly offered to put him up for the night. He accepted, and we got off the truck in Santo Spirito, leaving His Majesty's inebriated subjects behind. We made our way to my little apartment, where I arranged for him to sleep on the couch in my living room. Then we parted, as he was going to leave at the crack of dawn to return to his base.

When I woke up at about 7:30 the next morning, he was already gone. In the corner of the living room there was a chest of drawers in which I kept, among other things, a gold wristwatch, the only item of any value among my possessions. More as a matter of routine than out of suspicion, I pulled open the top drawer. To my horror, the gold watch was gone. I am ashamed to admit that the most common, racist prejudices swept through my mind: most Americans are obviously right in considering the blacks to be inferior, I thought to myself. I had let this fellow into my apartment, done him a favour by letting him sleep on my couch, and he had gone and stolen my valuable gold watch! I paced angrily around the room for a few moments and then returned to the chest of drawers. I rummaged in the top drawer again and suddenly the tips of my fingers felt something metallic: it was my watch. It had slid under the sheet of paper lining the bottom of the drawer. I instantly realized how wrong it had been of me to make sweeping generalizations about black people. And even if that soldier had in fact taken my watch, there was no justification at all for me to condemn all blacks as a group—as if we Jews had not suffered outrageously from such prejudices and generalizations. It was a lesson I never forgot.

The summer of 1940 passed very quickly. I divided my time between the sports club and private lessons with a teacher hired by Uncle Robert to give me a crash course in Serbo-Croatian grammar and Yugoslav history. In September, I was accepted into the eighth grade at *Druga Muška Realna Gimnazija*, a public high school for boys. I was fifteen and a half years old and should have been in the tenth grade, but I couldn't complain: I was finally back in school and could live a nearly normal life, free from the fear of arrest and deportation. Very soon, though, I began to suffer from my forced association with boys so much younger. I was two years older than they were, and my recent experiences had made me much more mature. It frustrated me that all the boys my age were in the tenth grade and that their sense of hierarchical superiority over me, a lowly eighth grader, made it impossible for them to even consider befriending me. To make matters worse, there was no chance of meeting any girls. The school was coeducational only from the tenth grade up, and tenth grade girls were even more unlikely to consort with an eighth grader. In my despair, I made one clumsy attempt to make friends with a young classmate of mine—with the sole objective of somehow meeting his attractive older sister, who was in the tenth grade. My plan failed miserably; she continued to look through me as though I were thin air.

Towards the end of 1940, Zagreb seemed like a calm and fairly safe place to be, compared to what was happening in the rest of Europe. But the war was in fact rapidly approaching. Although he was personally pro-Western, the Prince Regent Paul began to make appeasing gestures towards the Axis. In October 1940, possibly to placate Hitler, the Yugoslav government for the first time passed some anti-Semitic laws, limiting the number of Jewish students admitted to university (the *numerus clausus* law) and banning Jews from the food trade. Shortly afterwards, Winston Churchill noted memorably: "Prince Paul's attitude looks like that of an unfortunate man in a cage with a tiger, hoping not to provoke him, while steadily dinnertime approaches."

During the few months I spent in a Yugoslav state school between the autumn of 1940 and the spring of 1941, I never once experienced anti-Semitism, from my classmates or from my teachers. That I was Jewish was totally and reassuringly irrelevant. Zagreb was the capital of the province of Croatia, however, and Croatian nationalism was rising. I did become aware of the strong animosity harboured by the Catholic Croats towards the Orthodox Serbs, whom they accused of being unfairly dominant in the national army and government and of forcibly imposing the Serbian Royal Family on Yugoslavia. Nothing at all, however, suggested that this simmering hostility would degenerate into the horrifying, bloodthirsty fury that would be unleashed by the Ustashe, the Croatian nationalist extremists, on the Serbs, Gypsies, and Jews only a few months later.

3 INVASION

ON THE FIRST SUNDAY in April 1941, Germany and Italy attacked the Kingdom of Yugoslavia. I was vaguely aware of the dramatic political events taking place around us but did not imagine how immediate and drastic an effect they would have on my daily life.

Less than two weeks earlier, Prince Regent Paul had finally succumbed to Hitler's threats and Yugoslavia had adhered to the Axis Pact. But only two days later, Paul had been overthrown in a military coup led by high-ranking Serbian officers, who were opposed to the alliance with Germany. They arrested some government ministers and sent Paul into exile, replacing him with young Crown Prince Peter, whom they proclaimed king (although he was six months short of his eighteenth birthday and technically still underage). The new government went out of its way, however, not to provoke the Germans, even reiterating Yugoslavia's adherence to the Axis and offering compensation for any damage done to German property during the rioting that had accompanied the coup. But Hitler, who was planning an attack on Greece for 1 April, seized this opportunity to invade Yugoslavia as well. He postponed his attack on Greece by a few days and on 6 April struck both countries.

Early Sunday morning, Belgrade and other cities were heavily bombed and the Axis armies invaded Yugoslavia from all sides. The attack should really have been expected, but those like myself who had never lived through a war could not imagine that it would actually happen. We all realized that the Yugoslavs were in no position to repel the huge German and Italian armies on their own, but we hoped they would be able to hold out long enough for Great Britain and its allies to come to the rescue. It came as a terrible and quite unexpected shock to us when the Yugoslav soldiers of Croatian ethnicity simply laid down their arms and went home. The national army swiftly collapsed under the heavy Axis onslaught.

By Thursday, 10 April, the Germans had reached the outskirts of Zagreb and were expected to enter the city at any moment (the Italian army had moved in only in the west, along the Adriatic coast). At a time like this, naturally, I wanted to be with my mother, so I caught what turned out to be the last train leaving Zagreb before the Germans arrived. The train's destination was Belgrade, but I got off in the town of Slavonski Brod and caught a connection to Derventa, in Bosnia, where my mother and her husband and mother-in-law were living under "forced residence." I found them quite easily (Derventa was no more than a large village), and we settled down to wait. There was no possibility of escape, and although we were worried and frightened, we drew some comfort just from being together, unaware as we were of the terrible consequences that the German occupation would hold for us. Until then, the only member of our family who had ever been arrested by the Germans was Uncle Julius. He had been rounded up in Vienna in November 1938, during the *Kristallnacht* pogrom, and sent to the Dachau concentration camp. But after a few weeks' internment, he had been released, and had later joined us in Yugoslavia together with Uncle Ferdinand. Thus, in our minds, arrest by the Germans—let alone coming under their occupation—was not necessarily synonymous with death.

One or two days after my arrival in Derventa, the Luftwaffe bombed it, even though it was a small, predominantly Muslim town of no particular strategic importance. We were all in our rented apartment on the second floor of a little two-storey house when we heard the first explosions. Someone had told us that in case of a bombing attack—if one had no time to find proper shelter—the safest place to hide was in the corner of a room, where the floor intersected with the building's outer supporting walls. We gathered in a corner and huddled together while the aircraft roared overhead, dropping their bombs. Suddenly, our house was hit; we held on to one another tightly as everything came crashing down around us. When the dust finally cleared, we realized how precious that advice had been: the entire house had collapsed, save for the corners, which had indeed remained attached to the outer walls. We were practically unscathed, apart from minor cuts from flying glass and the shock of our first exposure to bombing. Our main problem was that we were stuck on the second floor and had no way of climbing down. We remained stranded for quite some time on that little island of bricks and cement until someone came by with a ladder and helped us down. We gathered up whatever was salvageable and found shelter elsewhere.

Shortly afterwards, I witnessed a sight that epitomized the totality of the Yugoslav defeat: a small group of senior officers, including two generals, all of them obviously Serbs (the Croats had long discarded their uniforms), walked silently and dejectedly through Derventa. They looked haggard, discouraged, and completely disoriented. I watched them as they turned south and shuffled away into the distance; it was the most poignant sight I had ever seen.

The next day, there were wild rumours that the German army was approaching and would be entering Derventa at any moment. And in fact, grinding, rattling sounds were soon heard coming from the direction from which the Germans were expected. Three tanks suddenly appeared and rumbled past our house. I observed them with fascination and fear—I had never actually seen a tank before—and noticed a small, triangular red-and-white flag flapping on the first tank. Everyone in town assumed that this was the vanguard of the advancing German troops, and in an instant, the supporters of the Croatian nationalist extremists, the Ustashe, came out of the woodwork. In the Kingdom of Yugoslavia, their association had been outlawed, but now about twenty of them quickly put on armbands marked with a large "U" and proudly assembled in the town's central square to welcome their liberators. As the tanks drove in, the Ustashe sympathizers raised their arms in the Nazi salute—whereupon the tanks immediately opened fire, mowing most of them down. The tanks were evidently manned by Serbs and were the very last remnants of the retreating Yugoslav army. The tanks then turned south and disappeared into the distance.

The next day, German troops did arrive, and before long nearly every Croat in Derventa, Catholic or Muslim, was wearing the "U" armband. The Ustashe took over the civilian administration and swiftly settled some local accounts, murdering a number of Serbs. The Jewish population of Derventa—a small Sephardi community (descendants of Jews expelled from Spain nearly 450 years earlier) and about two hundred refugees from Nazi-occupied Europe—was not immediately harassed. We were ordered only to report to the Ustashe police at regular intervals. At first, life seemed to continue as before—although I did hear of some isolated cases of assault and robbery.

Within a few days, Yugoslavia had been overrun. The Germans then swept into Greece, where they quickly defeated both the Greek army and the British Expeditionary Force. (Although the entire Balkan campaign did not take long, the large numbers of troops required for this *Blitzkrieg* had forced Hitler to postpone his planned attack on the Soviet Union by six to eight weeks. This prevented the Germans from conquering Moscow before the winter and may well have cost them a total victory over the Soviet Union.)

In the wake of the Axis victory, leaders of the Fascist Ustashe movement returned to Croatia from their exile in Italy, where they had for years been sheltered, financed and trained by Mussolini. Their leader, Ante Pavelić, was installed as *Poglavnik* (Chieftain) of a new Independent State of Croatia, which included both Catholic Croatia and predominantly Muslim Bosnia-Herzegovina. At first, this new regime seemed destined to remain a puppet of Fascist Italy, but it soon proved to be more similar to the Nazis in both ideology and methods. The Croats were given civil and administrative authority, although most of the country remained under German military occupation, with the Italians maintaining control only over some areas along the Adriatic coast.

Shortly after they took power, the Ustashe issued a decree ordering all Jews to wear a yellow Star of David on the lapel. As none were

supplied, making these badges became my main occupation for the next few days. I had meanwhile made friends with a boy named Franz Schulbaum, also a refugee from Vienna, who had been interned in Derventa with his parents. Together, we kept ourselves busy by making the badges for the entire group of foreign refugees. We obtained some cardboard, yellow cloth, safety pins, and black ink, and over the next few days produced some two hundred badges, with a Star of David and the letter "Ž" (for *Židov*, "Jew" in Serbo-Croatian) neatly printed in the centre.

Unaware as we were of their ominous significance as a first step towards deportation and extermination, we derived considerable satisfaction from being useful to the group and from the professional look of our handiwork.

Apart from our badge-making, life for the next few weeks continued without major events, although rumours abounded. We kept up our hopes and encouraged one another with talk of something drastic—a *deus ex machina*, such as a British invasion (the United States had not yet entered the war) that would save us from our predicament. Meanwhile, we tried to attract as little attention as possible. As there was no possibility of going to school and we were the only young people among the refugees, Franz and I whiled away our days together, spending most of our time fantasizing about one day becoming Americans and living freely in the United States. We did make the superficial acquaintance of a few local Muslim youths, but this never reached the level of friendship; our cultural and religious backgrounds were too different, and we had the uneasy feeling that most of the Muslims sympathized with the Ustashe. Like the Catholic Croats, they resented the Orthodox Serbs for their overbearing dominance of Yugoslavia, and they were receptive to the propaganda that the Jews—along with the Serbs and Gypsies—were mortal enemies of the new state.

We were able to follow the war's progress thanks to a small radio set that one of our fellow refugees had managed to conceal (there was an Ustashe ordinance forbidding Jews to possess radios). Although reception was very poor, members of our group would regularly assemble in secret to listen to the BBC's German-language broadcasts—a serious crime punishable by immediate arrest and deportation. They would take notes and later relay the latest news to the rest of us. Other refugees would stand guard outside the house to warn the listeners if anyone suspicious approached. Franz and I often volunteered for this task, loitering unobtrusively near the house where the radio set was situated and, if danger approached, whistling an agreed-upon tune as loudly as possible. The tune Franz and I had chosen was "British Grenadiers," an English military march that we had heard on the BBC. We were not fully aware of how serious a provocation this might constitute, but no Ustashe or German ever reacted to the tune when we whistled it; they were either insufficiently knowledgeable to recognize it, or, more likely, our whistling mangled the melody beyond recognition.

My only other pastime during those first eerily tranquil weeks was listening to the poetry of Alexander von Sacher-Masoch. He was not Jewish, but his wife was, which explains his presence with our group of refugees in Derventa. He was originally from Vienna, a journalist and writer, and the great-nephew of the novelist Leopold von Sacher-Masoch, who had given masochism its name (I had no idea at the time that such a term existed, let alone what it meant). From time to time he would tell me he had written a new poem and ask me whether I would mind listening to it. I did not mind, not having much else to do, and would sit quietly some afternoons while he declaimed his verses. I understood very little of his abstract and sophisticated poetry, so I could not make very many pertinent comments, but he enjoyed reading to me because I was, as he put it, "a good listener" (meaning that I did not interrupt and always looked as though I were paying attention).

> *Von Sacher-Masoch wrote several books, including a fiction-alized account of his war years in Yugoslavia titled* Die Ölgärten brennen (The Oil Gardens Are Burning). *He does not mention his brief stay in Derventa.*

After about two months of our *drôle de guerre*, during which nothing much seemed to happen, our relative tranquility came to an end. One day in late June or early July 1941, the Ustashe police ordered us to pack our personal belongings immediately and to stand ready for evacuation. A few hours later, policemen went through the village and rounded up the entire Jewish population, locals and refugees alike. They escorted us to the railway station, allowing us to take along only what we could physically carry. Once we were assembled at the station, we were ordered to climb into the cattle cars that were there waiting for us. We realized that the purpose was probably to deport us to a concentration camp, but a mixture of scanty knowledge and wishful thinking did not make this necessarily a frightening prospect. Under the illusion that concentration camps were nothing but work camps where families were permitted to stay together, we calmly climbed into the cattle cars. It was a hot summer day and the sun shone down relentlessly. The wagons were extremely crowded, packed with men, women, and children of all ages, and it soon became unbearably hot and stuffy. Several hours went by before the train set off, travelling slowly in a northeasterly direction. By this time most of us were desperate to relieve ourselves. It must be remembered that we were all pre-war Central Europeans, who would normally have chosen to suffer in silence rather than admit to needing to attend to bodily functions—let alone contemplate doing so in public. But it was impossible to hold out any longer, and eventually someone mustered the courage to suggest out loud that the ladies relieve themselves first, through a barred opening in the side of the carriage. The men huddled in a corner while they did so, looking the other way, waiting their turn. Then the women gathered in a corner while we relieved ourselves. It was quite a traumatic experience for all of us, but we tried to take it in as positive a spirit as we could.

Our slow-moving train stopped after about two hours in the town of Bosanski Brod, some 30 kilometres from Derventa. Bosanski Brod was at the end of the narrow-gauge Bosnian railway line. To proceed any further, we would have to transfer to another train on the standard-gauge Croatian network. In Bosanski Brod, however, things came to a standstill. We were kept in the cattle cars for two days and two nights, allowed out only for very brief periods to stretch our legs. The Ustashe gave us no food, but the local Jewish community was permitted to supply us with bread, water, and hot sausages. Then, on the third day, the train started up again and returned slowly to Derventa, where we were released without explanation. We never found out why we had been taken on this eerie excursion to Bosanski Brod, but the intention must have been to deport us to a concentration camp. Fortunately, the Ustashe were as disorganized as they were brutal; a last-minute logistical hitch must have arisen, forcing them to abort our deportation.

As the summer of 1941 wore on, more and more Jews living in the German-occupied part of the Independent State of Croatia were arrested and deported to concentration camps. For a long time, however, little or nothing was known of their fate. We always managed to find some reason to continue hoping for a turn for the better, telling ourselves that perhaps, as foreigners, we would be spared. In reality, even if we had known what was happening to the others and what was in store for us, there was little we could have done. We were trapped and felt quite helpless.

In such a context of impotence and worry, it may seem incongruous that in September 1941, Uncle Robert wrote to my mother suggesting that she send me back to Zagreb, where the Jewish community was organizing schooling for young people my age. Jewish children had been banned from all state schools by the Ustashe's anti-Semitic edicts (aping the Nazis, who had done the same in Austria three years earlier). These improvised lessons under the auspices of the Jewish community were my only chance of not losing another school year. For my part, I was eager to leave Derventa; I was not getting on at all with my stepfather, and the prospect of going to school again delighted me. I insisted that my mother allow me to return to Zagreb, and eventually she agreed. We parted in the autumn of 1941.

When I reached Zagreb, I discovered that the schooling was not exactly what I had hoped for. In the difficult circumstances, all the Jewish community could do was to organize a few lectures, held covertly in private homes. So as not to attract the Ustashe's attention, we would arrive one by one, at intervals, as unobtrusively as possible. The atmosphere at these lectures was very gloomy. Few Jewish children

were left in Zagreb by the autumn of 1941, and there were never more than four or five students in my study group. Some of my classmates' fathers had already been deported, with no news of their fate. The only glimmer of light in this sombre world was the personality of our principal lecturer, a medical doctor named Dr. Rechnitzer. He was a brilliant and eloquent man, capable of speaking intelligently and compellingly about an impressively wide range of subjects. At a time when everything was being done to crush us, he lifted our spirits with his inspiring and stimulating lectures.

Dr. Mirko Rechnitzer

He also reminded us, in an attempt to bolster our self-esteem, that the Jews Einstein and Freud, together with Moses, had influenced human thought more than anyone else in the history of mankind. Frightened and despondent as we were, his words gave us some solace.

Conditions continued to deteriorate rapidly. Increasing numbers of Jews, both local and foreign, were being arrested and sent to concentration camps. Towards the end of 1941, my stepfather, Friedrich Löbl, was deported to the death camp at Jasenovac, about 100 kilometres southeast of Zagreb. Nothing more was ever heard from him. We came to realize, reluctantly, that alarmingly few detainees were being released from the

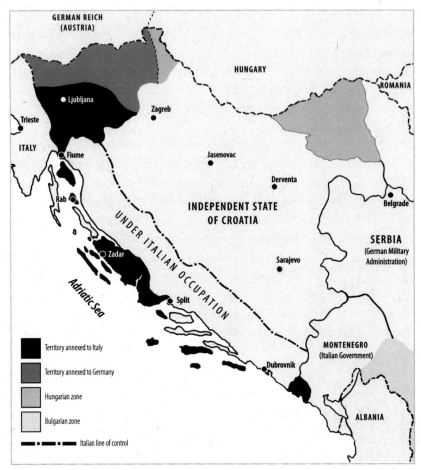

The partition of Yugoslavia after the Axis invasion of April 1941

camps (usually following the intervention of some foreign consulate) and that their tales of horror were probably true. For many months, Uncle Robert and Aunt Camilla had refused to see the writing on the wall. On more than one occasion I had heard them say: "If the Ustashe haven't touched us until now, why should they harm us in the future?" But now, even they were concluding that we had to flee.

The only place that might possibly be safe was the Italian zone of occupation. The Italian army controlled the entire Adriatic coast of Yugoslavia, from Rijeka (Fiume) in the north to the Albanian border in the south, including all the Adriatic islands. Some areas, including the town of Split, had actually been annexed by Italy. The rest was, at first,

merely under Italian military occupation, with the civilian administration in the hands of the Croats. However, when the Italians became
aware of the appalling atrocities being committed by the Ustashe against
Serbs and Jews, they had intervened, curtailing the powers of the Croat
administration in the Italian zones and in that way putting an end to
the horrors. News of the Italians' astonishing attitude quickly reached
the ears of the Jews still under German/Ustashe control. The fact that the
Italians treated the Jews like normal human beings was sufficient reason
to do everything possible to try and reach their zone of occupation. But
it was dangerous and difficult to escape the areas under German/Ustashe
control. In fact, it was a crime for a Jew to even attempt to leave; Jews who
were caught doing so faced immediate arrest and deportation to a death
camp. Also, there was no assurance at all that if we reached the Italian
zone, we would actually gain admission (a number of Jewish refugees
had been turned back at the border by Italian troops). According to our
information, however, once one was actually inside Italian-held territory,
one was comparatively safe. One might even be transferred to Italy itself,
where, according to rumour, living conditions were better, the local
population was hospitable, and one would be safer than in an occupied
zone of Yugoslavia, which the Italian Army might one day evacuate.

In preparation for our escape from Zagreb, Uncle Robert liquidated his
inventory of neckties and tried to dispose of whatever other assets could
be sold. The problem was how to make the proceeds liquid, portable, and
easy to hide. He bought a few gold coins on the black market but handed
over most of his money to Dr. Šik, who was being blackmailed and needed
cash. Dr. Šik was such a successful lawyer that over the years he had
accumulated quite a few enemies, mostly people against whom he had
won court cases (the usual outcome of his efforts); some of them—and
their lawyers—were now extorting money from him, threatening to
denounce him to the Ustashe if he did not pay them off. Any contrived
reason—even the simple fact of having won a court case against a
Gentile in the past—would have sufficed to have him arrested and sent
to a death camp. When Dr. Šik could no longer meet the demands of his
blackmailers, he turned to Uncle Robert for help: he promised that if my
uncle gave him cash in local currency, he would repay him after the war
from a dollar account he had opened in New York many years earlier.
He now had no access to it and, of course, had to keep it a secret (for a

Jew, maintaining a foreign bank account was even more dangerous than trying to escape). This offer was convenient for my uncle, and in view of the risks involved, a simple handwritten agreement was drawn up on a small scrap of paper. Uncle Robert handed over various sums to Dr. Šik, sometimes in my presence, and the amounts were always meticulously noted on that original piece of paper. In the ensuing months, however, the written record was lost and Dr. Šik was deported by the Ustashe to Jasenovac, where he was murdered.

> *After the war, a New York court ruled that Uncle Robert was entitled to reimbursement by Dr. Šik's estate. I was the only witness in Uncle Robert's favour, and the judge's decision rested entirely on whether or not he believed my testimony. I was very pleased that he did, and Uncle Robert received a few thousand dollars, which he sorely needed.*

By the end of 1941, our only thought was how to get out of Zagreb. It was impossible to travel anywhere in the new Independent State of Croatia without documents called *Propusnice*. These were special passes authorizing the holder to travel from one specified location to another. No one was allowed to travel without such a document, and Jews were not even permitted to apply for one. However, corrupt officials were selling them through intermediaries. We managed to purchase fake *Propusnice* entitling us to "return" from Zagreb to a village in German-occupied southern Croatia, supposedly our usual place of residence. We knew that in order to reach that place, we would have to pass through the town of Split, in Italian-held territory. Our plan was to somehow evade surveillance once we were in Split and to remain—illegally—in the Italian zone. Uncle Robert was going to attempt the journey first, on his own; if he managed to remain in Split, he would let us know and prepare accommodation for us. Then Aunt Camilla, her husband Oskar, and I would leave Zagreb. It was our hope that my mother and her mother-in-law, who were still in Derventa, would be able to join us later.

In late December 1941, Uncle Robert set out on his journey to the Italian zone. Within a few days, we received word that he had arrived safely and had succeeded in staying in Split. He urged us to join him there without delay. As public warehouses no longer accepted Jewish property, we quickly arranged to have our remaining furniture stored by private individuals, knowing full well that there was little hope of ever seeing our belongings again, even if we did return to Zagreb one day.

We planned to depart on 12 January 1942. In order not to arouse suspicion by being seen carrying luggage out of the house, we packed our bags the day before and sent them on ahead to the railway station. It was just a few days before my seventeenth birthday. I remember how carefully I folded the beautiful hand-tailored suit of English wool—grey with red pinstripes—that Uncle Robert had ordered for my birthday. It was the very first suit I had ever owned. It had been delivered on 11 January, together with a shiny new pair of handmade shoes. I was extremely proud of my new clothes and had packed them with special attention. But I never got the chance to wear them.

It was about noon on 12 January 1942. The apartment was empty and we were ready to set out for the railway station. As there was no longer any furniture, I had hung my overcoat on a window handle in the living room. Aunt Camilla and Uncle Oskar were already waiting for me by the front door. What happened next has remained engraved in my memory like a film in slow motion: I turned to face the window and walked towards it, reaching with my hand to take my coat. At that moment, the doorbell rang violently, three times. We opened the door and were confronted by two plainclothes detectives, who accused us of attempting to leave without authorization (as though we would have obtained it if we had asked for it). They said we were under arrest and ordered us to follow them.

4 PRISON

WHILE WE WALKED DOWN the two flights of steps, accompanied by the detectives, I wondered who might have denounced us. Perhaps one of the other tenants, who, despite our precautions, had noticed our preparations? Or perhaps it was the concierge, the usual—and most likely—suspect?

We stepped out into the street and were led towards a waiting police car. It was bitingly cold, and I dug my hands deep into my coat pockets. With the tips of my fingers I felt the edges of some sheets of paper and realized to my horror that I was carrying the false travel documents for all three of us. Only later would I discover that if you were a Jew, material proof of any "wrongdoing" was entirely irrelevant. At that moment I thought it desperately important to somehow get rid of them. Approaching the police car, I noticed that the detective holding open the back door was not watching me. As I slowly got into the car, I extracted the papers from my pocket and slipped them into the rain gutter. Settling into the back seat as nonchalantly as I could, I secretly enjoyed an intense—if short-lived—feeling of triumph.

The detectives drove us to the Ustashe police headquarters, in the large square only a few blocks away from our apartment.

The name of this important square has always reflected the current political regime. Under the Ustashe, it was called Independent State of Croatia Square; previously, under the monarchy, it had been King Peter Square. After the war, under the Communists, it was Square of the Revolution; today, in newly independent Croatia, it is Square of the Croatian Greats.

▲ *Ustashe police headquarters on Independent State of Croatia Square, where Uncle Oskar, Aunt Camilla, and I were imprisoned on 12 January 1942. This picture was taken in 1981, when the building was a dormitory for university students; by then, the building was named after Moša Pijade, the Jewish partisan leader who had been one of Tito's closest associates.*

The three of us were led into an office, where our personal information was taken down. We were searched and fingerprinted and our watches, belts, neckties, and shoelaces were confiscated. Then each of us was interrogated separately.

The Ustashe who conducted my interrogation accused me of trying to leave Zagreb without permission. I denied this strenuously, but he seemed completely uninterested in my answers. His questioning was perfunctory; he ignored my replies and made no attempt at all to get me to confess. It began to dawn on me that because I was a Jew, the question of my guilt or innocence was simply not relevant: I was now in the hands of the Ustashe, and it made no difference to them whether I had or had not committed the crime of trying to save my life by escaping. My fate, whatever it was, was a foregone conclusion.

I was led down a flight of stairs into the basement and locked into a tiny cell, about one metre wide and two metres long. For the first time in my life, eleven days before my seventeenth birthday, I was under arrest. I surveyed my surroundings. The cell was completely bare except for a narrow cot against one wall and a naked light bulb hanging from the ceiling. I could see a small window high up on the wall, but its glass pane was completely opaque, making it impossible for me to tell whether it was night or day. I sat down on the edge of the cot and stretched out my legs. The cell was so narrow that my feet easily touched the opposite wall.

I soon lost any sense of time; I had nothing to do or read, and the light bulb burned continuously. Every few hours someone brought me food. Whenever I needed to go to the toilet, I banged on the cell door and an armed guard would accompany me to the latrine, wait for me, and then accompany me back.

The door to my cell was made of heavy steel, with five rows of small holes drilled in at eye level, eight holes to a row. Because the walls of my cell were a uniform pale grey, the only patterns my eyes could focus on and play with were those provided by the forty little holes. I spent hours lying on my cot, my gaze fixed on them, counting them over and over in every possible direction, arranging and rearranging them into innumerable shapes and patterns. When I could no longer bear the monotony, I would get up and peer out through them into the hallway. Usually there was nothing to be seen except the cell door opposite mine, but I did occasionally catch sight of a prisoner being led away for interrogation. Sometimes I also detected the distant screaming of someone being tortured or beaten—although I myself was not physically harmed in this prison.

After a time, I was taken out once more for questioning, but it consisted only in the verification of my personal data and the repetition of the accusation that I had illegally tried to escape from Croatia. No one attempted to get me to confess, and no attention was paid to my denials.

One day, I somehow discovered that Aunt Camilla was locked up in the cell next to mine. Whenever we felt especially downcast or lonely, we would tap cautiously on the thick wall dividing us, just to let each other know we were still there. We had no code, never having contemplated finding ourselves in a situation like this, but that occasional, irregular little tapping was a source of comfort and encouragement to me during my solitary confinement.

Finally, after what seemed to be an eternity but turned out to have been only eight days, I was transferred—alone, without Aunt Camilla or Uncle

Oskar—from the cell in the basement of the Zagreb police headquarters to the prison at Savska Cesta, on the outskirts of the city.

My new cell was much larger than the previous one, but it was unbearably crowded: about thirty-five prisoners were packed into it. The cell was completely bare, with no bunks or chairs, yet there was practically no room to move. I was by far the youngest prisoner in the group and, as far as I could tell, the only Jew and the only foreigner. Cold, hungry, and despondent as we were, we barely exchanged a word, but I got the impression that none of my fellow prisoners were common criminals: they were either suspected Communists or political opponents of other kinds, imagined or real, of the Ustashe regime. It was in this cell that, on 23 January 1942, I turned seventeen.

Curiously, the only time we did not suffer from the cold was at night. We slept on the bare cement floor, had nothing with which to cover ourselves, and used our shoes as pillows—yet the tight quarters forced us to sleep so close to one another that our collective body warmth protected us against the freezing January temperatures. One disadvantage of sleeping so tightly packed together was that it was impossible to turn over during the night. There was no choice but to stand up, turn around, and lie down again. But that was the least of my troubles; we received very little food, and for the first time in my life I suffered the torment of hunger.

Now and then a few inmates would be taken out of the cell to perform chores in the prison. Fortunately, on one of these occasions, I was included in a small work party assigned to transporting some bags of onions and garlic from the courtyard to the kitchen storehouse. When the guards were not looking, we greedily plunged our hands into the bags, stuffing as many of those precious bulbs as we could into our pockets. For the next few days, I was able to still my hunger a little by eating an onion or a piece of garlic and then washing it down with great quantities of water.

One day, to my immense surprise, I received a small food parcel. It was from my cousin Blanka, who was still in Zagreb. She later told me that she had sent me a number of other parcels, none of which ever arrived; it was thus a miracle that I did receive this one. The prize item it contained was a 200 gram tin of salted butter. I devoured the other contents of the package immediately but decided to make that butter last as long as I could, eating no more than a single spoonful every day—or rather at night, to avoid being seen and envied by my hungry cellmates.

My strategy, however, proved a failure. After less than two weeks at Savska Cesta, during which I was never summoned or questioned, I was marched out one morning from my cell to an office on the ground floor of the prison building. A guard thoroughly searched me, found the tin—which was still half full of that precious, nourishing butter—and, to my despair, put it in his own pocket. I swore to myself that day that never again would I save anything edible "for later." I was handed a typewritten sheet of paper, which stated that "Imre Rochlitz, as a Jew, being dangerous to public order and safety, has been sentenced to two years' hard labour in the Jasenovac concentration camp." There was no reference to the accusation that I had illegally tried to escape—I had been sentenced simply for being a Jew. The document was shown to me, I was permitted to read it, and then it was taken away.

Until that moment I had still harboured the hope that somehow I would be released—either because I was not a Croat but a foreigner, or because I was still only a boy, or perhaps because someone, somewhere realized that in my case a terrible mistake had been made. I knew I was no threat or bother to anybody, although months and years of anti-Semitic propaganda and brainwashing had, I confess, begun to influence my own perception of reality. I had even wondered to myself at times whether there might not be some truth to Nazi claims about some Jews: that they were dishonest, parasitic, unclean, and afraid of physical work. During the first days of my imprisonment, I had tried to reassure myself that I certainly did not belong to those arguably reprehensible categories of Jews. Culturally and in my heart I was an Austrian—and moreover I did not even look Jewish! Surely my innocence would soon be recognized and I would be released.

My sentencing to hard labour in Jasenovac dealt a cruel blow to my hopes; it was the worst outcome imaginable. Everyone knew by then—as I did—that Jasenovac was the harshest of all concentration camps, and I had never heard of anyone as young as I being sent there. But this was now my fate, and as I stood in that office, trying to come to terms with what had happened, numerous thoughts raced through my mind: "I am only seventeen, I have never done anything wrong, perhaps if I work hard and obey all commands I will not be harmed; perhaps the scrupulous execution of everything that I am ordered to do is the key that will permit me to survive." These foolish thoughts and illusions would vanish quickly once I set foot in Jasenovac.

Twelve more prisoners were brought into the room, all of them Serbs, as far as I could tell. There were now thirteen of us. It was 1 February 1942; within three days I would be the only one still alive.

Ustashe guards led us to a police van and drove us to the Zagreb railway station, where we were told to climb into a cattle wagon. The village of Jasenovac is only about 100 kilometres southeast of Zagreb, yet the journey took several hours, perhaps because our wagon was hitched to a freight train that travelled very slowly and stopped frequently.

We arrived after dark and were not taken immediately to the concentration camp, which was a few kilometres outside the village. The Ustashe locked us up for the night in a room in the basement of a small building, which may have been the local police station. The room had a single, small, barred opening high up on the wall, at street level. Shortly after we were locked in, we noticed a small face peering down at us. It was a young girl, perhaps eight or nine, who seemed to be smiling sweetly. One of the prisoners had some money on him—I do not know how he had managed to keep it despite the repeated body searches to which we had been subjected—and he asked the little girl whether she would buy some bread for us. When she readily agreed, he threw the coins up to her. As soon as the money was safely in her hand, she started cursing and throwing stones down at us. She then ran off, and we, of course, never saw any bread. Ever since, unfortunately, the sight of a sweetly smiling little girl can awaken memories of this incident.

As the night wore on, it became colder and colder. We realized that the only way to avoid freezing to death was to constantly keep moving. As the room was quite small, we formed a circle and, shivering and beating our hands against our sides, shuffled behind one another for the entire night.

When morning broke, we were marched to the Jasenovac concentration camp, a few kilometres away. It was a terribly cold day, and the entire area lay under a cover of snow and ice.

5 JASENOVAC

A TALL BARBED-WIRE FENCE, punctuated by watchtowers, encircled the entire camp. We were marched through the front gate to the headquarters building and then led to the prisoners' quarters, which consisted of six or seven long, wooden barracks. The inmate in charge of my barracks gave me a bowl, a spoon, and a thin blanket and led me to my bunk. Two rows of triple-level bunks ran the entire length of the barracks, one along either side. In the centre was a small woodstove. Each bunk level, less than 1.5 metres wide, was the designated sleeping quarters for three inmates. There were well over two hundred inmates in my barracks alone.

I do not remember everything that happened while I was in Jasenovac. I was barely seventeen when I was interned, spent only three weeks there, and tried my best for the next sixty years to forget that infernal place. Yet some episodes and a general feeling of horror and loss of hope remain indelible.

The look and smell of excrement and death pervaded every aspect of the camp. The inmates were dressed in filthy, foul-smelling rags. They were emaciated, unshaven, and extremely weak, and despite the freezing cold and ice-covered ground, none had proper shoes. Their feet mostly wrapped in rags, they dragged themselves with difficulty from one place to another, a glassy, immobile gaze in their eyes. I was shocked by that look: it expressed nothing, not even fear. They were like living dead.

Within days, I became one of them. It dawned on me that what I faced was impending, painful, messy, cold death. I, and apparently everyone else, was certain to die—either by being shot, knifed, or clubbed to death by an Ustashe guard or by succumbing to exhaustion, malnutrition, disease, and cold. It was sure to be only a matter of days, and there was nothing anyone could do about it.

▲ *Jasenovac death camp (partial view)*

It was so cold that nobody ever undressed—I even slept with my shoes on. The blanket that each of us had received was so thin that it was practically of no use. At night, when I squeezed into my bunk, I and the two other inmates beside me would use our blankets collectively, spreading all three over our shivering bodies in an attempt to somehow keep warm.

There were, of course, no washing facilities of any kind. I very quickly became heavily infested with both body and hair lice, as did everyone else. Soon I also began suffering from severe diarrhea, the consequence of our single daily meal of watery bean soup.

The sense of utter helplessness and resignation was such that barely anyone ever spoke to anyone else. Although I was too downcast to pay much notice, I got the impression that my barracks contained a random mixture of Serbs, Croats, and Jews. I eventually recognized one inmate as a Jewish refugee from Vienna whom I had known in Zagreb. I immediately asked him whether he knew what had happened to my stepfather, Friedrich Löbl, who had been arrested in the village of Derventa only two months earlier, together with a group of other Jewish men, and deported to Jasenovac. The Ustashe had killed him, the man told me, they had killed the whole group upon their arrival in the camp.

Everyone I asked about was already dead, including Dr. Lavoslav Šik, the lawyer who had sheltered and protected me in Zagreb and who had been like a father to me.

I had arrived in the camp in a group of thirteen. Within a few days the other twelve were dead. Normally I would not have been aware of this, but three days after I arrived in Jasenovac I heard an Ustashe officer calling out a list of about fifty names. He ordered the inmates to assemble in marching formation, four to a row. We all assumed—I am not sure why, it may actually have been announced, or perhaps it was just hoped for—that this group was being transferred to another concentration camp, Djakovo, where conditions were supposedly better. It was rumoured that it contained tailoring and carpentry workshops, that one worked in huts and sheds rather than exposed to the elements, and that there was less wanton killing.

I screwed up my courage and asked the Ustashe officer—who, had he so chosen, could have shot me then and there for even daring to address him—why I was not on the list. I pointed out that my name must have been omitted by mistake since the names of the other twelve with whom I had arrived had just been called out. He lazily waved me away without replying.

The next day we found out that the entire group had been taken out and killed. Whether this had been the intention all along or whether they had been assembled for the purpose of being transferred and the guards had later changed their minds and decided to kill them, was not clear, nor did it matter. Many groups were marched out of the camp in this fashion and then killed nearby, their bodies thrown into the Sava River or into mass graves.

I would learn only later that "transfer to Djakovo" was in fact nothing but a frequently used, cynical euphemism for immediate elimination.

Very soon after my arrival I was assigned to a gravediggers' detail, a group of fifteen to twenty inmates whose job it was to go through the barracks every morning and gather up the corpses of those who had died during the night. Most people in the camp died during the day, murdered while carrying out forced labour or during the Ustashe's killing sprees; but many, weakened by maltreatment, starvation, and disease, simply died in their bunks during the freezing nights.

I had never seen a corpse before, nor had I ever seen anyone actually dying. Although I was already fourteen when my grandmother passed away in 1939, my family had kept me from her deathbed, and even from her funeral. After a few days in Jasenovac, corpses became commonplace and no longer affected me. On two occasions I woke up in the morning and discovered that the person lying by my side, under our shared blankets, had died during the night. My only surprise was that I had slept through their deaths unawares. I never knew their names, nor do I remember their faces. I do not remember that I was upset; I felt it made no difference. None of us was going to live much longer anyway.

Our job as gravediggers was to drag the corpses out of the barracks— we found ten to fifteen in each hut every morning—and load them onto a large sleigh. Once the sleigh was piled high, several armed guards would march us out through the camp gate to a nearby field.

We would spend the entire day in the field, digging mass graves in the frozen ground and flinging the corpses into them. Each grave was meant to hold about four hundred bodies. The digging was probably the hardest work in the camp, but it made little difference to me; I had accepted that this was where I was going to die. The earth was frozen hard, and the work was exhausting and painful: none of us had gloves, which had been taken from us upon our arrival. We were in an utterly weakened state but had to work without respite. How many of the gravediggers themselves

▲ *Jasenovac, 1942. An inmate (in the upper right hand corner)—possibly a gravedigger like me—and an Ustashe guard, standing among corpses.*

were murdered on any given day—under the pretext that they worked too slowly—depended entirely on the mood of the guards.

Before we were permitted to dump the bodies into the graves, the guards would search them for anything of value. Supposedly, all valuables (and even worthless objects) had been taken from us when we entered Jasenovac. However, the guards were particularly interested in the corpses' teeth, and if they found any gold bridges or crowns, they would eagerly yank them out. Once they had finished with the corpses, it was our turn to see if we could salvage anything. We occasionally removed a piece of clothing from a corpse, if it seemed warmer than what we possessed. I myself took some socks from a pair of dead feet, and also a spoon from a corpse's pocket, without feeling any revulsion or compunction.

One of the camp guards who often escorted us was a boy my age, no more than seventeen. As far as I could tell, I was the youngest inmate in the camp—and he was the youngest guard. I remember his face, but I do not think I ever knew his name; we were not supposed to know names. I do remember that he always wore a Muslim fez on his head, cocked to one side. Most of the camp guards were Catholic Croats (at one time, the commander of Jasenovac was a former priest), but some of them were Muslims, who were permitted to keep their distinctive headwear.

One day this guard began shouting at me that I was not digging hard enough. I still remember his expression, both primitive and cruel, empty of any humanity. I worked as vigorously as I could, but it was still not enough to satisfy him. He shouted that he was going to kill me.

He pushed me to the edge of the nearest grave, in which there were already over a hundred corpses, knocked me into it with the butt of his rifle, and placed the muzzle against my left temple. I pleaded with him not to kill me, although I knew it was no use. He pulled the trigger. I heard the gun's mechanism click, but no bullet came out. Perhaps the rifle was not loaded, although this is doubtful. Guards as a rule carried loaded rifles and pistols, and I had seen this particular guard shoot other gravediggers before.

He did not pull the trigger again but instead turned his weapon around and started to beat me with the rifle butt. I have no doubt that he was trying to break my back. He would certainly have succeeded had I not been lying on several layers of corpses, which absorbed some of the impact of his blows; I can still hear the air being squeezed from their dead lungs. After a time—he must have given me twenty or even thirty blows—he gave up. He ordered me to climb out of the grave and go back to my digging. I had better work harder than before, he said, or he would kill me at once. I do not know how, but I did manage to work harder. At the end of the day, as we marched back to the camp, he ordered me to sing Ustashe songs.

We received food only once a day, at around noon. We would return to the camp from the gravedigging and stand in line with our bowls and spoons while an inmate ladled out beans from a kettle. They were unsalted, and we received nothing else, not even bread. Afterwards, we would be marched back to resume our gravedigging. Within a short time, like almost everyone else, I developed a terrible case of diarrhea, which progressively weakened me. As a child I had always been a fussy and selective eater, forcing my mother to employ all manner of ruses to get me to eat nourishing food. How quickly this changed in Jasenovac. One day I noticed a piece of raw, bloody gristle, probably pork, discarded on a heap of garbage. Making sure that no one saw me (one could be shot on the spot for any reason), I picked it up and gnawed on it voraciously for a couple of hours.

About a week after my arrival, my uncle Oskar, who had been arrested at the same time as I, was also interned in the camp. But we barely spoke; we knew that there was nothing we could do for each other.

It was one of the coldest winters in memory. It snowed heavily and, it seemed to me, without interruption. I began to suffer from frostbite in my toes, which severely hindered my ability to walk.

One morning, instead of going out with the gravediggers' detail, I was ordered to shovel the freshly fallen snow from a path inside the camp. An Ustashe walked by me, holding a pistol in his hand. I shovelled as fast and as hard as I could; nevertheless, he cuffed me violently with his weapon. I fell over, but got up quickly and continued shovelling to the limit of my strength, aware that this was my only chance to avoid being shot on the spot. He hit me once more with his pistol; I fell again but got back on my feet and continued shovelling. Seemingly satisfied, he continued on his way. Another prisoner was shovelling snow a few metres farther on. The Ustashe struck him with his pistol, and the prisoner fell to the ground. He was either too stunned or too weak to get up immediately, and the Ustashe shot him in the head. I continued shovelling.

I returned to Jasenovac in the summer of 1981 and visited the small museum on the site. In one of the displays was an Ustashe document dated 12 February 1942, reporting the deportation of Jewish men to Jasenovac and Jewish women to a camp at Stara Gradiška. Uncle Oskar, a tailor by profession ("krojač"), is third on the list. This photograph was taken in 1981, through the glass display case. In 2005 I contacted the Jasenovac archives and asked for a better copy. They replied that the document had disappeared during the looting that accompanied the 1992 civil war. ▸

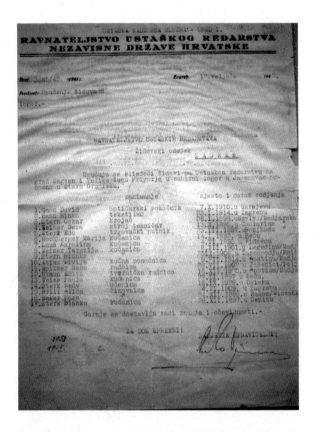

Despite the biting cold, the general stench from the living, the dying, and the dead was beyond description. It was clear to me from my rapidly declining physical condition that the cold and the exhausting work would finish me off within a week or two—if I was not murdered before then. I had no fear of death, nor did I look forward to it as an end to my suffering; it was just an inevitable, inescapable outcome about which I could do nothing. Any hope of salvation had been completely extinguished. And with the death of hope, so too died the possibility of the existence of God. Like all children, I had long entertained the fantasy of an all-powerful creator who watched over my life. After a few days in Jasenovac, I became certain that God did not exist, and I still am.

In the beginning, I did quarrel with my fate: Why am I in this death camp? Why will I die here? I have done no harm to these Ustashe or to anyone else. It must all be a terrible mistake. But everything is futile. My fate is of no concern to anyone. There is no God.

I also remember pondering the futility of earthly goods; many of the inmates had once been wealthy and influential people, and all that was of no avail to them now.

While I never seriously considered doing away with myself—there was no safe way of committing suicide, that is, with any assurance of quick success—I also did not think of trying to escape. It seemed that there was nowhere to go, even if I did succeed. Where could I hide, and how could I survive in the snow- and ice-covered fields and forests? I was certain there was no chance the local population would provide shelter or assistance. They were all peasants and villagers, brainwashed and terrorized by the Ustashe into believing that any prisoner must be a dangerous enemy of the state; most probably they would immediately turn me in. Also, I soon witnessed what was done to recaptured escapees.

We were woken up one night and ordered to assemble outside in the cold. It was announced that an inmate of our barracks had escaped. Two Ustashe walked by us, counting us off: "one ... two ..." The "twos" were sent back to their bunks while the "ones" were ordered to regroup in formation.

I was among the "ones." We were kept standing for hours in the freezing night. We tried to warm up by marching on the spot, stamping our feet as energetically as we dared in order to keep our circulation going. After a while, it became clear that we were going to be killed in reprisal for the escape. I was too cold, weak, and tired—and certain that I would die soon in any case—to care; I was completely resigned to my fate. The others must have been in a similar state, physically and mentally, because no one cried, fainted, or reacted in any way. We just continued to stamp our feet quietly on the icy ground.

Mass killings always took place outside the camp. At dawn, shortly before we were going to be marched out, we were informed that the escaped prisoner had been caught and that we had been reprieved.

All of the inmates were assembled, and the unsuccessful escapee was shown to us as a warning. He was naked, unable to stand, and supported by two guards. I was too far away to see him clearly, but I got the impression that his body was a dark, glistening colour, as though the outer layer of his skin had been stripped away. But I felt no pity or compassion; the only feeling I can remember is one of hatred. My hatred, however, was not directed at the Ustashe—it was directed at him. I found myself detesting him intensely, not for having caused me unnecessary suffering but for having broken camp regulations. I felt he was a criminal for having tried to escape and that he deserved to be punished. This was the horrifying extent to which my faculties and discernment had been reduced. The Ustashe had succeeded in brutalizing me both physically and morally; I had succumbed to camp logic and had adopted it as my own.

We buried him later that morning, together with the other corpses that had accumulated in the barracks overnight.

On my eighteenth day in the camp, I was late for the midday beans. The morning gravedigging had gone on longer than usual, and by the time we returned to the camp the ladling out was about to end. Desperate not to miss this single daily meal, I hobbled as quickly as I could to the barracks to fetch my bowl and spoon—my toes were badly frozen by then and I felt very weak—and then hurried back. By the time I returned, there was no longer a line of prisoners (one was never allowed second helpings), but an Ustashe officer was standing beside the kettle, calling out the name "Oskar Stern." I hesitated. I knew there were at least two other inmates by that name in the camp, and I doubted very much that it was my uncle they were looking for. He was an ordinary inmate, a tailor from Vienna who didn't speak a word of Serbo-Croatian, with no special skills like carpentry or engineering, which the Ustashe sometimes found useful. One could never foresee the consequences of addressing an Ustashe, so I weighed the officer's demeanour for a moment, decided that it did not seem particularly threatening, and approached him, saying that I had an uncle by the name of Oskar Stern. He asked whether my uncle was German, which I confirmed (he was in fact Austrian, but since the 1938 *Anschluss,* Austria had become a province of the German Reich). He then asked whether I knew someone by the name of Imre Rochlitz. It turned out that he had called my name several times while the beans were being ladled out and, since no one answered, had assumed that I was dead.

I told the officer that I was Imre Rochlitz. He replied that there was no time for me to eat, ordered me to fetch my uncle at once, and then led both of us to the headquarters building. Another Ustashe registered us in some sort of log and led us to a guardroom, where we were seated on a bench and chained to it. After a while I noticed that one of the guards was peeling an orange. I had missed my daily beans, and my uncle and I were both desperately hungry and weak, so I screwed up my courage and asked the guard whether he would permit us to chew on the orange peels. He laughed and flung the peels past us, ensuring, chained down as we were, that they landed beyond our reach.

We sat there through the entire night. At dawn a guard brought in some cleaner clothes, obviously taken from dead prisoners, and ordered us to change into them; our own clothes smelled unbearably and were tattered and charred from huddling around the little stove in the barracks. We obeyed this strange order, without a clue as to its possible meaning.

A heavy chain and padlock were brought in. Uncle Oskar and I were chained around the wrists and to each other, and then an officer marched us to the railway station, where we boarded a train. The officer took us into one of the compartments, sat down in front of us, opened a newspaper, and paid no further attention to us. The train started up. I observed the officer. He seemed quite detached and indifferent and to harbour no particular animosity towards us. After consulting with my uncle in whispers, I decided to take a chance and to address him. In as submissive a tone as possible, I asked him whether he would permit me to ask him a question. When he replied affirmatively, I asked him whether he could tell us where we were going. With a calm and indifferent voice, he said he had orders to take us to Ustashe police headquarters in Zagreb, where he expected that we would be handed over to the Germans for execution, in retaliation for the killing of a German soldier by the Partisans. He then turned back to his newspaper.

The journey back to Zagreb took several hours. To our amazement, from the Zagreb train station we continued by public transport, boarding a tram along the Zrinjevac, one of the city's main avenues. My uncle and I must have been quite a sight—gaunt, dirty, smelly, and chained to each other. Understandably, the other passengers shrank away from us. Their reaction, I felt, did not stem from hatred for Jews or for opponents of the regime, but from a basic instinct of self-preservation, as well as from simple horror at our appearance. They knew it was safest to distance themselves clearly from anyone under arrest, and I was not surprised to detect no sympathy coming from them.

Suddenly I noticed that one of the passengers seated in the tram was a former teacher of mine, whose star student I had been the preceding year at *Druga Muška Realna Gimnazija*, the Zagreb high school I had attended for a few months. Our eyes met, and I saw his look turn to shock as he recognized me. He quickly recomposed his expression and averted his gaze. I could not really blame him; there was nothing he could have done to help me even if he had wished, and any display of sympathy on his part could have endangered his own existence. (When I revisited Zagreb in 1981, I found that the tram still followed the same route; see photograph on page 57.)

When we reached police headquarters—the same building where I had been held in solitary confinement in the basement just over a month earlier—we were led up several flights of stairs, unchained, and locked into a small room.

Oskar and I spent the whole evening and the ensuing night there, without food or water. It was as though they had forgotten us. I had not eaten for nearly two days and was not only very hungry but also extremely uncomfortable, as my uncontrollable diarrhea had by now badly soiled my underwear. I knocked on the door and asked the guard to take me to a toilet. Once the toilet door was safely closed behind me, I removed the underwear and tried to flush it down the drain. To my horror, it got stuck in the plumbing. Water started rising in the toilet bowl and, knowing the Ustashe, I was gripped by fear that now they would kill me—for this, if for no other reason. I struggled with the underwear for some time before I somehow managed to extricate it from the drainpipe, unplugging the toilet. When I saw the water flowing freely again, I heaved a sigh of relief.

In the morning, Uncle Oskar was taken out of the room. Half an hour passed, and just as I was concluding that they must have killed him, they came for me. I was accompanied to an office several floors below, where for the second time in two days I was asked for my personal data. I could not help being taken aback when the Ustashe official interrogating me addressed me as "Mr. Rochlitz."

I was handed a piece of paper and told to wait.

After a while, I risked a glance at the paper: it stated that I was being released from Jasenovac because the remainder of my two-year sentence had been waived. I was completely stunned. I heard a voice say that I could now leave. Not quite understanding what was happening to me, or knowing how far I would get, I picked myself up and made for the exit.

Outside on the sidewalk I found Uncle Oskar waiting for me, together with Aunt Camilla, whom I had not seen since our arrest. We fell into one another's arms, incredulous and sobbing profusely.

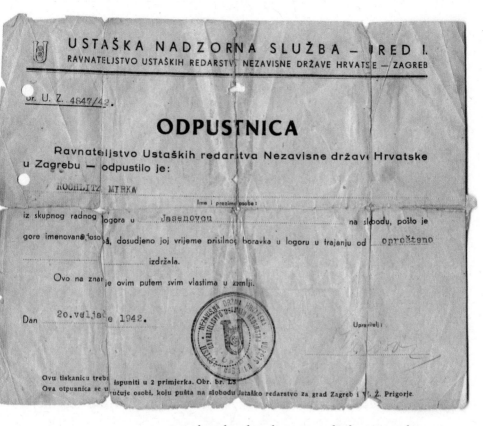

USTAŠKA NADZORNA SLUŽBA — URED I.
RAVNATELJSTVO USTAŠKIH REDARSTVA NEZAVISNE DRŽAVE HRVATSKE — ZAGREB

Br. U. Z. 4847/42.

ODPUSTNICA

Ravnateljstvo Ustaških redarstva Nezavisne države Hrvatske u Zagrebu — odpustilo je:

ROCHLITZ MIRKA

Ime i prezime osobe :

iz skupnog radnog logora u   Jasenovcu   na slobodu, pošto je

gore imenovana osoba, dosudjeno joj vrijeme prisilnog boravka u logoru u trajanju od   oprošteno

izdržala.

Ovo na znanje ovim putem svim vlastima u zemlji.

Dan   20.veljače 1942.   Upravitelj :

Ovu tiskanicu treba ispuniti u 2 primjerka. Obr. br. 13
Ova otpusnica se uručuje osobi, koju pušta na slobodu Ustaško redarstvo za grad Zagreb i V. Ž. Prigorje.

⬤ *My release form from the Jasenovac death camp, 20 February 1942*

6 RELEASE AND ESCAPE

I WEIGHED 44 KILOS when I was released from Jasenovac on 20 February 1942. At 1.8 metres tall, I was practically a walking skeleton— except that I could barely walk. My toes were so badly frostbitten that I was reduced to a slow limp. Uncle Oskar was only in marginally better condition, perhaps because he had been in the camp for a few days less than I had. Aunt Camilla had been interned in Stara Gradiška, a women's camp, where conditions had not been as terrible as in Jasenovac. She immediately organized our nursing back to health; she devoted herself to Oskar, while I was taken in by the family of Kurt Asner, a close friend who had been my schoolmate when I attended high school in Zagreb the previous year.

The Asners—father, mother, and sons Freddy and Kurt—were still living in their lovely apartment in the centre of Zagreb, even though they were Jewish. They enjoyed a sort of reprieve from persecution because Mr. Asner's position as managing director of a vegetable oil plant was considered vital to the Croatian economy. They were permitted to keep their property and continued living their lives practically undisturbed, free even from the obligation to wear the yellow star. The entire family was extremely kind and welcoming, taking me in without hesitation and doing their best to nurse me back to health.

My most serious ailment was frostbite. My fingers and toes— especially my toes—were completely numb and had started to turn black. Dr. Rechnitzer, the physician whose clandestine lectures on Einstein and Freud had so inspired me a few months earlier (and who, fortunately, was still alive and in Zagreb), was called in. His first diagnosis was that both my big toes would have to be amputated. He decided, however, to make a last-ditch attempt to save them, prescribing a long succession of alternating hot and cold baths, accompanied by careful massaging. Miraculously, the treatment worked. He succeeded in saving my toes but had to cut out part of my left heel—although this later had no effect on my ability to walk.

I stayed in bed for four or five weeks, mostly sleeping and eating. The only readily available food was horse sausages, which became the staple of my recovery. Mrs. Asner made sure that I ate as much as I wanted during the day and left several horse sausage sandwiches and glasses of milk by my bedside for the night. Hunger pangs would wake me up every two or three hours; I would devour a sandwich, gulp down a glass of milk—without getting out of bed—and then go back to sleep. By the end of five or six weeks my weight had returned to normal.

Uncle Oskar also recovered, as did Aunt Camilla. We began to piece together the story behind our incredible release. It turned out that we owed our lives first and foremost to Uncle Ferdinand.

When Camilla, Oskar, and I were arrested by the Ustashe in January 1942, Uncle Ferdinand was already in relative safety in the Italian zone of occupation on the Croatian coast, with his brothers Julius and Robert. They were waiting for us to join them. When we did not appear, they realized we had been arrested. Somehow, Uncle Ferdinand knew that one of the highest-ranking Nazis in Croatia was an Austrian, a former head of the Austrian War Archives by the name of Edmund von Glaise-Horstenau. Uncle Ferdinand hoped that General von Glaise-Horstenau, who had spent years directing the archives, would be receptive to the fact that he was an Austrian war hero and a recipient of the *Goldene Tapfer-keitsmedaille*, the highest decoration for valour. He wrote a letter to the general, pleading for our lives; incredibly, the letter had the desired effect.

I learned from Aunt Camilla, who had been released two days before Uncle Oskar and me, that she had been met at Ustashe police headquarters by the general's adjutant, a Major Knehe. The major had told her that from now on we were under the personal protection of General von Glaise-Horstenau. We should not try to contact the general directly, but in case of need could reach Knehe at any time of night or day. He had given Camilla a special telephone number for this purpose and had instructed her to keep one or two Gentile friends informed at all times of our whereabouts. If we were arrested again by the Ustashe, these friends were to contact him, and the general would again intervene to have us released.

◄ *General von Glaise-Horstenau (left) with the Croatian dictator Pavelić. In his dress and demeanor, Pavelić is obviously aping Hitler*

Major Knehe had also explained that the general had not directly asked the Ustashe to release us from the camps, fearing that they would kill us immediately and inform him that we had died of "natural causes" or been killed while trying to escape. Glaise-Horstenau had instead requested that the Ustashe transport us back to Zagreb, implying that we were to be executed by the Germans—and then exerted his authority to have us freed.

An Ustashe document pertaining specifically to our release was found in the Croatian State Archives in the 1990s by Dr. Menachem Shelah, editor of the Yad Vashem volume on the Holocaust in Yugoslavia (the document, dated 20 February 1942, is now published online by the Jasenovac Memorial Site). Following is the second page of the two-page document:

It bears the stamp of the Ustashe "Jewish Section" and states that Uncle Oskar, Aunt Camilla, and I were being discharged by "free decision" of Ustashe commander Eugen Kvaternik, on the initiative and recommendation of the German army command in Zagreb.

A handwritten note in red ink at the bottom of the page says: *"Rochlitz and Stern have not been traced."* Fortunately, we were.

In 2000, during a visit to the Austrian War Archives in Vienna, I was received by Dr. Peter Broucek, the biographer of General von Glaise-Horstenau (*Ein General im Zwielicht*, Vienna: 1980). We opened Uncle Ferdinand's personal file and found his military service record, with its various citations for bravery. We also found a typed report, deposited by Uncle Ferdinand in 1937, describing a First World War battle in which he had taken part. In 1937, von Glaise-Horstenau had been director of those archives and a well-known historian of the First World War. It is therefore possible that the two were acquainted, which could explain— aside from the fact that he was a decorated war hero—why five years later Uncle Ferdinand felt he could appeal for help directly to von Glaise-Horstenau, and that the general might respond.

These were the circumstances of my release from Jasenovac, the camp from which practically no one came out alive. It is still difficult for me to come to terms with the fact that I owe my life to a Nazi general, a man who previously had been second only to Arthur Seyβ-Inquart in the Nazi party hierarchy in Austria. But it is undeniable that it was his intervention that saved me. I have never heard of anyone else being saved in this manner, and there is no doubt that it was a highly unusual, if not unique, exception. From 1941 to 1944, von Glaise-Horstenau was the Supreme Representative of the German army in Croatia and in that capacity certainly shared responsibility for the unspeakable atrocities committed both by the Germans themselves and by their Ustashe cohorts. At the same time, he also found it in him to respond to Uncle Ferdinand's appeal. Historical research has shown that von Glaise-Horstenau protested on several occasions, in writing, against the abominations committed by the Ustashe against civilians (although not Jews) in Croatia. He was arrested by the US Army in 1945 and committed suicide in prison a year later, after testifying at the Nuremberg trials.

Paradoxically—and tragically—the false sense of security that the general's intervention had procured was to become, eighteen months later, a contributing cause of the deaths of Camilla and Oskar and of Ferdinand himself.

But this was still the spring of 1942. Camilla, Oskar, and I had more or less recovered physically from our camp experience. It was time to decide what to do next. Although we had assurances from the general's adjutant that we were now under protection, we realized that Zagreb remained a death trap. We knew, for example, that our own relative, the lawyer Dr. Lavoslav Šik, had been released a first time from Jasenovac upon the intervention of one of his former clients, a German company, which had claimed that it still needed his services. Although he had been assured that he would no longer be persecuted, the Ustashe soon arrested him again and sent him back to Jasenovac. When a new request for his release was made, they answered that he was no longer alive. No one ever learned whether he was indeed already dead or whether the release request itself had prompted his murder. His fate was a lesson we could not ignore.

The only possible avenue of escape remained the Italian zone of occupation on the Dalmatian coast, so we resolved to make another attempt to enter it. Travel restrictions were as severe as ever, but we succeeded again in obtaining forged travel documents, *Propusnice*, which entitled us to travel from Zagreb to a small town in German-occupied southern Croatia, supposedly our usual place of residence. The direct railway link from Zagreb to that town was regularly blown up by the Resistance (Chetniks or Partisans), and travellers were therefore forced to make the journey in a roundabout way, which took them through the town of Split in the Italian zone of occupation. That was where Uncle Robert was waiting for us and where we planned to "disappear" and remain illegally.

The Italians had become alarmed by the large numbers of Jews seeking refuge in their zone of occupation and had tightened their regulations. Now one had to obtain a special visa even to transit through territory under their control. I volunteered to go to the Italian Consulate in Zagreb and apply for transit visas for the three of us. I remember telling the consular official that the visas were "for my aunt, my uncle, and myself." He had no hesitation in granting a visa to me and to Camilla (whose papers still bore the surname from her previous, fictitious marriage)—but he refused one to Uncle Oskar on the grounds that "Oskar Stern" was a Jewish name. I was quite puzzled by his reasoning: if my uncle was Jewish, wasn't there a good chance that I and my aunt might also be Jewish? But the official asked no questions, and I went away with the clear impression that he was trying to apply his instructions as leniently as he could, refusing visas only when he felt he had no choice.

I went home very pleased with myself, even though I had obtained only two out of three visas. I was satisfied with the way I had dealt with the consular official, entirely on my own. The sense of achievement must have put quite a spring in my step, because when I arrived home, my pockets were empty: the documents had fallen out along the way. I was gripped by despair. It had been so difficult—and costly—to obtain them, and what would we do now? I raced out of the house and carefully retraced my steps. To my immense relief, I found the papers lying untouched on the sidewalk.

Despite Uncle Oskar's lack of an Italian transit visa, the three of us decided to attempt to enter the Italian zone. We were encouraged by the knowledge that the Italian border guards had the authority to issue transit visas on the spot, and in any case, we had no alternative. I said goodbye to the wonderful Asners and readied myself for departure. (All the Asners survived the war, except for Mr. Asner, who shortly afterwards was arrested and murdered in Jasenovac.)

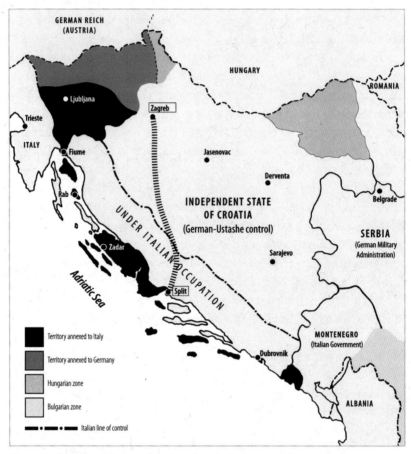

The route of pur planned escape from Zagreb to the Italian zone of occupation

One morning in June 1942, we boarded the train for Split. It was early evening when the train stopped at a checkpoint manned by the *Carabinieri* (Italian military police) on the demarcation line between the Ustashe-controlled zone and the Italian-controlled zone of Croatia. I hopped off and made straight for the command hut, where the young corporal in charge impressed me as bored and sleepy and—more important—completely uninterested in verifying identities. He stamped a transit visa onto my uncle's papers without question, and we were able to continue on to Split.

The train entered the Split railway station at about ten in the evening. It was the last stop on the line, and everyone had to get off. Our objective was to stay in Split, where Uncle Robert was waiting for us, but we knew that the Italians were on the lookout for refugees and that we would have to proceed carefully.

Passengers were being permitted to alight from the train from one door only, and Italian soldiers were checking all travel documents. I edged my way to the front of the line and saw that only residents of Split were being allowed to pass unhindered; the papers of those holding transit visas, like ours, were being withheld. The Italians were going to escort those passengers directly to the harbour (which was across the street from the railway station) and return the papers to them only after they were securely on board a boat departing their occupation zone.

I edged my way back to Camilla and Oskar. We quickly discussed this unexpected complication and concluded that our only chance was to attempt a ruse. We separated and mingled with the alighting passengers. I got off the train first and told the soldiers, mostly in sign language, that I lived in Split and that my parents, who were still on the train, had my documents. They let me pass. Uncle Oskar stepped off the train a few moments later and tried to explain that he lived in Split and that it was his wife farther back who had his documents—and they let him by. Finally, Aunt Camilla alighted with the last group of passengers and claimed that her husband had already presented her papers. The Italian soldiers—who seemed anything but motivated, and probably did not even understand what she was saying—simply waved her by.

As agreed, we reunited near the station's main exit. To our dismay, we were confronted with a new obstacle: all passengers were being obliged to leave through this exit and to show their papers to Italian guards, who this time were checking them far more thoroughly. After brief consultation, we agreed that it would be foolhardy to attempt the same ploy again; we needed time to think of something. We entered the small station restaurant and sat down as nonchalantly as we could—it was past 11 p.m., and we were anxious to avoid attracting attention. After weighing the situation, we decided that I—since I spoke Serbo-Croatian better than my aunt or uncle—would try to strike up a casual conversation with one of the two waiters, a middle-aged Croat. We guessed, and hoped, that he might be more concerned with daily bread for his family than with politics. I cautiously addressed him. He immediately understood that we were refugees and, when I saw that his reaction was not unfriendly, I came directly to the point: I asked him if he could help us get out of the station without having to show papers. I am fairly certain that I did not offer him compensation, nor did he request any. He seemed quite compassionate, and he willingly suggested a way. The station restaurant would remain open all night, he told me; we should spend the whole night sitting and napping unobtrusively at our table, as though we were waiting for an early train. A curfew for civilians was in force in Split between midnight and dawn, so spending the night in the restaurant would not necessarily arouse suspicion. There was a door leading directly from the restaurant to the street, which the Italians did not guard directly but watched from a distance, from their position at the main exit. Early in the morning they would be too busy with traffic through the main exit to pay much attention to the restaurant exit: at that time of day, the restaurant's customers were mainly local residents who stopped by for their breakfast coffee. We should mingle with the breakfasting locals and then walk out of the restaurant exit at intervals, without our luggage, and stroll away. Later, we would be able to send a local porter for our luggage.

That waiter helped us out of a tough spot. His advice proved entirely reliable, and all three of us got out of the station in precisely the way he suggested. We were now illegal residents in territory controlled by Italy, a founding partner of the Axis. For the first time, however, we felt that we were outside the immediate clutches of the Germans and the Ustashe. Or so we hoped.

7 SPLIT

UNCLE ROBERT HAD RENTED TWO ROOMS for us in an old mansion on the Marijan Hill, overlooking the town of Split. During peacetime the beautiful Dalmatian coast had been a favourite destination for holiday makers from central and southern Europe; now, under Italian military occupation and with tourism at a standstill, plenty of rental accommodation was available.

Our landlord was a frail, sickly old man, who lived with his much younger wife and two pretty daughters. They were part of a well-established local family impoverished by the war, and they rented two rooms to us while continuing to live in the rest of their large home. Although they were well educated and had once been quite wealthy, they were in many respects typical inhabitants of the Dalmatian coast: ethnic Croats and devout Catholics, with strong ties to Italian culture. The region of Dalmatia had for centuries been closely linked to Italy, in particular to the Venetian Republic, and Split prided itself in being the birthplace of Diocletian, one of the great Roman emperors. I was struck by the attachment of our landlords to Italian culture, which they considered richer and more sophisticated than their own; they read mostly Italian literature and sometimes spoke Italian among themselves. Yet like many Dalmatians, they faced a moral dilemma: as Croats, they were strongly against the forced imposition of Italian rule (the Fascists had annexed Split to Italy and renamed it Spalato) and kept their contacts with the Italian occupiers to a bare minimum; at the same time, they disagreed with the extremist policies of the barbarous Ustashe regime that claimed to represent them. As we grew to know one another, a deep bond of mutual respect and understanding developed between our two families. They empathized with the hardships we had gone through and with our anxieties for the future; we appreciated the way they navigated the treacherous waters into which the war had thrown them, doing their best not to endanger their present and future while seeking to live at peace with their consciences.

I, naturally, was particularly interested in the sisters. The elder of the two was in her early twenties, a few years older than I. She was a strikingly beautiful young woman with a fiery and independent temperament. She dreamed of becoming an opera singer, a profession for which she unquestionably possessed all the required attributes but one—a good voice. This did not deter her. She practised with discipline and determination, belting out scales and exercises at all hours of the day and night (unfortunately, particularly at night). We sometimes found it grating and exasperating but had to take it in good spirits; after all, we were in Split illegally and did not want to attract undue attention by changing lodgings.

I became good friends with the younger daughter, Carmen, who was seventeen and a half. I was enthusiastic at this opportunity to finally strike up a friendship with a girl of my age, particularly since Carmen was pretty, intelligent, charming, and lovely in every respect. She was already engaged to a budding local poet some ten years her senior, but despite this fact—or perhaps because of it (he was a little too old and serious for her)—our friendship blossomed. We would spend hours leaning against the fence in front of her house, talking about every imaginable subject and simply delighting in each other's company. Our relationship remained platonic, and her fiancé and parents never voiced any objections to it. That summer friendship with Carmen was as sincere and rewarding a relationship as I have ever known.

After the horrors we had experienced under Ustashe rule, life in Split was paradise. Although I was a little apprehensive at first—Fascist Italy was after all the main ally of Nazi Germany—I soon realized, to my amazement, that the Italian occupation troops represented no threat to us. There were no anti-Semitic restrictions, including no obligation to wear the yellow star, and the Italians seemed to make no effort to track down and identify illegal refugees. Most important, they prevented local members of the Ustashe from harassing anyone, Jew or Serb.

Still, there was considerable tension in the air. The attitude of our landlords was shared by most of the local people, who resented and were hostile to the Fascist occupation and annexation. Although only a small minority would have actually preferred the Ustashe regime, the opposition to the forced imposition of Italian identity was practically unanimous. This was perhaps one of the reasons why the occupying Italians felt unthreatened by and even comfortable with the Jewish refugees; we were all profoundly grateful for their humane attitude and protection and very much wanted them to stay, knowing full well that their presence was the only barrier between a brutal, certain death and a chance of survival.

For the first time in over a year, I felt free. Despite my illegal status, I went for walks into town with Carmen, strolled up and down the *Corso* (promenade), went to the beach, sat in outdoor cafés, and often went to the local cinema, which screened mainly Italian films (Vittorio De Sica was the young romantic idol, Beniamino Gigli the leading romantic tenor). Our only real problem was a scarcity of food; although there was usually an abundance of fruit, the availability of other foods was limited and irregular. But we never really went hungry, and we received some supplies and assistance from the local Jewish community.

One day in June 1942, a violent anti-Semitic attack did take place. Uncle Robert, who was present, told me what had happened. He had gone to Friday evening prayers in the ancient Split synagogue when suddenly a gang of thugs had burst in. To everyone's surprise, these were Italians, members of the local Fascist militia. They attacked the members of the congregation, robbed them of their valuables, and beat up several of them, including Uncle Robert, who was badly bruised. They ransacked the premises and set them on fire. A number of nearby Jewish homes and shops were also plundered, with the participation of some Italian soldiers as well as firemen and police. It was only the intervention of the Italian military police that put an end to the violence.

> *According to Yad Vashem's "History of the Holocaust in Yugoslavia," the local Italian military command strongly disapproved of this attack. It had supposedly been "provoked" by the defacing of the marble plaque commemorating Italy's occupation of Split. The involvement of rank-and-file Italian soldiers prompted the commanding general to threaten them with court martial, to cancel all leaves until further notice, and to issue strict orders forbidding future participation in "political demonstrations."*

Also, the Fascist militia was forbidden to repeat such actions. As far as I know, nothing of the kind happened again. Uncle Robert recovered completely from his injuries.

It was obvious that in reaching Italian-held territory, we had considerably increased our chances of survival. My mother, however, was still in Derventa, in Croatian territory controlled by the Ustashe and Germans. While we were planning our escape from Zagreb in June, we had written to her, pleading with her to join us. But she had replied that she could not abandon Mrs. Löbl, her mother-in-law. Before his arrest and deportation to Jasenovac, Mr. Löbl had made my mother promise that she would never abandon his mother—whom I remember as an unpleasant, cantankerous old woman, although my intense dislike for her son undoubtedly influenced my attitude towards her. Mr. Löbl had meanwhile been murdered and my mother, naturally, felt obligated to honour her commitment. She had considered the possibility of joining us together with Mrs. Löbl, but had decided against it, as her mother-in-law was simply too ill and feeble to embark on such a difficult train journey. Thus, when we escaped to the Italian zone, my mother had stayed behind. Once we were safely in Split, however, we continued to write to her, begging her to join us. Finally, towards the end of July 1942, she agreed. She wrote that she had found a reliable local family with whom to leave Mrs. Löbl and was now ready to attempt the journey.

My mother required forged travel documents, similar to the ones we had used when entering the Italian zone. We located someone in Split who was able to supply them, a meeting was arranged in a local café, and I was sent to pick them up. For some reason, I could not find the woman who was to sell me the documents; either I had misunderstood where I was to meet her or I had arrived at the wrong time. Only on our second appointment, a few days later, did I locate her and succeed in obtaining the documents. We mailed them immediately to Derventa, but by then it was too late: my mother—and her mother-in-law—had disappeared.

A short while later, I heard from my mother for the last time. Incredibly, she had been able to write a postcard from the German train in which she was being deported. She wrote that she was being sent to a concentration camp but not to worry, she would survive and we would meet again after all this was over.

There are records of several transports from Yugoslavia to Auschwitz in August 1942. My mother and her mother-in-law must have been on one of them. They did not survive.

I still blame myself for missing that first appointment; if things had gone differently, perhaps my mother would have received the travel documents in time. It is a doubt that will never cease to torment me.

‹ *Irene Rochlitz (1898—1942)*

When I think of my mother, murdered in Auschwitz at the age of forty-four, it is almost a consolation to remember that, as I write these lines several decades later, she would almost certainly have died of old age by now.

But what of her murderers? It gives me no peace that my mother, a young, good, kind, intelligent, loving person, who never harmed anyone, and who enjoyed life, was murdered in cold blood in Auschwitz, together with so many others—while her murderers may have enjoyed a self-righteous life of pleasure and prosperity for years afterwards, without punishment or even remorse.

I sometimes think it would be best if everyone who lived through the Holocaust, victims and criminals, were already dead, so that humanity could live free of the direct horror of that experience, and of the direct guilt for it.

8 NOVI

AT THE END OF AUGUST 1942, the Italian *Questura* (police) in Split announced an amnesty. Illegal refugees who turned themselves in and registered with the Italian authorities would not be arrested or deported, but relocated to other areas under Italian control. We eagerly seized this opportunity. We had heard that in the wake of previous amnesties the Italians had transferred many refugees to the Italian mainland, and we ardently hoped they would do the same with us. As the Germans and Ustashe were dangerously near the Italian-occupied Adriatic coast, there was a real risk that a change in the political or military situation might once again put us at their mercy. According to the rumour mill, which churned constantly, the Jewish refugees transferred to the Italian mainland had been settled in small villages, mainly in the north of the country. The marvellous (to my ears) term the Italians employed to describe the refugees' status was *confino libero* (free confinement). Conditioned as I was by my Germanic education, this concept baffled me. How could someone be confined and free at the same time? I soon found out: the refugees were indeed confined to the boundaries of the villages to which they had been assigned, but they remained free to go about their lives within them. They were lodged in private homes, families were allowed to remain together, and refugees received the same rations as the local population—which, we heard, was usually sympathetic. The only serious restriction the refugees faced was the obligation to report periodically to the local police station, to show that they had not absconded. How wonderful it would be, I thought, if we too were transferred to the safety of a secluded Italian village, to live out the war in peace and tranquility, as far as possible from the horrors of the Balkans.

Uncle Robert, who had been in Split since December 1941, had benefited from a previous amnesty and was therefore already "legal," as were Uncles Ferdinand and Julius, who were living undisturbed in the Italian-occupied town of Metković, to the south. Therefore, only Aunt Camilla, Uncle Oskar, and I reported to the Split *Questura* in August 1942. Our hopes to be transferred to Italy, however, were immediately dashed. We were told that reporting refugees would be concentrated in various locations along the Dalmatian coast, in areas under Italian control but not formally annexed to Italy. There was no possibility that we would be sent to the Italian mainland.

A few days later, I bade farewell to my dear friend Carmen and climbed into an Italian military truck, together with Aunt Camilla and Uncles Oskar and Robert. We were driven for hours along the winding coastal road, until the truck finally stopped in a small village, Novi Vinodolski, some 300 kilometres north of Split.

The voyage from Split to Novi Vinodolski, where the Italians placed us under "free confinement"

Novi, as everyone called it, had been a popular summer resort during peacetime; with tourism now at a complete standstill, there was plenty of room to accommodate refugees. We were assigned two rooms in a small cottage and got our first taste of *confino libero*. The Italians granted us complete freedom of movement within Novi, the only restrictions being the observation of the nightly curfew, which applied to the local residents as well, and the obligation to report periodically to the *Carabinieri* post in the village.

Novi was very small and dull compared to Split, and I soon began to feel bored and isolated. As the local population was not particularly friendly, I kept my dealings with them to a bare minimum. I could sense a coldness bordering on hostility emanating from them, perhaps because we were not the moneyed holiday makers to whom they had been accustomed. I also got the impression that they were more sympathetic to the Ustashe regime than the more cosmopolitan citizens of Split. On several occasions I overheard expressions of outright support for the murderous Croatian Fascists.

My stay in Novi would have been an unhappy one had it not been for an extraordinary encounter that was to have a profound effect on my life. Within a few days of my arrival, I began to notice strange comings and goings in the vicinity of a small villa not far from our cottage. Animals of every kind, agricultural and domestic, were being taken to it at practically all hours of the day. Intrigued, I approached the villa and spent the next few days watching the procession of animals. I soon met the couple who lived there: Vlado Horvatić, a man of about thirty, and his pretty wife. Despite the big difference in our ages (I was not yet eighteen), we quickly became friends. I learned that Vlado had been a student of veterinary medicine at Zagreb University; when the Ustashe seized power, he had abandoned his studies and fled with his wife to Italian-held territory. When we got to know each other better, Vlado confided that he had been forced to abandon his studies because he was half Jewish (his wife was Catholic).

There were no veterinarians in Novi or anywhere else in the vicinity. Word spread quickly of Vlado's training and abilities, and soon villagers and peasants from miles around were bringing him their cattle, pigs, sheep, goats, horses, chickens, cats, dogs, and birds for treatment. As Vlado had abandoned his studies before his final exams, he was not formally qualified and therefore could not accept money for his services.

Fortunately, his patients' owners always brought along gifts with them—most of them edible—which he often shared with me.

Vlado spoke with a severe stutter, and his manner could sometimes be brusque and aloof. Some people found him unpleasant and even arrogant, although it was obvious to me that this behaviour stemmed from his disability. The most remarkable transformation would take place, however, whenever he dealt with animals: his stutter would miraculously disappear, enabling him to speak with confidence and fluency, in a steady, soothing voice. Dogs, cats, cows, parrots, and even mice would suddenly appear to understand Serbo-Croatian. They would nuzzle up to him affectionately and allow him to tend their wounds or give them injections without ever resisting or biting. Vlado would sometimes use his moustache to elicit the animals' confidence: he would slowly approach their snouts and rub his whiskers gently against theirs, sniffing and snorting the way they did while emitting short, reassuring grunts. The effect he had on animals—and they on him—was riveting to watch.

I spent hours observing Vlado at work. As I had been hoping to study medicine after the war, aside from the sheer pleasure of the experience, I thought it might also come in useful. To my delight, after a short while Vlado allowed me to assist him while he performed minor operations. I was thrilled at the trust this extraordinary person placed in me.

There were no more than a dozen refugees living in Novi, none of them my age. Therefore, even when Vlado was not working as a vet, I would spend my time with him and his wife, who were as socially isolated as I. The three of us became inseparable; we would go swimming together, play table tennis, or listen to Vlado's collection of American jazz records. Sometimes we would make cardboard cut-outs of the silhouettes of jazz musicians playing their instruments and paste them on the walls of the house. We often just sat on the rocks near their villa, which was perched on a cliff, gazing out over the Adriatic while we talked about our hopes.

We all shared the dream of one day making it to the freedom and safety of America, and we tried to imagine the excitement of living there. At the same time, deep down, we doubted that we would ever reach its shores.

The tranquil, pleasant weeks I spent in Novi were marred by my great anxiety over my mother's fate. Fear began to set in that I might never see her again. I felt helpless and tried to avoid thinking of what she might be going through; I did not yet know that she was already dead.

I was less worried about my brother Max, although I had not heard from him for nearly a year and a half. The last I knew, he was in England, undergoing agricultural training under the auspices of a Zionist organization. Communications with England had been interrupted since April 1941, when the Axis invaded Yugoslavia, but I was comforted by the knowledge that at least he was free in the West.

The Italian garrison in Novi was very small, only a handful of soldiers. We had practically no contact with them, as my uncles and aunt spoke no Italian and were not sociable by nature. But I had picked up some Italian by now and could communicate with them when necessary. This was useful mainly during the visits of one of the corporals stationed in the village. About once a week, he would come to see us, bringing us bread and marmalade from his personal weekly ration. He wanted no compensation beyond our heartfelt thanks. I felt that these small acts of kindness— which obviously meant so much to us—meant a great deal to him too. They were his way of defending his own humanity against the brutalization of war. He once took me aside and told me that he was moved to help us because Aunt Camilla reminded him of his mother. Other refugee families, particularly those with young, attractive women among their members, enjoyed more attention than we did from the gregarious, extroverted Italians, who were obviously uncomfortable in those inhospitable surroundings and who missed their homes and families.

The Italians were always courteous and friendly, but it worried us that they claimed not to know what was in store for us. Indeed, they were telling the truth: neither they nor we could have imagined that our fate, and that of some four thousand other Jewish refugees under Italian occupation in Croatia, was at that moment the subject of intense diplomatic activity between the German and Italian governments.

> *A startling document from the archives of the Italian Foreign Ministry illustrates what was going on. An internal report to Mussolini, dated 21 August 1942, informed "Il Duce" that the Germans were requesting Italian collaboration in the deportation of thousands of Jews from the Italian zones of occupation in Croatia. The report indicated clearly that those thousands would be destined for elimination and liquidation (the underlining in the document is mine).*

Ministero degli Affari Esteri
Gabinetto

APPUNTO PER IL DUCE

Bismarck ha dato comunicazione di un telegramma a firma
Ribbentrop con il quale questa Ambasciata di Germania viene
richiesta di provocare istruzioni alle competenti Autorità
Militari italiane in Croazia affinchè anche nelle zone di
nostra occupazione possano essere attuati i provvedimenti
divisati da parte germanica e croata per un trasferimento
in massa degli ebrei di Croazia nei territori orientali.

Bismarck ha affermato che si tratterebbe di varie mi-
gliaia di persone ed ha lasciato comprendere che tali provvedimenti tenderebbero, in pratica, alla loro dispersione
ed eliminazione.

L'Ufficio competente fa presente che segnalazioni della R.Legazione a Zagabria inducono a ritenere che, per desi
derio germanico, che trova consenziente il Governo ustascia
la questione della liquidazione degli ebrei in Croazia sta-
rebbe ormai entrando in una fase risolutiva.

Si sottopone, Duce, quanto precede per le Vostre deci-
sioni.

Roma, 21 agosto 1942-XX

Mussolini was evidently not perturbed, because he scribbled
"Nulla Osta" (No objection) in the upper right-hand corner,
signing with his characteristic stylized "M." He had effectively
sentenced us to death. Historical research published after the
war has shown that high-ranking Italian soldiers and diplomats
reacted sharply to Mussolini's authorization of our deportation.
They vehemently protested that such an action would be contrary
to Italian values and damaging to Italy's prestige. Faced with firm

opposition within his own ranks to collaborating in the "Final Solution," Mussolini was obliged to relent. The Italian army and Foreign Ministry then coordinated their efforts to save us, adopting delaying tactics and inventing excuses to placate the Germans.

We had no idea that our fate was of interest to anyone. It was therefore very alarming when, on 1 November 1942, the *Carabinieri* knocked on our door at five o'clock in the morning. Politely but firmly, they gave us one hour to pack our belongings and to prepare ourselves for transfer. I asked the *Carabiniere* in charge where we were being taken and was deeply troubled by his insistence that he did not know. But we had no choice and readied ourselves to leave.

At six o'clock an open truck drew up in front of our cottage, carrying a few other refugees and their luggage. I tried to question the driver about our destination, to no avail. With heavy hearts, we climbed onto the truck. Two more vehicles then appeared, bearing all the other Jewish refugees from Novi—except for my friend Vlado, who evidently was not registered as a Jew.

We set out in a northerly direction. The little convoy drove through the town of Crikvenica, where several more trucks bearing refugees joined it, and continued northwards. We were aware that soon there would be a fork in the road: if the trucks turned right, the Italians were delivering us to the Ustashe or the Germans, thus abandoning us to certain death; if the trucks turned left, we were remaining in the Italian zone and possibly being taken to Italy itself. As we neared that fork, the tension among us rose rapidly, nearly turning to panic; the refusal of the *Carabinieri* to provide any information or to reassure us in any way had made us fear the worst.

I vividly remember the enormous wave of relief that swept through us as our convoy turned left at the fork. We began to hope we might even be on our way to Italy. As the truck trundled on, I began to fantasize that I was already in a remote Italian village, far from the Ustashe and the Germans, studying English and Italian and awaiting the war's end in seclusion and safety.

But that was not to be. After driving on for a few more kilometres, our convoy turned into the village of Kraljevica, very near the Italian border but still in the Italian zone. The trucks drove through a gate in a tall barbed-wire fence and stopped. It took us only a few moments to realize that we were now enclosed in what ominously resembled a concentration camp, complete with wooden barracks, watchtowers, armed guards, and searchlights.

9 KRALJEVICA

MY FIRST LOOK AT THE ITALIAN CAMP for Civil Internees in Kraljevica brought back sinister recent memories. There were four large wooden barracks and eight smaller ones clustered together in a sloping field, already turned into a muddy bog by the autumn rains. Powerful searchlights beamed down on us from the ramparts of the ancient castle that loomed over the camp.

When our little convoy drove in on 1 November 1942, there were already hundreds of people milling around. As we climbed down from the trucks, Italian soldiers divided the men from the women. Men were assigned to the four large barracks (which, I later learned, had previously served as stables for the Yugoslav cavalry), while the smaller barracks were designated to house the women and children. As I carried my luggage to my barracks, I noticed that a tall barbed-wire fence, patrolled by sentries, surrounded the entire camp, and that a fence also ran between the barracks, dividing the men's from the women's quarters.

But the resemblance to Jasenovac ended there. It quickly became obvious that this was a concentration camp where the inmates were meant to survive. The camp guards were ordinary Italian soldiers, not members of the Fascist militia, and their outlook on the world patently did not include hating Jews. Their hatred, if they harboured any, was directed against the war and the havoc it was wreaking on their lives. After a very brief period of caution, I came to take their civility for granted.

This was still a concentration camp, however, and there were hardships to be faced. The primary discomfort was overcrowding. As every inmate was entitled to an individual bunk and straw mattress, to accommodate all of us the Italians had crammed row upon row of double-decker bunks into every available space in the barracks, leaving practically no room to move.

▲ *The Italian camp in the shadow of Kraljevica Castle, where*
I was interned in November 1942

Another difficulty was the shortage of food. We were provided only with reduced Italian army rations, consisting of a cup of black liquid (bearing some resemblance to coffee) in the morning and a minestrone-like broth containing a lump of pasta, beans, or other vegetables at noon and in the evening. We also received a small daily ration of bread and 100 grams a week of either salami or Parmesan cheese, which we tried to stretch out over two or three days. I would try to make the Parmesan cheese last a little longer by roasting its hard and unappetizing outer crust over a hot stove until it became soft and edible. The task of ladling out the broth from the huge, steaming cauldrons was assigned to inmates on a rotation basis. When I lined up for a meal, I was always very hungry. As my turn approached, I would concentrate all my mental energies on the person distributing the food, in an attempt to mesmerize that person into scooping down to the bottom of the cauldron, where the precious, more nourishing solids usually settled. I sometimes got the impression that this technique actually worked, although what undoubtedly worked better was being on friendly terms with whoever was holding the ladle. Unfortunately this was not always possible, as these people were rotated frequently.

About 1,200 Jewish refugees were interned in Kraljevica (or Porto Re, as the Italians called it) in early November 1942. Most of them were from the former Yugoslavia, but there were also Austrians, Czechs, Hungarians, and other nationalities. The camp population did not represent a normal cross-section of society, Jewish or otherwise. A disproportionately high number were middle-aged and elderly (when the Ustashe took power, the first to be murdered were young people), and the level of education as well as pre-war economic standing was well above average. Many were doctors, lawyers, teachers, industrialists, bank directors, or businessmen.

Nothing had been confiscated from us on arrival—we had not even been searched—and some inmates still possessed cash or gold coins. They were able to supplement the meagre camp diet by ordering in food from the townspeople of Kraljevica. I sometimes watched enviously as wealthier inmates had delicious-looking cooked meals delivered for their private consumption. Although this commerce was technically in breach of camp regulations, the Italians found a way to tolerate it by approving it on "medical grounds." The bellies of the rest of us were never quite full, but we never suffered from real malnutrition. Ironically, for some inmates these conditions even turned out to be beneficial. Some overweight, middle-aged refugees, who had long suffered from a variety of physical ailments and had never mustered the discipline to respect a diet, were "miraculously" cured in the camp. The scarcity of food and the very liquid, non-fat diet caused them to slim down rapidly, with the result that many of their health disorders—in particular liver ailments—simply vanished together with their bulging waistlines.

A few days after I arrived, elections were held in the camp. The Italians had requested that we choose a three-member Governing Committee to represent us in all dealings with them. A list of candidates was drawn up, all adult inmates—male and female—were given the right to vote, and with the assistance of the Italians, a secret ballot was organized. In the winter of 1942, the "Kraljevica Camp for Civil Internees" was probably the only entity in all of Axis-occupied Europe with democratically elected representatives. Once we had elected the three, however, the camp commander insisted on ceremoniously "appointing" them to the Governing Committee.

The fence dividing the men's from the women's quarters was soon dismantled, and two additional wooden barracks were erected, one for mothers with small children, and another to house the infirmary, camp administration, camp court, a barber shop, a tailor shop, and a chapel for Gentile spouses and converts to Christianity (there were a few among us).

One of the centres of social activity, particularly at night, was the latrines. As our very liquid diet provoked a need to urinate frequently, nearly everyone—not only the aging and the incontinent—had to get out of bed at least once during the night for this purpose. Some kept night pots or bottles beside their bunks, but most preferred to stroll over to the shed where the latrines were situated. As a result, night-time traffic was constant and at times quite intense, which provided the opportunity to meet family members and friends along the way. At first, these encounters were awkward and even embarrassing. Central European Jews like ourselves were strongly conditioned against any allusions to physiological necessities, particularly in the presence of members of the opposite sex. With time, however, I overcame my inhibitions and began to look forward to the nightly routine of making my way to the latrines, bumping into friends, exchanging gossip for a while, and then sauntering back to bed.

The latrine barracks was divided into a men's and a women's section, the division consisting only of a wooden partition suspended between the ceiling and the floor, touching neither. Consequently, it was easy to hear voices and noises coming from the other side. One evening, someone on the ladies' side loudly let some wind. After a brief moment of embarrassed silence, a wit on the men's side inquired: "Is that you, Sara?" There was a roar of laughter, and the story spread like wildfire through the camp, becoming a favourite joke.

Another event centred on the latrines became a talking point for a while. One evening, the cash-stuffed wallet of one of the wealthier inmates fell into the latrine pit. He was very distressed and offered a substantial reward to anyone willing to venture down to retrieve it. After some hesitation, one young man decided to take the plunge. He was not particularly popular among us before his descent, and by the time he emerged, his popularity had plummeted even further. But he had earned his reward.

The latrines also provided us with an opportunity to appreciate the extent of the Italians' concern for our well-being. The camp was practically on the edge of the Adriatic Sea, and with the approach of winter, cold winds and heavy rains began to make our nightly excursions to the latrines more difficult. After some people complained that they had fallen ill because of their nightly exposure to the elements, we appealed to the camp commander for help. He responded at once, ordering his troops to construct covered wooden passageways that led directly from our barracks to the latrines. They were completed within a few days.

Sheltered from the inclement weather, we were able to pursue our nightly routine in relative comfort.

I—and everyone else—was puzzled by our sudden internment. What could it mean? Could this be a first step towards handing us over to the Ustashe and the Nazis, or were other forces at work? Throughout the war, US President Franklin D. Roosevelt was revered as a Messiah by practically all persecuted Jews in occupied Europe, and we were no exception. Thus, the prevalent theory making the rounds in Kraljevica was that Roosevelt in person was responsible for our humane treatment by the Italians; in return, he had probably promised to treat them leniently once the war—which the Allies were certain to win—was over.

In my conversations with Italian soldiers, I had often detected their sympathy towards the United States. Many had relatives living there or had dreamed of immigrating themselves. Like us, they viewed the United States as the Promised Land, and it was obvious that Mussolini's propaganda had not succeeded in persuading the Italians to hate the United States or to love the Germans.

It was a chilling disappointment for me to learn, years later, that the Allies—both American and British—could scarcely have been less concerned with our fate. According to some historians, the Italian soldiers and diplomats who protected us did so primarily for humanitarian reasons. They were horrified by the atrocities being committed by the Ustashe and were opposed to becoming accomplices in the Final Solution. As those Italians saw it, we had "taken refuge under the Italian flag" and they considered it contrary to their honour and reputation to abandon us. Other historians have suggested that the Italian protection of Jews in Croatia (as well as in France, Greece, and elsewhere) was primarily a political move, designed to enhance Italy's prestige, protect its economic interests, and strengthen its imperial aspirations. The truth may lie somewhere in between. What is clear, however, is that our arrest and concentration behind barbed wire in November 1942 was nothing less than an attempt to pull the wool over the Germans' eyes: they were to be induced into thinking that this might be a first step towards our deportation, while in reality the Italians' objective was the opposite. Towards the end of 1942, the commander of the Second Army in Croatia, General Mario Roatta, visited Kraljevica and met with our Governing Committee. Later, the committee members told us that according to

▲ *Venice, 1941—Italian Foreign Minister Ciano speaking at the ceremony marking the adherence of Croatia to the Axis. Seated at left, the Croatian dictator Ante Pavelić. Seated at right, German Foreign Minister Joachim von Ribbentrop. Circled: the Marquis d'Ajeta (l.) and Count Luca Pietromarchi (whose wife was of Jewish descent); these two senior Italian officials played a central role in thwarting our deportation. Pietromarchi, who became Italian Ambassador to the Soviet Union in the 1950s, left a detailed private diary in which he described the efforts he and others made to save us.*

Roatta, German pressure to hand us over was intense. The general had told them that he wished he could put all of us in a submarine for the next six months, until the storm over our heads subsided. In any case, Roatta had promised that as long as he was in command, no one would be permitted to touch us.

> *General Roatta was later accused of war crimes, for atrocities committed by troops under his command in Slovenia and Croatia against civilian populations. Under his orders, Italian soldiers had torched villages, tortured prisoners, executed hostages and imprisoned thousands of "rebellious" Slovenes: men, women, and*

children had been deported to concentration camps, where many perished from abuse, malnutrition, and disease. Roatta was apparently allowed to escape from his prison cell in Rome in 1945, thus preventing a trial that would have been politically embarrassing for the Italian government. He went into exile in Franco's Spain but later benefited from an amnesty and returned to Italy, where he died in 1968.

A number of officials in the Italian Foreign Ministry participated in the effort to circumvent Mussolini's agreement to hand us over to the Germans. According to the seminal study of this episode by the Israeli historian Daniel Carpi (Yad Vashem, 1977), pressure to protect us came from two other sources: the DELASEM, *an Italian Jewish refugee aid agency that repeatedly appealed to the Italian authorities to treat us humanely; and, astonishingly—at least to me—the Vatican. From the very beginning of our ordeals caused by anti-Jewish persecution, my family had deeply resented the Church's silence. In Vienna, we were distressed—although not really surprised—when Cardinal Innitzer welcomed the Nazis and encouraged his faithful to do likewise. Later, in Zagreb, the very visible association of Archbishop Stepinac with the Ustashe regime further disheartened us. I have little doubt that many of those who perpetrated atrocities interpreted the absence of explicit condemnation by Church leaders as acquiescence in their deeds. The Church had the moral authority to stay the hand of many murderers and chose not exercise it. The Vatican, for its part, has justified its silence by arguing that it was working behind the scenes to contain the persecution. I have always questioned the validity of this argument, considering it essentially an excuse for cowardice and bigotry. When evidence crops up, however, that substantiates Vatican claims, it is right to acknowledge it. The following document, which appears in Carpi's study, relates directly to us—the few thousand Jewish refugees under Italian occupation on the Croatian coast.*

It is a dispatch from Italy's Ambassador to the Vatican, Raffaele Guariglia, to his superior, Foreign Minister Ciano. The document is dated 5 November 1942, five days after we were rounded up and interned at Kraljevica. Guariglia reports that Vatican officials

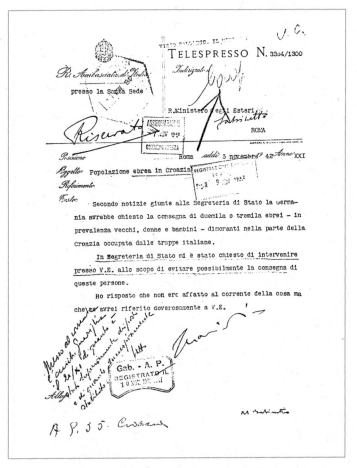

had learned of a German request that the Italians hand over two or three thousand Jews—mainly old people, women, and children—living under their occupation in Croatia. Guariglia conveys a Vatican request that the Italians refrain from doing so, "if possible." Historian Jonathan Steinberg writes in his book All or Nothing—The Axis and the Holocaust, 1941–43 (Routledge, 1990) that there is no evidence that Vatican intervention on behalf of the Jews affected Italian policy in the matter of consignment in October and November 1942. Nevertheless, he adds, Vatican influence was certainly "a presence in the background." To me, whether or not it was Vatican intervention that hindered our deportation, this tangible evidence that they did make an effort to help us makes a world of difference.

Inside the camp in Kraljevica, we tried to find comfort in General Roatta's reassurances to our Governing Committee that no harm would befall us. Yet we knew very well that the Fascists had introduced harsh anti-Semitic legislation in Italy in 1938. Italian Jews were not yet at risk of deportation and extermination (this occurred only after the collapse of Italy in September 1943), but they were already the victims of shameful discrimination and persecution. Although Italy had not extended its anti-Semitic legislation to its occupied territories, we were aware of our very shaky status: we were refugees from occupied Europe, most of whom had entered Italian-occupied territory illegally. War was raging, and we realized that we could not count on Italian protection indefinitely.

We felt at least temporarily safe, though, and tried to get on with our lives. Our Governing Committee began to raise funds for the purchase of extra food supplies from outside the camp by levying taxes on the wealthier inmates. It also set about organizing a school, with both primary and secondary divisions. Although I had finished only the eighth grade and then missed two years of schooling because of the war, I was admitted to the eleventh grade—which was then combined with the twelfth for lack of pupils. Under the circumstances, this makeshift little high school boasted a teaching staff with extraordinary credentials. Many of my teachers were prominent former university professors who, rather than sit around all day doing nothing, eagerly seized this opportunity to teach again. The language of instruction was Serbo-Croatian, but we also studied Latin, Greek, and Italian. We did not study English, which the commander would not have tolerated, or German, which we could not have stomached. There were no more than a dozen students in my class, with very few textbooks among us, but nothing could dampen our enthusiasm to get on with our studies, which had been truncated by the war.

Since fleeing Vienna over four years earlier, I had led the disrupted life of a refugee on the run, unable to socialize normally with young people my age, let alone forge meaningful friendships with them. A long period of social isolation is difficult to cope with at any age, but for a teenager it can be practically unbearable. My joy at finally being back in the company of my peers was therefore immense. I was thrilled at this opportunity to make both female and male friends, and some of the ties I formed in the camp would last for years.

My best friend was Ivo Herzer, who was eighteen, like me. Ivo was originally from Zagreb and was in the camp with his mother and father. Although we had many interests in common, the bond that united us most profoundly was the dream of a new life in the United States. Determined that someday, somehow, we would make it (we both eventually did), we began preparing for our future life as best we could. Our immediate objective was to learn English. We succeeded in laying our hands on an English–German pocket dictionary and systematically set about memorizing all of its 12,000 entries, from A to Z. This rudimentary little dictionary provided only one German translation for each English word and gave no indication at all as to what the correct English pronunciation might be. We often had to guess, therefore, how words were pronounced, and probably produced some very funny sounds in the process. But these minor drawbacks presented no obstacle to us: we ploughed with methodical determination through the volume's tattered pages, convinced that we were cleverly preparing for our future. I doubt, however, that a native speaker would have understood a word of our English.

Our Governing Committee began to promulgate a series of internal rules and regulations. It decreed, for example, that those who were able to work would carry out duties for the benefit of the camp and its inmates. My work duty, as a student at the camp school, was to help carry the large cauldrons from the kitchen to the barracks at mealtimes. We would eat sitting on our bunks or, when the weather was fine, outdoors.

Although no one was required to perform services of any kind for the Italian army, we were expected to stand smartly to attention whenever the Italian flag was raised or lowered. We obliged, usually with some giggling and shuffling of feet, although the camp commander, who was often present at this little ceremony, did not seem to mind. He was an army captain of about forty-five, always immaculately dressed, who sported an impressively well-tended goatee (Italian officers each had an individual orderly who cared for their personal needs). A true gentleman of the old school, he always behaved in a civilized manner towards us—although it did no harm that he soon became infatuated with one of our fellow inmates, a lovely young woman, who seemed flattered by his attentions. When we celebrated Passover, in the spring of 1943, we organized a traditional Seder meal, which he and members of his staff attended as our guests of honour.

▲ *Kraljevica inmates wearing Italian*
uniforms, 1942–43.

All the Italian military personnel we encountered in Kraljevica, including those who were not in love with detainees, treated us decently. It was not uncommon for officers to take leisurely strolls through the camp, making the occasional remark about order to be kept or garbage to be removed. I noticed that their comments were often thinly veiled pretexts to strike up friendly conversations with us, on a wide variety of topics. I understood that they were bored and lonely and simply looking for someone to talk to. In all of Axis-occupied Europe, we Jews were worthy only of death; here in this godforsaken camp on the shores of the Adriatic, we were sought-after conversation companions.

The Italians continually sought to improve our living conditions. They provided us with medicines, blankets, kitchen utensils, and even pieces of military clothing.

Only one Italian ever behaved discourteously towards us, and unfortunately, he may have paid dearly for it. A certain Lieutenant Santangeli sometimes addressed inmates less politely than his fellow officers, on occasion even raising his voice and employing harsh language. One day, an inmate was sufficiently offended by Santangeli's behaviour to register a formal complaint with the camp commander. Within days, the lieutenant was transferred out of the camp. There was a subsequent rumour that he had been dispatched to the Russian Front—although I sincerely hope this is untrue, as it would have constituted disproportionately harsh punishment, which he did not deserve.

Once it had dealt with our primary needs, our Governing Committee turned its attention to more trivial pursuits. An "internal security service" was established consisting of only one inmate, whom we jocularly came to call our Chief of Police. No one quite knew what his duties were—he least of all—but his appointment may have been intended to reassure the Italians that law and order reigned within the camp (which it did in any case, with or without him). Through no fault of mine, I became one of the very few inmates to provide grist for his mill. One morning, while drinking my coffee from my personal bowl, I bit on a hard object. I extracted it from my mouth and discovered, to my amazement, that it was a broken razor blade. I dutifully reported this bizarre occurrence to the Chief of Police, who, having nothing better to do, immediately embarked on a full investigation of the affair. In his attempt to discover who might have had a motive to kill or injure me, he followed leads of envy and unrequited love, as well as an imaginative array of other hypotheses, all as exciting as they were unrealistic. Our sleuth searched doggedly for clues and interrogated suspects—most of them my fellow students—but unearthed no evidence of foul play and failed to identify a culprit, if there ever was one. He finally conceded defeat.

It must be said to our sleuth's credit, however, that he did render himself useful as a calming influence during the arguments that often flared up between inmates, usually the consequence of our overcrowded living conditions. The prolonged, excessive intimacy forced upon people who were for the most part total strangers, aggravated by almost unlimited free time, was a constant source of tension—although this state of affairs also encouraged an almost unnaturally intense social life. Love affairs bloomed (although I have no idea where they could have been consummated), couples broke up, and others were formed. Several of the new family alignments and relationships established in the camp lasted well beyond the war.

Boredom was our greatest enemy. Some played cards or chess, some studied foreign languages, as Ivo and I did, and some spent their days in conversation and gossip, commenting on the latest rumours about the progress of the war or discussing aspects of our daily life. Occasionally, and without warning, we would be treated to a Gottlieb—Kraus debate. Dr. Hinko Gottlieb and Dr. Hans Kraus, both lawyers, were two of the most outstanding personalities in the camp. Dr. Gottlieb had been a well-known poet, writer, and Zionist leader in Zagreb before the war. He was a very distinguished-looking gentleman who enjoyed wide respect as a cultured and profound thinker. His speaking style was grave and solemn. Dr. Kraus, on the other hand, was an impish character, somewhat resembling the actor Peter Lorre. Kraus was a typical between-the-wars Viennese café intellectual, loquacious and provocative, who relished scandalizing his listeners with unconventional views. Although Kraus seemed like the quintessential Viennese Jew to me, he claimed not to be Jewish at all, alleging that he had abandoned Vienna of his own free will, in solidarity with his persecuted Jewish friends. Some believed him, although I suspected that this was just another example of his delight in being provocative. The Gottlieb–Kraus debates, which were conducted in German, would erupt spontaneously. They became a staple of camp life and came to cover a wide range of topics—literary, artistic, political, and philosophical. They never failed to be both amusing and instructive. Although the dignified Dr. Gottlieb did not seem to take Kraus too seriously—Kraus didn't take himself excessively seriously either—he obviously enjoyed the cut and thrust of the arguments, and he respected Kraus's broad erudition and debating skills.

> *Dr. Hinko Gottlieb published a fantasy novel after the war titled* The Key to the Great Gate *(Simon and Schuster, 1947). One of the book's main characters is Dr. Hans Strauss, an argumentative little lawyer from Vienna. The character is obviously based on Dr. Hans Kraus, Gottlieb's debating partner in Kraljevica.*

In an attempt to keep busy, some inmates established a puppet theatre. In the spring of 1943 we even organized "Camp Olympiads," with competitions in a variety of sports. But the most popular camp activity was music making. We were lucky to have several good musicians among us, in particular a Mr. Nadasi, who had been a small-town orchestra conductor before the war. Although the only instruments available were a few violins and violas—and one accordion—Nadasi succeeded in transcribing several classical works for this modest and unusual ensemble, on note paper provided by the Italians. The result was amazing, sounding—to my untrained ear—very much like a full symphony orchestra. The star violinist in this orchestra was Erwin Glasner, a bachelor of about fifty from Vienna (who later managed to reach the United States and join the New York Philharmonic). My friends and I were duly impressed by his musical skills, but what particularly entertained us was his unshakable pessimism. There was no item of news, no rumour, no snippet of information in which he could not detect signs of our imminent doom. Whenever a report reached us about the progress of the war, he always succeeded in interpreting it in a way that foretold the worst possible consequences for all of us. At the same time, he almost constantly wore a smile on his face—although a second glance was sufficient to discern that this was the unmistakable smirk of grim certainty.

Our music making was enriched by the presence of a number of good singers: a professional soprano (Nadasi's wife), a good amateur tenor, and a competent if somewhat academic basso, who treated us to recitals of lieder by Schubert and Wolf. Three teenage girls, Dora, Rena, and Mira, formed the Do-Re-Mi trio, which performed the latest popular songs (mostly Italian) in beautiful three-part harmony.

The Italians were enthused by all this musical activity, and whenever concerts were held (at least once a week), music-starved Italian soldiers and officers from the entire area flocked to the camp. The classical repertoire at first included only short orchestral pieces, but then, with the establishment of the camp choir, came to include excerpts from operas as well. Despite my very modest vocal talents, I joined the choir, together with several other tone-deaf companions.

One day, a performance of the *a bocca chiusa* or "humming" choir from the opera *Madama Butterfly* was on the program. As the piece was composed by Puccini to be sung from the wings of a theatre or from behind the scenery, the Italians obligingly erected a large backdrop made of canvas tenting, to enable us to perform unseen by the audience. When our turn came, we took our positions behind the tenting and began to hum. Someone suddenly noticed that the tent material was covered in one of the camp's scarcest and most precious commodities: buttons. As the "humming" choir lasts only a few minutes, we knew we had to act quickly. Out of sight and continuing to hum as musically as we could, we descended on the buttons. Some inmates had penknives, others used their bare hands, and in a matter of moments we had stripped the tenting completely bare. It was fortunate that we did not cause the entire structure to collapse. At the end of the piece, when we came forward to take our applause, our pockets were bulging with tent buttons—although none of our Italian guests seemed to notice. To this day, when I hear Puccini's "humming" choir, I invariably think of buttons.

Despite the occasional amusing moment, the generally tranquil atmosphere, and the return to a semblance of normal life, there was no avoiding the deep personal tragedies caused by the war. Most of the internees had a son, brother, father, or other close relative who had been deported to Jasenovac and disappeared. As a result, I was the object of frequent, insistent questioning by anxious family members desperate for news of their loved ones. But I had lived in Zagreb for only three and a half years, most of that time illegally, and had not made the acquaintance of many people. I could truthfully claim that I did not know whether this or that individual was still alive when I was in the camp. It was also true that my senses had been numbed by the sheer horror of Jasenovac: I had barely had the strength to drag myself forward, let alone speak to other inmates and exchange information. Faced with the distress of the relatives, I did my best to be as encouraging and optimistic as I could without telling outright lies, knowing full well that the chances of survival in Jasenovac were practically non-existent.

There was one especially painful situation, which haunts me to this day. It involved only two people but exemplified the thousands of similar tragedies that were taking place. A frail old woman, hard of hearing and barely able to fend for herself, was among the camp inmates. She was accompanied only by her grandson, a little boy of four or five, whose parents had been deported and killed by the Ustashe or Germans. The little boy was an intractable, rebellious child, whom even a vigorous adult would have found difficult to handle. The old woman, of course, was quite incapable of coping. Whenever she felt overwhelmed, she would call on me to take over; for some reason, I seemed to be the only person in the camp who could calm the little boy down. He was always happy to see me and very affectionate, perhaps because I reminded him of his father. He would settle down almost immediately, take my hand, and go for a walk with me around the barracks. Very soon, a close bond developed between us. At one point, I even considered adopting him, but the obstacles were too many: I was only eighteen, practically still a child myself. How could I adopt a five-year-old boy, while both of us were inmates in a concentration camp? It was impossible, yet I felt he would be lost if I didn't; both he and his grandmother were totally cut off—not only from the rest of us but from reality as well. She had lived her life, but what chances did he have? It was a difficult decision, but I did not adopt him. I do not know the boy's fate. I do not even remember his name. I am afraid that he did not survive, and I still feel that I might have saved him.

The spring of 1943 turned to summer. We knew very little of the progress of the war, as the only news sources available to us were some Italian and Croatian newspapers—which, of course, carried only official Axis news and propaganda—and the wild, unsubstantiated rumours that occasionally swept through the camp. We realized that the Italians were keeping us interned for our own protection, but we could not be certain that they might not eventually give in to German pressure and hand us over. Mr. Glasner—and he was not alone in this opinion—was quite convinced that one day the Italians would in fact do so.

As the months passed, however, I increasingly appreciated how safe a place the camp was to wait out the war; I even turned down an opportunity to escape. A corporal with whom I had become friendly suggested that I don an Italian uniform—which he would supply—and walk out the main gate while he was on guard duty. I was convinced that he was sincere and that this was no trap or provocation, but had to explain to him that I was not at all tempted to leave the camp. Where could I go? I had no desire to join the Communist Partisans or the Royalist Chetniks, and I certainly did not want to risk being caught and sent back to a death camp.

After all I had seen and experienced, I longed to stay where I was, sheltered from the Ustashe and the Nazis, and to wait until the war ended or until we were liberated by the Allies.

10 RAB

IN EARLY JULY 1943, the Italians evacuated all 1,200 of us from the camp in Kraljevica. We were trucked some 80 kilometres south along the Adriatic coast and ferried to the island of Rab (Arbe in Italian). The Italians interned us in a camp a few kilometres from the island's principal town, also named Rab, which had been a flourishing tourist resort before the war. The new camp contained several rows of small wooden huts, rendering the overcrowding even worse than it had been in Kraljevica; as many as ten people were forced to squeeze into a single hut. The only advantage of the new accommodations, as opposed to the large men's and women's barracks in Kraljevica, was that family units could now live together, two to three families per hut. I was able to move into one hut with Aunt Camilla and Uncles Oskar and Robert—and five or six others. Facilities for washing and cooking were very rudimentary, the weather was almost unbearably hot and humid, and, as before, we were encircled by a barbed-wire fence, which was constantly patrolled by armed Italian soldiers. But the humane attitude of our "captors" did not change; on particularly hot days, whoever so wished could go for a swim at a nearby beach—albeit under armed guard—and two vacant hotels in the town of Rab (the Adria and the Imperial) were transformed into hospitals for sick inmates.

Over two thousand other Jewish refugees had been living under Italian occupation in various localities along the Adriatic coast; they too were transferred to Rab in early July 1943, and interned in a camp near ours. Although there was no direct communication between the two camps, I soon learned that my uncles Ferdinand and Julius, who had spent the past eight months under "free confinement" in southern Dalmatia, were now on the island with us.

My most vivid memory of the camp on Rab is linked, perhaps surprisingly, to a literary competition. I was now eighteen and spent most of my time with my friends, a group of eight or nine young men between seventeen and twenty-three. Although we shared interests and ambitions, there was also a considerable degree of intellectual rivalry among us, often rendering our discussions very animated. One day, someone proposed that we hold a short story competition. We convened and, by majority vote, selected a topic for it: paraphrasing Lord Byron's "We will each write a ghost story," which he declared one rainy day in 1816 in Geneva (a suggestion that resulted in Mary Shelley's *Frankenstein*), we determined that "We will each write a gruesome story." A two-week deadline was set, after which we would assemble and each contestant would read his story out loud to the others. Then there would be a vote. The meeting would be moderated by a literature professor, a member of our group who was a little older than we were. Each contestant was required to contribute a two-*kune* coin (worth very little) to the prize money, and the winner would take all.

I was gripped by panic. I had never tried my hand at writing anything, let alone a short story, and I was unable to get started. I was also daunted by the strength of the competition, in particular by Vlado Gottlieb, son of the master debater and author Dr. Hinko Gottlieb. Vlado was one of the most brilliant and bitingly sarcastic people I have ever known. He already had some writing experience and towered over us all intellec-tually—although my friends Ivo Herzer, Zdenko Kronfeld, and Vlado Granski were also very bright and talented. I decided to drop out of the competition. The ignominy of being called a coward seemed preferable to the ridicule I expected for submitting an inferior story. I tried to withdraw under the pretext that the requirement of writing in Serbo-Croatian, the mother tongue of all the contestants except me, placed me at an unfair disadvantage. But my friends were unyielding; they agreed that I could write in German, a language all of them understood well.

I was cornered. The evening before the deadline, I finally summoned the determination to write the story. I wrote a basically simple but very contrived story of two sisters working in a travelling circus who fall in love with the lion tamer. Each sister plans a sticky end for the other, hoping to get away with murder without being suspected. One of the sisters manages to poison the other, but as she lies down to sleep, an axe suspended in a contraption above her bed falls and beheads her. The innocent lion tamer is then accused of the double murder, found guilty, and executed.

The next evening we met in a small, empty hut on the camp grounds. We lit candles, and each of us read out his gruesome story in the flickering candlelight.

Vlado Gottlieb's story, "Sassafras," was undoubtedly the best (afterwards, in the cold light of day, there was unanimous agreement on this). It was about a green seaweed (or was it really a ghost, or a being from outer space?) called Sassafras that devoured humans, including, eventually, the author himself.

Ivo Herzer's story was also marvellously spine-tingling: a bleeding apparition in a passing elevator disappears without a trace by the time the narrator, racing down the stairs to overtake it, manages to pry the elevator open.

To my astonishment, I won. I did not think that my story was the best and felt that my exemption from having to write in Serbo-Croatian had probably given me an unfair advantage over the others. Most people who know both languages would agree that German is far richer and more expressive than Serbo-Croatian, and certainly more suited for the writing of gruesome stories. Nevertheless, I remember the outcome of that competition as a moment of sweet, unexpected, triumph.

As the summer of 1943 progressed, it became increasingly obvious, even from official Italian news reports, that the tide of the war had resolutely turned against the Axis. But although Mussolini had been overthrown on 25 July, Italy continued to be allied with Germany. Isolated as I was on that little island in the Adriatic Sea, it seemed to me that the war would go on forever. I wondered whether I would ever be free and able to live without being hunted.

The capitulation of Italy to the Allies on 8 September 1943 came as a complete surprise. All of a sudden, Tito's Partisans appeared on Rab, the Italians laid down their arms, and the gates of our camp were flung open. There was no combat. The Partisans allowed the disarmed Italians to retreat to some troop transport vessels that were cruising in the vicinity. We were left behind, although the Italians withdrew in such disarray that I doubt they could have taken us with them even if they had wanted to.

The Partisans did arrest the camp commander, Colonel Vincenzo Cuiuli. In addition to the three camps for Jewish refugees on Rab, where conditions were humane, there was also a large prison camp for Slovenian "rebels." The Italians, who had been trying for two years to crush Slovenian resistance to their occupation and annexation, had imprisoned thousands of men, women, and children in the camp. Conditions were extremely harsh, malnutrition and disease were rampant, and as many as four thousand may have perished and been buried there in mass graves. There was a rumour that Cuiuli was going to be transferred to Slovenia to be tried by a Slovenian People's Court. He allegedly committed suicide in his cell a few days after his arrest. Although Cuiuli deserved a fair trial to ascertain his responsibilities, my own knowledge of Communist "popular justice" meted out on the island makes me doubt he could have obtained one—and raises questions about the genuineness of such convenient suicides. Shortly after they landed, the Partisans also arrested four young Jewish women who were among my fellow internees and executed them. They were accused of spying on the Partisans for the benefit of the Italians. Only years later did I learn some of the background to this story. I heard it from Fausto Bacchetti, an Italian ambassador to Israel and later to Austria, who had served as a junior officer in the occupation army in Yugoslavia during the war. According to Bacchetti, a colonel in the Italian occupation army in Croatia had a Jewish mistress (not an unheard-of occurrence). She wanted to be able to meet with two Jewish girlfriends who had been interned by the Italians somewhere on the Adriatic coast. To oblige his mistress, the colonel had provided the girlfriends with special travel papers stating that the two were assisting the Italian army in its struggle against the Partisans. These special papers exempted the women from limitations on the movement of refugees, such as the curfew, and enabled them to visit the colonel's mistress whenever they wished. There was not the slightest truth to the far-fetched assertion that they were helping with the war effort—that had been an invention of the colonel's to justify the travel papers. Unluckily, the documents somehow fell into the hands of the Partisans. When they landed on Rab, "popular justice" was dispensed in the form of summary execution.

I do not know the circumstances of the execution of the other two women, both of them camp inmates, although the accusation that they were spies is no less absurd.

▲ *Rab, 8 or 9 September 1943. I (circled) head for the camp exit,
together with 1,200 other inmates. Directly behind me, in the
dark shirt, is my friend Ivo Herzer. There were then about 3,500
Jewish refugees on Rab. I saw this photograph only after the
war and am still amazed that the moment was captured. I do
not know who took it.*

With the opening of the camp gates, Robert, Oskar, Camilla, and I were
reunited with Ferdinand and Julius, who had been interned in an
adjacent camp.

Within a few days, the Partisans had ordered several dozen of us to
move into a former school in the town of Rab. They decided that the
school was to be guarded around the clock; for this task, they selected
three eighteen-year-olds: my friends Ivo Herzer and Vlado Granski, and
me. Each of us was given a Partisan cap (with the red star on it) and a
single rifle for the three of us. We had never undergone army training
and had no idea how to use a gun, but this did not matter much, as we
were not provided with ammunition either. We received strict instructions to provide a twenty-four-hour "armed" guard of the school premises.
I can remember few occasions when I was more afraid. Every time a gust
of wind rustled through the leaves or a bird settled on a branch, particularly at night, I was certain the Germans or the Ustashe had landed

on the island and were attacking us. To carry an unloaded gun was far more frightening than to have no gun at all. Instead of standing guard in shifts, Ivo, Vlado, and I spent most of the time awake and together, trying to comfort and reassure one another.

Able-bodied Slovenes were rapidly enrolled into the Partisans and sent to the mainland to join the war against the Nazis and the Ustashe. Jews from the former Yugoslavia who were of fighting age at first formed a Jewish Partisan battalion. It was disbanded shortly afterwards and its members integrated into regular Partisan units. Jewish refugees from countries other than Yugoslavia, like my family and me, were allowed to try and reach southern Italy, which was already under Allied control.

We had been fortunate that the Partisans had been the first to arrive when the Italians surrendered. Word reached us now that the Germans were approaching fast and that it would be wise to abandon Rab. It was obvious that the Partisan presence could only be temporary and that they would be unable to prevent the German army, with its tanks, armoured vehicles, and complete control of the skies, from retaking the area at will.

We designated the distinguished and well-spoken Dr. Gottlieb to represent us. He managed to contact the Allied Liaison Officer to the Partisans in Croatia, a British officer by the name of Captain Hunter. Our request was that the Allies ensure the evacuation to Italy of at least the women, children, and elderly, who were the least able to fend for themselves and who also constituted a burden on the Partisans. The British captain promised an answer within two or three days and was as good as his word: it was swift and it was negative. He replied that the Allied bases were too far away and that a boat could not be provided for the journey.

Most of us still believed—because we desperately wanted to—that the Allies were anxious to save us. It took some time for us to become disabused of this illusion. In fact, many of us felt after the war that the Italians, who were the allies of the hated Germans and who had little to gain from protecting us, were more concerned for our well-being and did more to ensure our survival than the Allies.

Unable to obtain help from the British and Americans, many tried to reach Italy on their own. Several hundred former inmates managed to hire *trabakulas*—small local fishing vessels—in which they island hopped down the coast to the island of Vis, 200 kilometres to the south.

◄ A trabakula, *the type of fishing vessel used by many refugees in their attempt to reach southern Italy*

The island was reportedly in Partisan hands and under the protection of Allied ships. Their hope was that from Vis it would be easier—and safer—to cross the Adriatic to Bari, in southern Italy, perhaps even with Allied help. Island hopping was very risky, not only because of the exposure to storms and to strafing by German aircraft, but also because several of the small islands along the way were already under Ustashe control. In addition, boat owners were not above blackmailing or betraying their passengers. Yet as far as I know, most of those who attempted this route—including my friend Ivo and his parents—succeeded in reaching Bari. They made it with not much more than the shirts on their backs, but they were finally free and safe.

Vlado Gottlieb, author of the Sassafras short story (and son of Dr. Gottlieb), whose wit and intellect I so admired, also made the crossing to Bari with his mother and father. But soon thereafter, he was killed in a motorcycle crash. During the year I knew Vlado, I had come to realize that he was tormented by guilt for having survived his beloved younger brother Danko, who had been murdered in Jasenovac. He sometimes gave me the feeling that he found life so unbearable that he was subconsciously seeking a way to end it. Dr. Gottlieb dedicated his book *The Key to the Great Gate* to the memory of his two sons.

My relatives and I also decided to take our chances island hopping. We found a *trabakula* that was prepared to take us and made our preparations to leave. Suddenly, I fell ill with a very high fever, which forced us to postpone our departure by several days, and by the time I recovered, it was too late. There were reports that the Germans had taken control of the sea lanes, and the owner of our *trabakula* was no longer willing to take the risk. We were left with no choice but to ask the Partisans to evacuate us to the mainland, which was only two kilometres away. Many other Jewish refugees who were still on the island also asked for the Partisans' assistance. The Partisans responded admirably; they spared no effort in evacuating scores of elderly people, families with children, and others to the mainland and then into the mountains, placing them out of the Germans' immediate reach.

About two hundred Jews remained on the island, for a variety of reasons: old age, poor health, or false optimism. One family, the Wollners, stayed behind because a local friend whom they knew from before the war promised to hide them. As it turned out, the Germans landed on Rab only in March 1944. They immediately rounded up the two hundred remaining Jews, including the Wollners (betrayed by their "friend"), and shipped them to Trieste. In Trieste they were loaded onto cattle wagons, together with inmates of the Trieste insane asylum, and deported to Auschwitz. According to one of the survivors, all except five teenage girls were gassed on the day of arrival.

11 LIKA

AS SOON AS THEY DEPOSITED US on the mainland, the Partisans advised us to distance ourselves from the coast as soon as possible. They suggested we make our way some 100 kilometres inland, to a hilly area called the Kordun. In the ongoing fighting, some areas often changed hands between the Partisans and the Germans or Ustashe, but the Kordun was considered more or less firmly in Partisan hands. Moreover, food was not in such short supply there as on the coast.

There were six of us: my uncles Ferdinand, Robert, and Julius, my aunt Camilla and her husband Oskar, and me. We decided that our best bet was to join up with the Levingers, a large family of Croatian Jews with whom we had become friendly in the camp on Rab. As we were foreigners, we felt that we stood a better chance of facing what lay ahead if we joined forces with them. The extended Levinger family consisted of two brothers in their forties, their wives and children, and an assortment of other relatives. Apart from their general warmth and liveliness, they had the striking characteristic of all being unusually tall—leading my uncle Robert, who specialized in coining nicknames, to dub them "The Levinger Travelling Circus." For my part, I was perfectly happy to join this "circus" because one of the girls, Nada, was a close friend of mine.

The Levingers had left Rab before us and had found shelter in the coastal village of Novi Vinodolski (where I had lived for a time under Italian "free confinement" eighteen months earlier). Local Partisans had warned them that the area was unsafe and urged them to leave as quickly as possible. The Levingers had therefore moved south to the town of Senj, which was where we joined up with them. I later heard that Jewish refugees who had remained in Novi Vinodolski were subsequently caught by the Germans and deported.

Senj turned out to be unsafe too. The town had been used by the Italians as an arms and ammunitions depot, and in their precipitous withdrawal following the capitulation of 8 September 1943, they had left practically everything behind. The Partisans were now busy transporting as much as they could of this war booty inland, to be recycled for their own use. It was obvious that the Germans would try to put a stop to this as soon as they could, and there were reports that they were already sweeping into the formerly Italian-occupied areas from the north and south, in an attempt to seize the entire coastline and cut off supply lines from the Allies to the Partisans. From a military point of view, everyone knew that the mechanized German army would have little difficulty in capturing and defending the coastal road from the lightly armed Partisans.

Retreat into the hills became urgent, and after only a few days in Senj, we departed. The Levingers hired a horse and cart to carry everyone's luggage, and we set off eastwards into the mountains, on the only road, which climbed steeply from the coast. The Levinger Travelling Circus, of which we were now full-fledged members, was quite a sight: a horse-

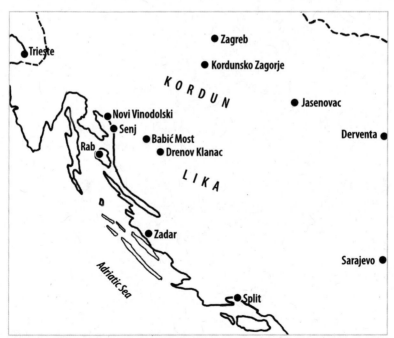

The Lika and Kordun regions of central Croatia, where we withdrew with the Partisans after the Italian capitulation

drawn cart heaped high with bundles and suitcases, followed by a group of about twenty refugees, many of them unusually tall. I remember thinking to myself that this was what it must have felt like during the Exodus from Egypt.

We pushed on for days, spending the nights in barns. At one point during our trek, we heard that the town of Senj, which we had just left, had been razed by German bombers.

It was already the beginning of January 1944 when we reached the village of Babić Most, in an area called the Lika, on the way to the Kordun. The weather had become very cold and it had started to snow heavily. We were lucky to find some peasants who allowed us take shelter, in return for payment, in a very small but warm barn. We unloaded the cart, piled all the luggage into the barn, and squeezed in ourselves. It was extremely crowded; when night fell there was barely enough room on the ground for all of us to lie down. It snowed during the entire night, for the whole of the next day, and during the following night as well. When we woke up on the second morning, the small windows of the barn, which were about a metre above ground, were completely covered. We dug a little trail through the snow and looked around: the countryside was blanketed in white, and no roads or paths of any kind were visible. We realized that it would be impossible to continue on our eastward trek and decided to stay where we were until conditions improved, assuming that the Germans too would find it difficult to advance in such deep snow.

Babić Most was a typical Yugoslav village, consisting of two rows of simple houses lining an unpaved country road, with a few barns and shacks in the vicinity. The atmosphere was cold, unfriendly, and threatening. The entire Lika area had a distinctly inhospitable air about it; temperatures were freezing, food was scarce, the countryside was forbidding, and even the population was not particularly welcoming.

Within a few days, however, I made a thrilling discovery: there was an American in a house at the other end of the village. I could hardly wait to meet him. The only American I had ever seen in my life was Jimmy Lyggett, the boxing coach in Zagreb, but I had never mustered the courage to actually speak to him. I thought of Americans as supermen, as charmed beings from another planet, so it was with great excitement and trepidation that I approached that little house in Babić Most. I found the American sitting in the dark, morosely staring into a void. I will never forget the way his face lit up when, instead of the expected local gibberish of which he understood nothing, he heard sounds that vaguely resembled English. Even though I had studied English with great diligence—particularly with my friend Ivo in Kraljevica—I had never actually conversed with a native English speaker. It was immensely satisfying for me to discover that I could communicate with him—although I was a little perplexed at first when he told me that he was based in "Idlee." I told him I thought the American bases were in "Italy." "Yeah, that's what I said," he replied.

The American was Horace A. Hanes, a twenty-eight-year-old US Air Force major, who had been a math teacher before the war. Flying a P-38 fighter bomber, he had been shot down by the Germans over Yugoslavia. Luckily, he had been picked up by the Partisans. He was now snowed in at Babić Most, like we were, and was anxiously waiting to be evacuated to Italy so that he could resume flying.

Major H. A. "Dude" Hanes (r.), November 1943 ▸

Major Hanes was suffering from a bad cold; somehow I managed to obtain some aspirin for him. My excitement at being able to speak to an American was so great that I visited him every day for the next few days. Very quickly, however, the local Partisans began to eye me with suspicion: in their view, all Westerners were possible counter-revolutionary spies, so anyone befriending them was a potential traitor. It was

January 1944 and the Partisans still strongly resented the fact that the Allies had been providing most of their support to the Royalist Chetniks, the rival Yugoslav underground in the struggle against the Germans. But before the uneasy atmosphere caused by my visits could turn into a problem, Hanes was whisked away and returned to his base in Italy.

> *The day I knocked on the door and found Hanes's house empty, I assumed I would never see or hear from him again. But his name stuck in my mind, exotic-sounding as it was to my Central European ears. More than a decade later, I was driving at night through Wisconsin, en route to New York. It was about three a.m. and I was keeping myself awake by listening to a local all-night radio station. The news came on, and I heard that Colonel Horace A. Hanes had just set a new supersonic world speed record in a flight over the Mojave Desert. I was astounded to hear his name and for a moment almost thought I was back in Yugoslavia. I wrote him a letter, congratulating him, and for a while we corresponded. He retired from the Air Force in 1973, with the rank of major general, and died in 2002.*

After a few days, the snow finally stopped falling. Reports reached us that the Germans were resuming their advance and that it was dangerous to stay any longer in Babić Most. I and the five other members of my family separated from the Levingers—probably because we realized it would be difficult to continue to find lodging large enough for all of us—and moved inland for a few more kilometres, to the village of Drenov Klanac. Just as we were entering the village, we encountered a peasant who offered to rent us a good room with *tekuća voda,* "running water." This amenity seemed unusually advanced for such a remote and backward area, and we immediately agreed without even seeing the room, paying the rent in advance by handing over some of the few remaining clothes from our luggage. When we reached the room, we discovered that the peasant had, in his way, spoken the truth: the water was indeed running, but it was in a brook a few hundred metres from the house. The room itself, however, was comparatively warm and comfortable; the six of us moved in, bartered away a few more clothes for potatoes and other food, and spent the next few days resting and waiting.

One afternoon, word arrived from the Partisans that German troops were approaching and could enter Drenov Klanac within hours. I insisted that we pack our rucksacks immediately and leave before nightfall, continuing our march in the direction of the Partisan-liberated region of Kordun. Uncle Ferdinand, who at fifty-five was the eldest in the family and whose opinion was respected by all, disagreed. He thought that the dangers of proceeding into Partisan territory were too great. Moreover, he said, the weather was still bad and we were all very tired. Most important, he was convinced that the German troops would not harm us. After all, he reminded me, he possessed correspondence with General von Glaise-Horstenau, who had personally intervened to have Oskar, Camilla, and me freed from Jasenovac. Apparently, the approaching column was not made up of savage Ustashe but of disciplined German troops. They would not dare to harm people under the personal protection of such an important general. Everyone except me agreed with Uncle Ferdinand. They were exhausted from fleeing endlessly into the mountains and hoped and trusted that the general's protection would save them. But I was adamant, and announced that under no circumstances would I remain: I refused to run the risk of falling into the hands of the Germans or the Ustashe again, and I was anxious to join up with the Partisans and begin fighting back.

The argument went on for quite some time and became very heated, but no one could be swayed. Finally, I simply picked up my rucksack and headed for the door. Only then did Uncle Robert decide to go with me. He said that although I was almost nineteen, I was still too immature for him to permit me to go off alone; he was sure I would do reckless things, and he had promised my mother that he would take care of me until I was grown up. He admonished me for being so childish and stubborn and for giving him no choice but to follow me out into the snow. At that point, Uncle Julius, who throughout his life usually followed Robert's lead, announced that he was joining us; the three of us departed.

About a year later, I found out that the SS Division "Prinz Eugen" had shot Ferdinand, Camilla, and Oskar when it swept through Drenov Klanac.

I cannot forget that, in a sense, they died because I was saved. If Ferdinand had not previously succeeded in obtaining von Glaise-Horstenau's help in freeing me from Jasenovac, he and the others would not have dared to stay behind.

▲ *The village of Drenov Klanac, where I parted from my aunt and uncles in January 1944. This photograph was taken in the summer of 1981, from the roadside; I could not bring myself to get any closer.*

12 JOINING THE PARTISANS

ROBERT, JULIUS, AND I trudged through the snow for several days until we finally reached the village of Kordunsko Zagorje in the Partisan-controlled area of Kordun. My most ardent desire was to get out of Yugoslavia, to reach southern Italy and join the American army—or if that was not possible, the British army. But there was no hope of that in the snowed-in Kordun in late January 1944. My remaining option, if I wanted to enlist in a fighting force, was to join the Partisans.

As soon as I arrived in Kordunsko Zagorje, I made a welcome discovery: my good friend Vlado Horvatić, whose veterinary skills I had so admired eighteen months earlier in Novi Vinodolski, was in the Partisans. He was Chief Veterinarian (and the only veterinarian) at the Partisan animal hospital, situated in the village itself. We were very happy to see each other and agreed that it would be ideal if I were to be stationed there with him. To increase my chances, Vlado advised me to tell the local Partisan command that I had been a veterinary student before the war.

Thus, in early February 1944, I became a Partisan. There was no formal signing up or swearing in; I simply reported to the local commander, who told me to wait in the village for orders. Robert and Julius, who were in their fifties and no longer of fighting age, would be allowed to lodge in the vicinity, together with several other Jewish refugees, mostly women and elderly men.

I spent a few days waiting and hoping that I would be posted to the animal hospital when, out of the blue, a dream opportunity to get out of Yugoslavia presented itself: word had arrived that Partisans with flying experience of any kind were to report to Corps Headquarters. I managed to find out that the Allies were for the first time going to provide Tito's forces with aircraft. A number of Partisans were going to be sent to liberated southern Italy and then onward to North Africa, to undergo pilot training.

Flying was comparatively new to Yugoslavia; there had been few trained pilots even before the war, and it was unlikely that many would now be with the Partisans. Technically trained people with much knowledge of aviation were not numerous either, and I assumed that the Partisans would be hard put to find suitable candidates. Although I had no relevant knowledge or experience at all, this seemed like a perfect opportunity to try and get out of the country and, once I was out, to "defect" and volunteer for the American army.

I was so desperate that I was prepared to stop at nothing, certainly not at a bit of innocent forgery. I had been a member of the International Boy Scouts in Vienna and had passed the test for semaphore signalling, Morse code, and marine knots. Although I had lost most of my personal documents, by an inexplicable stroke of luck I still had that certificate. I got my hands on a typewriter and artfully added a note stating that I had taken a course in glider piloting as well. I sent this "annotated" document to General Headquarters, accompanied by a letter in which I embellished my flying achievements.

As I had hoped, very few other Partisans could show any connection at all with aviation. I was selected for the pilot training program and ordered to report at once to a small regional command post in the Lika. I said goodbye to Robert, Julius, and Vlado and set out for the command post, where I met up with the nine other Partisans who had been chosen for the mission. We were briefed and each issued a *Schmeisser*, a small but vicious German submachine gun. These weapons had been salvaged from German corpses and were highly prized by the Partisans. I got further confirmation of our importance when each of us also received a supply of canned food—a rare and precious delicacy at the time.

Our instructions were to make our way to a location near the coastal city of Zadar, where a British submarine would pick us up at an appointed time. We were to move only at night and would have to cross two roads travelled and defended by the Germans. This represented the major danger to be faced, but it did not seem insurmountable. We were a very small group, and we knew that the Germans could not control the entire length of the roads at all times.

Our departure was set for midnight. As it was still early in the evening, I used my time to write a bitter and recriminatory letter to a girl with whom I had been in love in the camp on Rab. I had been heartbroken to discover, when I arrived in Kordunsko Zagorje, that she had meanwhile become the girlfriend of another Partisan. She was three years older than I and had never been my girlfriend. I was suffering from nothing more serious than a case of puppy love but nevertheless felt deeply disappointed and offended by her behaviour, and told her so in no uncertain terms. I sealed my dramatic farewell letter, entrusted it to the Partisan mail courier, and readied myself for departure.

Shortly before midnight, we were summoned to the command post for last-minute verification and briefing. Each of us was again submitted to detailed questioning as to our political reliability and personal background. As we had already been thoroughly interrogated during the previous phases of our selection, I was convinced that this questioning was only a routine, final pep talk. The officer interrogating me, however, was very surprised to hear that I had been studying veterinary medicine before the war. He informed me that he was cancelling my participation in the mission, as the Partisans needed veterinarians more urgently than they needed pilots. I was shocked by this unexpected obstacle and did my best to minimize my connection with veterinary medicine (which was not difficult). When I saw that the officer was not swayed, I reminded him that I had already been chosen for pilot training by superior order, a decision he was not in a position to overrule. But he called my bluff; as I watched in disbelief, he contacted the Partisan General Staff for Croatia on the field phone and obtained official authorization to keep me back.

I can remember few occasions in my life when I was as crestfallen as I was then. I had already been savouring the sweet taste of freedom in the West and now had to face this shattering setback. It was as though I were fated never to succeed in escaping to the West.

To make things worse, there was the farewell letter I had written to my "unfaithful" girlfriend. As I had been certain that I was leaving forever, never to return, I had written things that rendered it impossible for me ever to face her again. Now that I was condemned to remain in Yugoslavia, however, it was very likely that we would indeed meet again soon. The courier had nearly a six-hour lead, yet I raced out into the freezing night, in a desperate attempt to prevent him from delivering my letter. I chased him for hours, leaping through the deep snow for most of the night until finally, as day was breaking, I caught sight of him. I retrieved my letter and heaved a sigh of relief. At least my disappointment at having been excluded from the pilot program was not compounded by the need to explain my very embarrassing letter.

My regret at failing to leave Yugoslavia was mitigated somewhat by my subsequent posting to the animal hospital as Vlado's assistant. Then, about a month later, news reached me that all nine of my former companions in the pilot training program had been killed on their way to the coast while trying to cross one of the roads under German control.

13 VETERINARIAN

IF I FAILED IN MY ATTEMPT to flee to the West, being reunited with
Vlado Horvatić was undoubtedly the next best alternative. My admiration
and friendship for him were profound, and I looked forward to spending
time with this extraordinary man and assisting him in his work. Vlado
was not only head of the *marvena bolnica* (animal hospital) but also Chief
Veterinarian of the entire 8th Partisan "Assault" Division (the title
"Assault" was awarded as a collective decoration to units that had distinguished themselves in battle, an even higher accolade being "Proletarian").
The 8th Division, which belonged to the 4th Corps, consisted of some five
thousand combatants (men and women) as well as eight hundred horses
and mules. The division also possessed a few run-down and unreliable
trucks, but the animals were the primary means of transportation and of
moving heavy equipment; as such they were of vital importance.

I grudgingly came to admit to myself that the officer who had held
me back from the pilot training course (inadvertently saving my life) was
probably right: the Partisans did desperately need anyone with even the
slightest notions of veterinary medicine. Although my scanty knowledge
came only from observing Vlado at work a year and a half earlier, he, with
typical impudence (and sense of humour), appointed me his deputy and,
shortly afterwards, second-in-command at the animal hospital. His
justification for this decision was that I, unlike most other Partisans in
the Animal Hospital Unit, could read and write.

The stream of injured or ill animals to the hospital was constant, and
I was immediately plunged into frenetic activity. We were desperately
short of medicines, instruments, and medical reference books, and the
hospital itself consisted merely of a cluster of huts and wooden shacks,
but Vlado's talents and common sense enabled him to achieve astonishing

results. Apart from sewing up wounds and applying plenty of camphor and other disinfectants, his main course of action was to ensure that the horses and mules were kept clean and properly fed and that they were allowed to rest and convalesce for as long as possible. Vlado's motto was: "Coat clean, hoofs dry." I was amazed to see how many weak, sickly, and even moribund animals recovered under the proper conditions of hygiene and nutrition, permitting us eventually to send most of them back to their units. Although I was at first quite scared of horses and mules, finding myself on the receiving end of a number of hard and painful kicks while trying to treat them, I gradually developed a fondness for them. They were highly prized beasts in the Partisan world, and I counted myself lucky when I was issued with a mare myself (I was even luckier that she happened to be very tame and docile). I had almost no experience horseback riding, and as there were no saddles or stirrups available, I— and the considerate animal—had to make do with a blanket and ropes.

At various different times, between ten and forty Partisans were attached to the hospital, to help with cleaning and general maintenance and to man the various activities we organized, such as a blacksmith's shop for horseshoes and a workshop that made horse brushes from horsehair. There was also an area where horses and mules that were too severely injured or ill to be treated were shot, to be transformed into sausages. Most of our Partisan assistants were hard-bitten combat veterans, many of whom had already killed at least one enemy soldier or would have done so given half the chance, but when it came to putting a bullet through the head of an injured horse or mule to release it from its misery, they simply could not bring themselves to pull the trigger. It was usually Vlado or I who had to carry out this unpleasant duty.

I could not imagine that within a few months I would be forced to take Vlado's place, but as I was considering the possibility of studying medicine after the war, I tried to participate as fully as I could in everything he did and I listened attentively to his explanations. I often accompanied him on his periodic visits to the various units in our area, during which he inspected the conditions in which animals were being kept and gave instructions for changes or improvements. I also helped him organize a special course at the animal hospital for veterinary assistants, who were then placed in charge of the animals in the different constituent units of the 8th Division. They were responsible to Vlado, the

The staff of the animal hospital in the village of Kordunsko Zagorje, late 1944. By this time, Vlado had mysteriously disappeared, but I did not yet know what had happened to him. I am sitting on the ground in the first row, second from the right. The bushy-haired fellow next to me is my good friend Paolo, a former Italian soldier who had joined the Partisans after Italy's capitulation. When I returned to the area in the summer of 1981, I stopped in the village and showed this photograph to the first peasant I encountered. He pointed to the little boy wearing the grey waistcoat in the front row and said: "That's me."

He is the man in the blue cap standing next to me. His name (if I am not mistaken) is Milan Vukovratović. He was the son of our "landlady," the peasant woman around whose farmhouse the animal hospital was centred. On the left is his sister, Dragica, seen kneeling by Milan's side in the 1944 photograph. The man in the checkered shirt also appears in the 1944 photograph, kneeling to Milan's left. Ten years after this 1981 encounter, civil war broke out in Yugoslavia. These villagers were ethnic Serbs, living in a part of Croatia that, tragically, was again the theatre of fierce fighting. I hope they fled in time.

Chief Veterinarian, for maintaining levels of care and hygiene. Within a short time, the state of the animals in the combat units had improved noticeably; indeed, it was often better than that of the men.

This was the first time in my life that I came into close, continuous contact with animals. I had always lived in big cities, and as a child I had never been allowed to keep a pet. Only once, as small boys in Vienna, were my brother Max and I permitted to adopt an unwanted kitten, which we had rescued from drowning at the hands of its owner. Our mother allowed us to keep it as a reward for our good deed, but after a short while it disappeared. Then, for a time, we had some goldfish (as one of my uncles put it, "at least fish make no noise and cause no damage")—but they did not live long. Now that I was in the Partisans, I could finally have my own pet, and when a little white dog trotted into the veterinary hospital grounds one day, I adopted him and named him Rommel, in "honour" of the German general. Although I was very fond of my new pet, my choice of name reflected the local attitude towards dogs, which was one of disdain. Rommel kept me company for several months, but eventually he too disappeared.

There were no other veterinary services in the entire area, and as a result we also found ourselves caring for the livestock of the peasant population, in whose midst we lived and whose produce fed us. A peasant's prize possession was usually a pig (lard was very highly valued). These were fattened to enormous dimensions—I saw a few weighing 300 kilograms and more—before being slaughtered. To accelerate the fattening, the pigs were usually castrated, an operation I helped Vlado perform many times, and then, on occasion, even performed on my own. These operations, carried out of course without anesthetics, were invariably successful and never gave rise to complications. As soon as it was untied, the pig would scurry to the nearest trough and start eating.

I did have one harrowing encounter with a pig, however, the thought of which still makes me cringe. One day, while I was alone at the animal hospital—Vlado must have been out on an inspection—a group of peasants appeared, accompanied by the most gigantic pig I had ever seen. The animal had a bone lodged in its throat and was obviously choking. I had once assisted Vlado in a similar situation and had seen him use a twig to prod the bone deeper into the pig's throat until it slid into the stomach. Naturally, I was not at all eager to give this a try in his absence, but the pig's owner and his companions were quite desperate, certain as they were that the poor animal was on the verge of choking to death. I reluctantly agreed to try to help. The pig was so huge that it took seven or eight peasants to hold him down and to force open his mouth. I picked up a twig that happened to be lying nearby and tried to emulate what I had seen Vlado do; after a bit of prodding, the bone dislodged; to my great surprise and relief, the pig began to breathe normally and recovered rapidly. Profoundly grateful, the peasants returned to their village with their precious possession. Later that day, when Vlado returned, I proudly recounted my exploit. His reaction, however, chilled my enthusiasm: it turned out that I had taken a very grave risk. The only twig to be used in such cases, he told me, was the soft, flexible twig of a willow tree. The one I had randomly picked off the ground was far too hard and brittle and could have caused irreparable damage to the sensitive inner lining of the pig's gullet. Fortunately, for both them and me, pigs are very hardy creatures.

Vlado let on to no one that I knew so little about veterinary medicine. On the contrary, he delighted in telling tall tales and especially enjoyed persuading anyone who would listen that I had studied veterinary medicine for a number of years before the war (I was only nineteen, how could I have?). Although it startled me somewhat at first, I soon got used to being addressed as "Doctor," both by the local peasants and by my fellow Partisans. It was true that Vlado and I often found ourselves caring for them and their families too: there were very few medical doctors in the area, so we were often approached for the dispensing of first aid, the changing of bandages, and general medical advice.

Word that there were "doctors" at the animal hospital eventually reached Division Headquarters, and I soon found out that our superiors were not amused. The commander of the 8th Division, to which we belonged, was Colonel Miloš Šumonja, a man in his mid-twenties. I came to know him quite well, as he often galloped into the animal hospital and inspected our facilities. He was better educated than most Partisans, having been a schoolteacher before the invasion of Yugoslavia, and he seemed to enjoy the opportunity to converse with Vlado and me about topics not strictly related to the war. I felt that the primary reason for his visits, however, was his fondness for his horse; he wanted it to be well looked after and properly shod in the blacksmith's shop attached to the animal hospital.

One day, while Vlado was busy elsewhere, I accompanied Šumonja on one of these inspections. When it was over, he turned to me and said, "Comrade, I have received reports that you not only care for animals but also practise medicine on humans."

I tried to explain that Vlado and I had never volunteered to provide medical assistance to humans, but that it was difficult to refuse treatment in a real emergency, particularly when there was no one better qualified or equipped within a radius of many kilometres.

"I forbid you to care for humans," he replied, "without exception."

Naturally, I assured him that from then on we would scrupulously obey his order. But just then, by the most uncanny coincidence, a peasant girl ran breathlessly into the hospital grounds, shouting, "Doctor, Doctor, come quickly, Captain Jovanović is bleeding to death!"

Captain Jovanović was a local Partisan hero, small in stature but giant in valour. A Serb from a nearby village, with no pre-war military training of any kind, he had become a specialist in defusing the unexploded bombs and grenades that littered the countryside. No mishap had ever befallen him during these highly dangerous activities, but while jumping over a brook on his way to visit his family, his small Beretta pistol had fired accidentally and the bullet had gone right through his penis.

I told the girl that unfortunately I could do nothing because I was under strict orders not to attend to humans—but before I could finish my sentence, Šumonja ordered me to hurry to the injured captain's assistance, adding, rather sheepishly, that I could also provide first aid in the future, whenever there was no alternative (there practically never was).

Luckily, Jovanović merely had a flesh wound. The urinary tube was not injured, and I was able to stop the bleeding and evacuate him to the Partisan field hospital in Petrova Gora without much additional loss of blood. Later, I was able to provide him with tranquilizers in order to prevent erections, which could have reopened the wound. As far as I know, he made a full recovery.

Treating humans, however, was the exception in my work: my main contribution as a vet's assistant turned out to be battling equine scabies, a disease caused by mites that burrow under the skin of horses and mules, causing extreme itching and discomfort. The animals become very restless, rapidly lose weight, and if untreated, can die. Equine scabies is extremely contagious among the animals themselves and can even be transmitted

▲ *Treating a horse at the animal hospital in Kordunsko Zagorje:*
I am at the far left, taking notes. In early 1945, our unit received
a visit from "Agitprop," the Partisan department in charge of
morale-boosting propaganda. This photograph and others were
staged to illustrate "Partisan successes." The man seen treating
the horse, his back to the camera, was Dr. Adamović, then my
superior. The Partisans shot him shortly afterwards as a spy.

to humans. The fact that I had sometimes helped Vlado treat the disease was obviously known to headquarters, because when a dispatch reached the animal hospital in August 1944, requesting an "expert" to deal with a severe outbreak of scabies in the Turopolje-Pokupsko region, it named me. I felt confident that I could tackle the disease because, to a great extent, treatment was more a question of organization than of medical knowledge. As Vlado had taught me, all you needed was sulphur powder and a wooden hut.

I set off on foot to the Turopolje-Pokupsko region, about 100 kilometres away. When I arrived, I found a group of Partisans waiting, ready to assist me. I supervised the construction of a rectangular wooden cabin, just large enough to contain a horse. One of the narrow ends of the hut was a door, the top half of which was made of canvas. A horse or mule would be backed into the cabin, a bowl of smouldering sulphur would be placed beside it, and the door would be closed. The animal's head would be passed through a slit in the canvas, permitting it to breathe. An hour of exposure to dense sulphur fumes was enough to kill the parasites on the horse's body; those on the head and upper part of the neck protruding through the canvas were eradicated by the application of a salve made of sulphur powder and pig lard. I had a second cabin built and kept both in operation for twenty-four hours a day, as we passed all the horses and mules in the area through them. Within a few days, the scabies epidemic had been wiped out—at least for a few weeks. This is the experience as a Partisan vet that I remember with the greatest satisfaction; I felt that I had really made a difference, helping restore the operational capabilities of Partisan units, which could have been crippled because their animals were diseased.

14 A COMMUNIST REGIME

I WAS VERY PLEASED to be a member of a fighting force dedicated to the defeat of my mortal enemies, the Nazis and the Ustashe. But as the animal hospital was situated in the rugged hills of the Kordun region, at a distance from the main combat zones, for the first few months I was not directly involved in the fighting. I went about my business as Vlado's assistant, while my uncles Robert and Julius lived in a farmhouse nearby, slowly bartering away their personal belongings in exchange for food.

When I first joined the Partisans, I was enthusiastic about what I knew of Communist ideals. The prospect of a society in which equality and justice were guaranteed to all and where discrimination on the basis of ethnicity or religion was proscribed was very appealing to me. Within a short time, however, my starry-eyed zeal turned to bitter disappointment, as I came up against the realities of a Communist regime, in particular the ideological tyranny imposed by the Communist Party on our ranks. Examples ranged from the brutally ruthless to the utterly idiotic. As a rule, there was an atmosphere of servile adulation of anything Soviet, accompanied by suspicion bordering on outright hostility to anything emanating from the Western Allies—even when those prejudices were glaringly contradicted by facts on the ground. A typical example of the relentless Communist propaganda effort was the manipulative treatment given to supplies from the West. During the last few months of the war, the Western Allies provided us with regular (if insufficient) supplies of arms and ammunition. Our superiors thought it politically inconvenient, however, that we rank-and-file Partisans should know we were being aided by the contemptible Western capitalists rather than by the infallible Soviets. We were therefore told as a fact that all this aid actually came from Soviet Russia. American planes were bringing in the supplies? Oh yes, the Americans are just supplying the transportation because their bases are in nearby southern Italy. The flour is packed in bags marked "Product of Canada"? Oh yes, the Canadians are providing the bags, but the flour itself is Russian.

Among the items we received were tins of ham labelled in Russian; for the benefit of those who could read, the tins were clearly marked "Made in USA"—albeit in Russian Cyrillic characters (which are almost identical to their Serb equivalents). Perhaps these supplies had been packaged in the United States for delivery to the Soviets, and then in part been rerouted to us. Despite the labelling, we were told in no uncertain terms that the ham itself was of Russian origin—and it would have been very unhealthy to express any doubts.

In my everyday experience, all middle- and high-ranking Partisan officers were members of the Communist Party. Party members also had absolute preference when it came to manning posts that required specific professional knowledge, such as communications and administration. Whether a Partisan was professionally competent or even intellectually qualified for a particular position was always a secondary consideration. By favouring party members so ruthlessly and systematically, the party succeeded in attracting ambitious people into its ranks, offering them promotion in exchange for devotion. Belief in Communism, let alone familiarity with the writings of Marx and Engels, rarely had anything to do with it; the objective was to guarantee strict obedience.

To my amazement, I discovered that I still had to reckon with anti-Semitism; in fact, my personal identity placed me in triple jeopardy. First, as a Jew: centuries of religious indoctrination that the Jews were the "killers of Christ" had left their mark on the villagers and peasants who made up Partisan ranks; although they knew we shared a common enemy, many of them—including some in leading positions—were blatant anti-Semites. Second, I was of German mother tongue and education: those same villagers and peasants could not always fully appreciate the difference between a German-speaking Jew and a Nazi. Third, my first name is Imre, a typically Hungarian one: at the time the Hungarians were allies of the Germans and therefore thoroughly detested by the Partisans. I concluded that I needed to invent a more secure identity for myself, to be used whenever I sensed danger. I therefore "Slavicized" my name from Imre Rochlitz to Mirko Rohlić and claimed, when asked, that

I was a Slovene. I chose this nationality because Slovenia (where I had set foot only once, as a child) had been part of Yugoslavia before the war. Its inhabitants were not particularly hated by either the Serbs or the Croats, who were busy hating each other. Also, the Slovene language is closely related to Serbo-Croatian, which would satisfactorily explain to any suspicious or hostile Partisan why I could speak Serbo-Croatian fluently.

Under my new identity as Mirko Rohlić, I tried to navigate the treacherous Partisan terrain of suspicion, paranoia, and arbitrary justice. A curious consequence of this atmosphere of distortion and suppression of the truth was that on the one hand, we believed nothing we were told; on the other, we lost the ability to dismiss even the most outrageous rumours. One rumour circulating widely at the time was that Marshal Tito, our Supreme Commander, was not a real person but a radio transmitter that relayed orders received directly from Moscow. Some of my companions, on the other hand, were certain that they had deciphered the real meaning of T.I.T.O., suggesting that it was in fact an acronym for *Tajna Internacionalna Teroristička Organizacija* (Secret International Terrorist Organization). I even heard the rumour that Tito was a woman.

Undoubtedly, the unspeakable horrors the local population had to face played a significant role in forming some of their suspicious, uncompromising attitudes. The hilly area where I was stationed, the Kordun, was formally part of the Independent State of Croatia, ruled by Ante Pavelić and his Ustashe thugs. But ethnically, it was a Serbian Orthodox enclave within the Catholic Croatian state (about one-third of the pre-war population of the Croatian state were in fact Serbs). Immediately on the proclamation of the new state in April 1941, these Serbs were targeted for genocide by the Ustashe. Hundreds of thousands of "Schismatics," as the Orthodox Serbs were disparagingly referred to by the Catholic clergy (first and foremost by Alojzije Stepinac, wartime Archbishop of Zagreb, beatified by Pope John Paul II in 1998), were savagely massacred between 1941 and 1945. I myself witnessed some of these horrors in 1942 in Jasenovac, where Serbs were by far the most numerous victims of the Ustashe, followed by Jews and Gypsies. But the Ustashe not only murdered their victims in concentration camps; they also rampaged through the countryside, slaughtering Serb villagers and peasants with a barbarity that defies the imagination.

For Serbs living in the Kordun, the Lika, and other areas within the Croatian state, there was little choice but to go underground and join a resistance movement if they hoped to escape physical elimination. Almost all those I knew in the Partisan 8th Division—which was composed primarily of Serbs from these Croatian areas—had lost close relatives to the Ustashe. At the same time, it was fairly obvious that political doctrine and belief had very little, if anything, to do with their joining a Communist formation. I often received the impression that many of my "comrades" would have preferred to join the other main resistance movement, the Royalist Chetniks. Under the command of a former Yugoslav army colonel, Draža Mihajlović, the Chetniks (or "troopers") were fighting for the re-establishment of the Serb-dominated Kingdom of Yugoslavia and for the return of King Peter and the Royal House of Karadjordjević. The traditional Serb nationalism and Orthodox faith of the Chetniks had a greater appeal to the basically conservative peasants and villagers than did the revolutionary ideals of the Communist Partisans. But the Partisans were better organized than the Chetniks and, most important, were usually the first to arrive in the Serb villages, where they quickly enlisted all able-bodied (and not so able-bodied) peasants, no questions asked. Men and women of fighting age were expected to join, and once a villager was a member of an armed organization, especially one as well controlled as the Partisans, it was almost impossible—and certainly extremely dangerous—to attempt to switch allegiances. The formations themselves, however, did sometimes change alliances: the Chetniks and Partisans sometimes fought together against the Axis and at other times attacked each other. For a time, the Chetniks even sided with the Italians and Germans in combating the Partisans. Most shocking (to me), however, was that in March 1943 some high-ranking Partisans met with the Germans and offered to fight side by side with them against any Allied attempt to land in Yugoslavia. This was at a time when the Allies were still supporting the Partisans' rivals, the Chetniks; the Partisans apparently viewed the Allies as dangerous potential adversaries—even more dangerous than the Germans. But Churchill switched his support to the Partisans in late 1943, and by the time I joined in early 1944, there was no longer any question that the Germans were the primary enemy.

I only learned of these Partisan–German negotiations decades after the war (in S. K. Pavlowitch's Hitler's New Disorder *[London: 2008]). It dawned on me that had Churchill not switched his support when he did, I might have found myself under orders to fight alongside the Germans against the British! What would I have done? How could I have escaped this terrible dilemma? I have no idea and am grateful I never had to face it. It is intriguing to me that the German who negotiated in 1943 with the Partisan delegation (which included Milovan Djilas and Vladimir Velebit) was none other than Edmund von Glaise-Horstenau, the general who a year earlier had personally obtained my release from Jasenovac. One agreement that the Partisans and Germans apparently did reach and carry out in these negotiations was a limited prisoner exchange—until then, both sides killed all captured prisoners.*

The toll that the contradictions of wartime Yugoslavia took on the population was truly tragic: I know of one Slovene family in which a father and his three sons belonged to four distinct armed groups. At different times during the war, each group fought against the other three, and by the war's end, the father and his three sons were all dead.

In the Partisans, Communist Party control over the rank and file was achieved through political commissars. These were party officials assigned to the various units and ostensibly charged with supervising adherence to Communist precepts; in practice, their function was simply to ensure unquestioning obedience. Every Partisan unit, all the way down to platoon level, had both a commanding officer and a political commissar. In theory, the commander and the commissar had equal powers; in practice, the commissar was more equal than the commander. Any order signed by a unit's military commander had to be countersigned by the political commissar, while an order signed only by the political commissar was considered fully valid.

In the late summer of 1944, I received my first invitation to join the Communist Party. The political commissar whose signature appears on the following document (and whose name I do not remember) had been replaced by Milić Hajdin, a young Serb from a nearby village. Most of Hajdin's family had been massacred by the Ustashe, and Hajdin himself had escaped death by fleeing and joining the Partisans. He found

▲ *This unexceptional document, dated 25 June 1944, authorized me to move freely within the territory controlled by the 8th Partisan Division. There were no preprinted forms available (due to a chronic shortage of paper), so I wrote it out myself. I indicated my name as Mirko Rohlić and made sure to end the document in the mandatory form, with the letters "S.F-S.N," the initials of the Partisan motto: "Death to Fascism—Freedom to the People." The document is signed at the bottom right by my direct commander, Vlado Horvatić. To be valid, however, even this simple pass required the countersignature of our political commissar, at the bottom left.*

comradeship and comparative safety in their ranks, and he soon became a member of the Communist Party. He was certainly a good and reliable party member who would unquestioningly follow party instructions to the letter—even though he was practically illiterate and knew or understood nothing of Communist ideology. But notwithstanding his unquestioning loyalty to the party, he remained a kind-hearted, basically decent fellow. We respected each other and got along very well.

One of the commissar's functions was to vet and propose new party members. It was considered a special honour to be proposed for membership, and one was expected to accept with profound gratitude. When Commissar Hajdin took me aside one day and informed me that he felt that I deserved to join the Party, I became alarmed: I had no desire at all to join, but I also knew that a refusal might have serious consequences. Fortunately, though, Hajdin had decided to speak to me before proposing my name to his superiors. It took quite a bit of effort on my part to persuade him that, although I was deeply honoured by his confidence in me, I felt that joining the Party at this time would be inappropriate. I was a foreigner, I reminded him, and very uncertain about my personal future. This was neither the time nor the place for me to accept such an honour, I said with regret. Fortunately, he accepted my reasoning. Most important, I managed to elicit a promise from him not to report my reluctance to his Party superiors. I was aware that I was skating on very thin ice; the slightest suspicion of "political unreliability" could trigger a sudden transfer to the infamous "13th Battalion," a unit that (so it was said) was always assigned to mount desperate attacks on the Germans and the Ustashe, in which death was the certain outcome. (I later learned from friends in other Partisan units that "transfer to the 13th Battalion" was a common euphemism for summary execution.)

Hajdin remained true to his word. Although he repeated his offer on later occasions, and I always refused it, he never reported or denounced me.

I rapidly came to realize that in addition to the three jeopardies linked to my identity, I faced a fourth, unexpected peril: I knew too much. Despite my fragmented schooling, I was more educated than most Partisan commanders and political commissars. In the oppressive, anti-intellectual atmosphere that reigned, knowledge and learning were viewed as dangerous weapons wielded by the bourgeoisie to oppress and exploit the working classes. So I had to be very careful never to give the impression that I knew too much about anything. I did my best to keep a low profile, but this state of affairs always needled me; I chafed under the arbitrary rule of these people who had the power of life or death over me, without possibility of appeal, and who wielded their absolute authority, both administratively and intellectually, simply because they represented the Party. Their word was the law, and many of their fateful decisions depended simply on whether they liked you or not.

A friend of mine lost his life as a result of personal animosity, almost certainly anti-Semitic in origin. I had known the two Breslauer brothers since we had been inmates together in the Italian camps; they had later both joined the Partisans. The younger of the two, Albert, took the veterinary assistant's course we gave at the animal hospital and sometimes worked with me, while the elder brother was a medic in an infantry battalion. I had heard on occasion from Albert that his brother was unhappy in his unit, as his commander was a rabid anti-Semite. One day, during combat with German troops (who were actually Circassians, former Russian soldiers in German uniform), the elder Breslauer was ordered by his commander to retrieve the body of a companion who had been cut down very near to enemy lines. Breslauer had no choice, even though the commander's purpose was clear. As he approached the body, a Circassian slaughtered him with his bayonet.

15 FRIENDSHIPS AND HARDSHIPS

I HAD FEW CLOSE FRIENDS in the Partisans; the general atmosphere of suspicion and mistrust, compounded by anti-Semitic prejudice, forced me to be very cautious about fraternizing too closely with anyone. Several of the young Jewish men and women who had been interned with me in the Italian camps in Kraljevica and Rab had also joined the Partisans and remained my friends, but they were in other units and I rarely saw them.

With Eva Deutsch, a former fellow inmate in the Italian camps, who was stationed with another Partisan unit ▸

Apart from Vlado Horvatić, my best friend was a former Italian soldier by the name of Paolo. He was a dark, curly-haired Sicilian who had somehow made his way into the Partisans after the Italian debacle of 8 September 1943 (he is sitting next to me in the photograph at the top of page 133). He was not the only former Italian soldier in the Partisans; there were several others who had chosen to join rather than surrender to the Germans or attempt to return to war-torn Italy; there were also some Dutch and Belgians.

I cannot remember Paolo's last name—perhaps I never knew it—but I will never forget him. He had been posted at the animal hospital on the basis of his claim that he had cared for horses in his native Sicily and later in the Italian army. He was no better educated than the average local Partisan (i.e., he was illiterate)—but none of the Slavic melancholy and folk pessimism for him! He had the Italian quickness of mind, joy of life, and sense of humour. I enjoyed listening to his stories about Sicily before the war, how he would drive his father's orange-laden horse cart to market, singing arias from operas, in particular the cart driver's song from *Cavalleria Rusticana*. It was very easy to imagine him doing so; he often sang loudly and melodiously as he went about his work at the animal hospital.

Paolo confided to me that when he was fourteen, his parents had placed him in a Jesuit boarding school in preparation for the priesthood. All had gone smoothly until he discovered that a fundamental requirement for the priesthood was celibacy. Certain that this would be no life for him, he ran away. Although he knew only a few words of Serbo-Croatian, Paolo amused the entire unit with his singing, clowning, and practical jokes. I later lost touch with him and sincerely hope he made it safely back to Italy.

In addition to the military threat from the Germans and Ustashe (and occasionally the Chetniks), and the "political" menace posed by Communist rule, there were the arduous and primitive living conditions to contend with. The hilly Kordun area where I was stationed had been very backward even in peacetime; in wartime, conditions became even harsher. For most of us, the main problems were very basic: finding food and shelter. But for those like Max Hamburger, a highly intelligent young man who had been an inmate with me in the Italian camps, the situation became desperate. A diabetic, he had somehow been able to obtain insulin (perhaps with the help of the Italians) while in the camps. Under the difficult and isolated conditions in the Partisans, this became impossible, and he died.

The countryside around the animal hospital was devastated; with the front lines moving back and forth over the preceding months and years, artillery shells and bomber raids had wrought complete havoc. Many of the houses and buildings (most of them wooden) had been badly damaged if not destroyed, and the agricultural workforce as well as the livestock had been decimated. As a result, food was very scarce. For the Partisans, a meal generally meant a bowl of beans or polenta, sometimes with bread. Although we were not far from the Adriatic coast, combat with the Germans and Ustashe often interrupted supply routes, which led to to a chronic shortage of salt. It did not bother me, personally, to eat unsalted beans or polenta, so it amazed me that some of the local villagers were willing to barter meat—which was extremely scarce—for salt, often on the basis of ten kilograms of meat for one of salt.

There was no electricity—there had been none in peacetime, either— and water had to be brought from the nearest well or brook. For bodily needs, dilapidated, malodorous outhouses were sometimes available, but nobody liked to use them. I much preferred to find a secluded spot in the nearest cornfield—where I discovered that maize leaves were a very reasonable substitute for toilet paper, a non-existent luxury at the time (any kind of paper at all was very scarce).

I was lucky to be sharing a small room with Vlado at the animal hospital. Accommodation, particularly when on the move, usually meant sleeping on the ground in a barn or, if the weather was good, on a haystack. For units on manoeuvres, the Partisans had devised an original and efficient method for finding shelter and supplies. In every liberated village, they would designate a local elder, often against his will, as the person responsible for assisting the Partisans. Whenever a unit entered the village, the elder would be summoned and ordered to single out the villagers who would supply food and those who would provide accommodation. It was assumed that he would know best how to distribute the burden fairly (naturally, there was never any question of payment). These elders were not at all popular with the peasants; so much had been destroyed that the local people often could hardly feed themselves. But despite the occasional angry outburst, the system generally worked— perhaps, also, because refusal of any kind was severely punished.

The most distressing physical discomfort was lice; we were almost permanently infested with both body and hair lice (they are of different varieties). They not only cause unbearable itching but also spread typhoid and other diseases. Whenever possible, we attempted to delouse our clothes by boiling them and our hair by dousing it with gasoline. But we were never free of the parasites for long; they were omnipresent, and it was impossible to isolate oneself.

Until the last few months of the war, when the Allies started sending in more supplies, we were not entitled to any regular issue of clothing. There was a very good reason for this—the lack of a hinterland where Partisan uniforms could be manufactured. Except for the green cloth cap with the red star, which somehow was available to everyone, every Partisan was free—or rather, forced—to wear whatever clothing he could find, steal, or liberate (i.e., take from the enemy). This photograph, taken in 1944, shows me in a civilian shirt, an Italian army jacket, British army pants, an Ustashe belt with a US Colt 45 pistol, and German infantry boots.

◄ *This picture does not show that I had wrapped my feet in old rags, as I had no socks. By now, however, I was already a well-clad Partisan. Many possessed no shoes at all and had to wrap their feet in scraps of canvas or tarpaulin for months on end, even during the winter.*

Life was somewhat easier for Partisans who were born in the surrounding area. They were sometimes able to obtain extra food or the odd piece of clothing from family or friends. But for those from other parts of Yugoslavia—in particular, from the larger cities—and who were accustomed to more modern conveniences, it was difficult to subsist. I did have my uncles Robert and Julius nearby, who provided precious moral support, but they had no local connections and faced great difficulties in finding food and shelter. We had fled from Drenov Klanac, the village in the Lika, with only our rucksacks on our backs; my uncles were now slowly bartering away our few belongings, mostly clothes, in exchange for beans, potatoes, a chicken, and so on. We knew that our possessions would not last forever.

My Italian friend Paolo, probably thanks to his engaging personality, generally had reserves of extra food, which he sometimes shared with me. He was also by far the most popular man in our unit with the women.

Whenever I mentioned to friends, years later, that there were women in the Partisans, I invariably elicited knowing winks and suggestive elbow prodding. But the reality of it was quite sobering. Most of the peasant women from the Kordun and the Lika who joined the Partisans much resembled the men; they were sturdy in body, coarse in language, and rough in behaviour. They also shared the strenuous life, deprivations, and lack of hygiene of their male comrades. Try as I might, I was rarely able to find any of them in the least attractive. It is revealing that one of the meanings of the Serbo-Croatian word *fina*, when applied to women, is "fine," "beautiful"; the other meaning, however, particularly in Bosnia, is "strong," "sturdy," "fat." It amused me that the two meanings were essentially equivalent and complementary, testifying to local canons of feminine beauty.

▲ *Partisan women combatants of the 8th Division*

Most of the women I knew in the 8th Division performed non-combat duties such as first aid, nursing, administration, communications, propaganda (publication of news bulletins), and cooking. No women, as far as I know, were forced to join fighting units as combatants—but a number of them volunteered, performing the same duties as the men and displaying the same ruggedness and courage as their male counterparts.

There was an official directive that severely prohibited romantic liaisons within the same unit. As soon as a commissar found out that a couple had been formed, he immediately separated them, transferring one of the lovers to another unit. This was one of the very few Partisan regulations that was generally accepted as justified—by everyone except the couple concerned. Naturally, these rules were not always observed, particularly when it came to senior officers and commissars, who formed a caste above and beyond the law. My own unit commissar, Milić Hajdin, conducted a passionate affair with our cook, a young woman whose husband had been killed by the Ustashe and whose baby had disappeared in the first days of the German–Italian invasion (she found the child after the war). We teased them good-naturedly about their relationship, but they blushingly denied it and on occasion even became quite distraught, fearing that word would reach the higher echelons and that they would be separated. But they succeeded in remaining together, for three principal reasons, none of them linked to the man's position as commissar: they were lucky; they were both well-liked by all members of the platoon so that no one denounced them; and the cook, who was a fine person and outstanding at her job, was not sufficiently attractive to arouse desire or envy among the other men.

There were very few opportunities for relaxation and socializing, and when they did crop up, I seized them. One evening, I gathered with a group of Partisans and a few local peasant girls around a campfire. Someone brought out a harmonica; we formed a circle and spent several hours dancing the *kolo*, a traditional folk dance similar to the *hora*.

By midnight, I had befriended one of the peasant girls and was immersed in conversation with her when she suddenly announced that she and her friends had to leave. Although none of these girls were uniformed Partisans, they were about to go into action. After dancing vigorously for five hours, they intended to carry explosives to a railway line some 20 kilometres away and blow it up. My new acquaintance

▲ *Partisans dancing the* kolo

explained that she had to leave at once because it was a long walk over the hills to the railway and then back to her farm, and she wanted to be home by dawn because there were cows to milk and fields to plough. I was deeply impressed by her hardiness and bravery, and told her so in the most glowing terms. As we spoke, I heard a splashing sound on the ground near my feet. I glanced down and realized that she was urinating where she stood, arms folded, while continuing to converse with me.

The Germans didn't stand a chance.

16 AIRMEN

THE ASPECT OF MY YEAR as a Partisan that fills me with the greatest pride is my participation in numerous "search and rescue" operations to recover downed Allied airmen.

For the first few months of 1944, my only direct view of Allied operations came when the weather was good: I would look up and sometimes discern formations of little silver birds glistening in the sun, making their way majestically across the sky. For the most part, these were squadrons of US warplanes: four-engine Liberators (B-24s) and Flying Fortresses (B-17s) on their way from their bases in North Africa and Italy to bomb targets in Austria (now part of the German Reich) and Romania— in particular the oil fields at Ploesti. To me, they were spaceships from another world, the free world; I gazed at the silver birds longingly and wished that I could somehow transport myself into one of them.

On especially clear days, I could also distinguish tiny dots, which I assumed to be fighter planes, escorting the bombers. But as far as I was aware, neither the fighters nor the bombers took part directly in Partisan–German hostilities; I never saw them challenged by German planes or attacked by anti-aircraft fire. Once they reached their targets, however, the planes were engaged by the Luftwaffe and shot at by German anti-aircraft batteries, often suffering hits. If an aircraft was severely damaged, its crew had instructions to attempt to make it back over Yugoslavia and crash-land or bail out over Partisan-held territory. Certain areas changed hands frequently, so crews were briefed before every mission as to which areas had come more or less securely under Partisan control. My region in the Kordun was considered one of these, and Allied aircraft in distress often headed towards us. Everyone at the animal hospital was therefore constantly on the alert for the sound of low-flying aircraft or for the sight of descending parachutes. As soon as there was a sighting, the race against the Germans to reach the downed airmen would commence. The Germans and Ustashe had mechanized means of transportation and always made a special effort to capture or kill these airmen, often firing at them as the parachutes were coming down; it was vital that we locate them first and whisk them away as quickly as possible.

As I was the only Partisan in the immediate area who knew some English, I was placed in charge of the search parties for airmen bailing out in the vicinity. I was also made responsible for caring for others rescued nearby until they could be evacuated from Yugoslavia to the Allied bases in southern Italy. Between April and December 1944, I was able to rescue or assist approximately fifty downed airmen, as well as some Allied prisoners who had escaped from German or Ustashe captivity. I was so happy to meet these emissaries of the West that I asked them to leave me their names and addresses, in the hope that one day, if and when I finally made it to the free world, I might already have a few friends there. As there was practically no paper available, certainly not for private

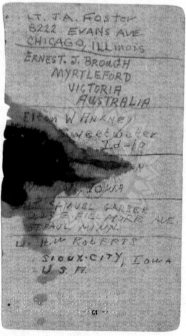

▲ *Pages from my passport where rescued airmen and escaped POWs left their names*

use, I asked the airmen and others to write down their names on the only sheets I possessed: the pages of my expired Hungarian passport. I have treasured that document and its sixty-some names to this day (see Appendix for full list).

I was always fascinated by the apparent innocence and bright-eyed naïveté of these Allied airmen, in particular the Americans. No matter how exhausted or ragged they were when we picked them up, they seemed to preserve a sort of immaculateness that insulated them from the harsh realities into which they had descended. They were brave, technically skilled professionals who executed their missions without flinching, many of them losing their lives in the process; but if they made it back to base unharmed, they could take a shower, change into clean clothes, and eat and sleep in peace and relative comfort, never having to contend with the destruction and suffering faced by those on the front line. Thus, if and when they had to bail out, and they landed in Partisan territory, it seemed to them—and to us—that they had dropped in from another world.

Naturally, they were elated at having been rescued, and their enthusiasm was sometimes overwhelming. They thought that Tito and all his Partisans were great heroes, and some became quite angry at their own authorities for not giving the Partisans more military and economic support. They were not with us long enough to become aware of the shortcomings of the people or of the system. Sometimes, in private conversations, I tried to describe a few of the injustices I had witnessed, to tell them of the relentless Communist propaganda to which we were subjected, and to warn them of the mistrustful, almost inimical attitude of the Partisan leaders towards the Western powers and even towards them as individuals. They listened to my criticisms politely, but blinded as they were by their gratitude, I usually felt that they did not believe me; most were complete political ingenues who knew nothing of the undemocratic traditions, the intrigues, and the suspicions that were endemic to the Balkans.

> *A year later, I found myself engaged once again in an attempt to open the eyes of an American soldier to the darker sides of Communism; this time, however, the American was himself a convinced Communist. It was in 1945, in the city of Bari, in liberated southern Italy. I was one step closer to realizing my dream of emigrating to the United States. I could finally wear a US uniform and had*

a job with the UN Relief and Rehabilitation Administration. Ivo Herzer (whom I had met again in Bari) and I made friends with a US army private by the name of Junius Irving Scales. At twenty-five, Junius was five years older than we were and culturally and intellectually far more advanced (he had been to college, while we had not even finished high school). Nevertheless, strong bonds of friendship developed. We formed a threesome, going to bars and shows together, engaging in long conversations about our experiences, and discussing our dreams for the future. I soon realized that Junius was perhaps the individual with the strongest personal qualities whom I had ever met: he was generous, compassionate, and learned; he had the sharpest of minds; and he was deeply loyal, both to his friends and to his country. He also happened to be a member of the US Communist Party, a fact that he hid neither from us nor from his superiors in the US army. His main objectives, he told Ivo and me, were to combat racial discrimination and social injustice in the United States and to improve the lot of ordinary working people through political action. Although he believed our hair-raising accounts of Communist totalitarianism, he was sure that these were only aberrations. He could not understand why Ivo and I so fervently wanted to get to the United States instead of seeking to build a future in one of the new "socialist" Eastern European countries. As he later wrote in his autobiography, Cause at Heart: A Former Communist Remembers *(University of Georgia Press, 1987), referring to Ivo and me: "I sought to destroy their illusions without success. They tried to destroy my illusions about Communism with equal unsuccess." Although our political views were sharply divergent, our friendship was profound, to the extent that he convinced his mother in North Carolina to provide Ivo and me with an "affidavit of support," an indispensable document for obtaining a US immigration visa.*

In late 1945, Junius was transferred back to the United States. When he came to bid us farewell, he advised us to sever all ties with him. He intended to pursue his activities with the Communist Party, he told us, and any association with him could jeopardize our chances of ever becoming US citizens. With deep regrets, we sacrificed our unique friendship.

◂ *Junius Scales
arrested by the
FBI, 1954*

Nine years later, Junius was arrested by the FBI and sentenced
to six years' imprisonment for being a member of the Communist
Party. He was not accused of any violent or subversive activities; he
was the first—and only—American ever to be convicted simply for
being a Party member. He spent several harrowing years fighting
his conviction, during which he resigned from the Communist
Party when Stalin's crimes were revealed, but in 1961 was sent to
jail. Junius spent fifteen months in prison, until President John F.
Kennedy, responding to public pressure, commuted his sentence.

I met Junius once more, in New York, in the late 1960s. We
talked about old times and regretted the loss of so many years of
friendship. But he was no longer the Junius I had known, and I
came away with the feeling that his spirit had been broken—both
by his disappointment with Communism and by the disgraceful
legal persecution to which he had been subjected.

17 SEVENTH OFFENSIVE

FROM TIME TO TIME the Germans tried to wipe out Partisan resistance by launching major offensives. Although the Partisans were becoming progressively stronger and controlling ever larger areas of Yugoslavia, they had no heavy weapons or aircraft and could not hold on to major population centres or roads for any length of time. With their superior weaponry, including tanks, artillery, and aircraft, the Germans and their allies could reconquer these practically at will.

The number of German troops pinned down in Yugoslavia, including non-Germans under German command, was substantial. According to German figures, at the end of 1943 there were fourteen German army divisions and two SS regiments, as well as five non-German divisions (manned by Russian ex-prisoners, Hungarians, French and Scandinavian fascists, and others), totalling over 200,000 men. In addition, the Germans could count on 160,000 Bulgarians and Croat and Serb fascists, for a grand total of over 360,000 men. The Germans estimated the Partisan force at the time at 110,000. Despite their numerical and material advantages, the Germans were unable to keep all areas under occupation simultaneously or even to secure the lines of communication (roads, railways, telephone lines) between them. Their tactic was to mount sudden offensives in an effort to encircle and wipe out major Partisan units—in particular, to eliminate the Partisan leadership.

The offensive that I witnessed took place in late May 1944, when the Germans unleashed their Seventh Offensive, code-named *Rösselsprung*, or "Knight's Move" (derived from chess). The primary goal of this offensive was to capture or kill Marshal Tito. An SS paratroop battalion parachuted into the town of Drvar, where Tito's headquarters were situated, but failed to capture him. They did seize his gleaming new marshal's uniform, however, which they later triumphantly exhibited in Vienna. The British succeeded in evacuating Tito to Bari, in southern Italy; he subsequently established his new headquarters on the island of Vis, in southern Dalmatia.

At the same time as the parachute drop on Drvar, there was a concentrated German attack on the Kordun area, where my Partisan unit was stationed. The attack began with heavy bombing and strafing from the air, followed by artillery and tank shelling and an infantry advance. As we had no anti-aircraft guns, we were ordered to shoot at the planes—which were flying very low—from every barrel available, including pistols. A small-calibre machine gun was set up near the veterinary hospital, and on several occasions we shot back at the planes strafing us, although they caused no casualties among us and I doubt we hit them.

By chance, an American airman happened to be holed up with us at the animal hospital. His rescue, which had taken place only a few days earlier, had been particularly dramatic. A US bomber had been seen flying low, obviously about to crash. Unfortunately, most of the crew (usually ten men) had been seen bailing out over German-held territory; only one parachute seemed to be coming down near the animal hospital. Knowing that the Germans or Ustashe would certainly go after him, I had rushed out with a group of four or five Partisans to try to locate him. We moved quickly and in about fifteen minutes had reached the area where I expected to find him.

We were searching the bushes, fearing that he might be lying somewhere unconscious, when suddenly I heard a loud shout behind me: Hands up! Recognizing a distinctive American accent, I raised my hands, turned around slowly, and came face to face with the muzzle of a pistol. I tried to reassure the airman that we were on his side, but at first he was very reluctant to believe me. I pointed to the red star on my cap, warned him that the enemy was probably on its way, and finally convinced him to lower his weapon. As we scrambled away through the trees, I mused on the young man's courage: totally outnumbered (there were several of us), he had been unafraid to challenge us single-handedly. Had we indeed been Germans, I doubt he would have got very far.

The airman's name was Lieutenant James E. Lackey, of Buffalo, New York. He was First Pilot and therefore commander of the plane that had been shot down; as such, he had bailed out last. As luck would have it, he was the only member of the crew to have come down over Partisan-held territory. The other nine crewmen landed in German areas, and I have no knowledge of their fate.

In view of the special circumstances under which we had become acquainted, Lackey and I quickly became friends. He told me of his concern for his wife in the United States: on the very day he was shot down, she was due to give birth to their first child. It worried him that the Air Force would inform her that he was missing in action and that she would be unduly distressed. I was arranging his transfer to Corps Headquarters, which maintained contacts with the Allies and organized the evacuation of downed airmen, when the Germans launched *Rösselsprung*. It became impossible to evacuate Lackey.

Enemy troops began to advance along the roads leading into our territory. As we stood no chance in face-to-face combat against their superior numbers and weaponry, our entire Veterinary Hospital Unit was ordered to withdraw into the hills. The order to move came suddenly, just as night was falling. There was no time to contact my uncles Robert and Julius, who were living with peasants in a farmhouse about 3 kilometres away; I could only hope they would retreat with the Partisans stationed near them. There were several other Jewish refugees living in the immediate vicinity of the animal hospital whom I managed to warn of the impending retreat. They attached themselves to our unit, and together with them—and Lackey—we moved into the hills. One of the Jewish refugees, an elderly lady who had been in the camp on Rab with me, was unable to keep up with us. I turned to one of the Partisans in our group and asked him to help her, but he cursed and refused. Although I was unaware that I held any rank at all (I discovered only several months later, by pure chance, that I had become a second lieutenant), I decided that my position as Vlado's deputy gave me some clout. I grabbed one of the elderly lady's bags and ordered the Partisan to pick up her rucksack and to assist her. When he rebuffed me again, I pulled my pistol and threatened to shoot him. Fortunately, he fell for my bluff, because I would never have used it.

In complete darkness, we made our way for a few kilometres into the hills, taking with us all the horses and mules that were able to walk. When we felt we had put sufficient distance between us and the Germans, we stopped and set up camp. When daylight broke, we positioned ourselves at the top of a ridge and observed the main road that cut across the countryside below. Only a few hundred metres from our hideout, I saw a column of soldiers and armoured vehicles winding its way forward. The soldiers were in German uniform—although I found out later that these were in fact Russian Cossacks, probably former prisoners of war whom the Germans had coerced into the *Wehrmacht* (although some of them may have volunteered). The Germans used former prisoners against "bandits," as we were called, in Yugoslavia, but did not trust them enough to send them into battle against the Allies or even the Soviets.

The column advanced slowly. Then, just as it was passing directly below us, two small aircraft appeared over the road, flying rather low. We were very alarmed. Their characteristic twin-boom indicated that these were probably German Focke-Wulfs, which had attacked us in the past. There was little likelihood that they might be Allied planes, as the only ones we had seen until then were high-flying bombers and fighters that had not directly taken part in the hostilities in Yugoslavia. The German troops below us evidently identified them as Focke-Wulfs too; as the planes swooped down over them, the soldiers waved and cheered enthusiastically. We realized that we might easily be spotted by the pilots and rushed to take cover as best we could under nearby trees and bushes.

At that moment, the two planes opened fire on the German troops. They swooped over the column repeatedly, letting loose a terrifying barrage of machinegun fire and violent explosions. Then, as suddenly as they had appeared, they vanished. We crept back to the edge of the ridge and saw that the column had been destroyed; the mangled bodies of the dead and wounded were strewn about everywhere. It was a gruesome sight. We withdrew and moved deeper into the hills. Only later did I learn that the twin-boom aircraft were in fact American P-38s, which greatly resembled the German model.

None of us—nor, evidently, the Germans—had ever seen one before. It was the same type of aircraft in which Major Hanes, the airman I had met a few months earlier while snowed in at Babić Most, had been shot down. But he had flown cover for the high-altitude bombers and had not participated in the local Yugoslav battles. I was never able to find out whether the pilots of these P-38s were Americans or, as our commanders and commissars "briefed" us, Partisans flying Allied planes.

After four or five days, the enemy withdrew and we returned to the little farmhouse and the surrounding huts and sheds that served as the veterinary hospital. Contrary to the Germans' normal custom, this time

Lockheed P-38

Focke-Wulf 189

they had not burned everything down. Apparently they were puzzled as to the purpose served by these structures; on one of the walls, someone had painted the word *Tiersammelplatz* (animal collection point) in large white letters, followed by a question mark.

Strewn about the premises were booklets that the Allies had apparently air-dropped into German-occupied areas. These booklets, written in German, tried to convince soldiers in the German army that the war was already lost for them and that they might as well try to save their skins. One of the various suggested methods was to feign tuberculosis. The following instructions were provided: obtain some lead powder, mix it with a salve, and apply it to several areas on your chest; this will show up on X-rays as spots on the lungs. Then, collect some smegma, the white substance that accumulates under the foreskin (the booklet correctly assumed that most German soldiers would not be circumcised). Just before being asked to expectorate, mix some smegma into your saliva and bite your tongue. Under a microscope, the bacteria in your saliva mixed with blood would be indistinguishable from tuberculosis bacteria.

One of the first things I did was search for Robert and Julius—and I was relieved to find that they were safe. For the duration of the offensive (about a week) they had remained hidden in a barn near the farmhouse where they had been lodging, undiscovered by the enemy.

During the time we spent hiding in the hills, Lackey and I had come to trust each other. I had confided to him that my greatest dream was to become an American and that I yearned to be fighting the Germans as a soldier in the US army rather than with the Communist Partisans. Lackey stunned me with the most amazing of proposals: he offered to let me assume his identity. He would give me his US Air Force uniform and identity papers so that I could pretend to be First Lieutenant

James E. Lackey of Buffalo, New York. For his part, he would pretend to be an airman with a different name who had lost all of his papers. Together, we would get ourselves evacuated to southern Italy in one of the Allied DC-3s (Dakotas) that were already flying in supplies for the Partisans, and flying out downed or escaped Allied military personnel (if any empty space remained, they also took badly injured Partisans).

Lackey assured me that he would have no trouble getting evacuated even without US papers, since he was obviously an American (and really could not be mistaken for anything else). I was very tempted to seize this opportunity, but the risks were immense: my English was still very poor, and I was painfully aware that I did not possess any of the typical American mannerisms that might make my impersonation convincing. It was easy to tell Americans from non-Americans before they even uttered a word, from the easy, relaxed way they carried themselves— from their ambling walk, the way they put their hands in their pockets and slouched, and their generally healthy complexions. The pathologi-cally suspicious Partisans were likely to verify identities very carefully; if caught, I would probably be shot on the spot. I strongly doubted that I could pull it off and regretfully refused Lackey's bold and generous offer.

Once the Germans had retreated, we were able to escort him to Corps Headquarters; from there he was safely evacuated to southern Italy. I briefly corresponded with him after the war and learned that he, his wife, and their baby were healthy and well.

A few days later, a Partisan mechanic in charge of the truck repair shop near the animal hospital came looking for me. He was very excited and insisted that I follow him. He led me to his repair shop and pointed to a figure sitting forlornly in a corner, his hands tied behind his back. It was a captured German soldier, who had evidently straggled away from his unit during *Rösselsprung*. I was quite good friends with the mechanic, who knew that I had been in the Jasenovac death camp. Convinced that he was doing me the greatest of favours, he offered to let me execute the German. The prisoner was a man in his mid-thirties (I remember being surprised by his relatively advanced age), visibly exhausted, and terrified. I had no desire to take revenge on such a pitiful and helpless being. Aware that my standing in the mechanic's eyes would plummet, I politely declined his offer. I do not know what happened to the prisoner; I think he was transferred to another unit and executed later.

▲ (l. to r. standing) Lt. Henry Flesh, Lt. Dale O. Davidson, Lt. Dale E. Martz, Lt. Warren F. Mugler. (l. to r. kneeling) Andrew E. Reis, S/Sgt. James H. Melanson, S/Sgt. Carl M. Thorberg, Sgt. Richard Kemmerle, Jr., Fernando O'Dell, Sgt. Wesley A. Roberds

IN MID-OCTOBER 1944, my platoon picked up the entire crew of an American B-24 (Liberator) bomber.

They had bailed out from their crippled aircraft while returning from bombing the Ploesti oil fields in Romania. While they were descending with their parachutes, the enemy had fired on them, but fortunately all ten landed in Partisan-controlled territory. Only one, O'Dell, was slightly injured. He had a sprained or broken ankle (my veterinary knowledge did not extend that far).

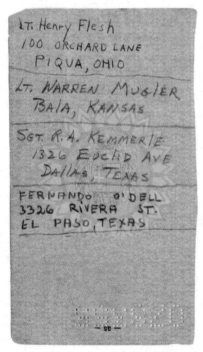

▲ *The crew of the downed B-24 left me their names and addresses*

Like all US airmen, they were equipped with handsome escape kits, containing, among other things, a beautiful map of Yugoslavia printed on silk, painkillers (morphine, I believe), concentrated chocolate, and some $50 in cash. The gratitude of these ten young men was overwhelming; knowing that they would be evacuated within a few days, they generously shared the contents of their kits with us. The silk maps went to the women, who wore them as headscarves, and the chocolate to the children. As I had been in charge of the rescue party and was also the only Partisan who spoke some English, they credited me with having saved them and tried to persuade me to accept some dollars. They would not be able to keep the money anyway, they explained, as these were army funds to be used only in an emergency; whatever was brought back to base would have to be returned. I must admit that I was very tempted to accept. I had no money at all, and my uncles were rapidly running out of items to barter in exchange for food. But I was so proud of having recovered an entire ten-man crew (the first and only time) that I felt that accepting money would cheapen the occasion, and refused.

The airmen wore beautiful Air Force clothing. I was particularly impressed by their warm leather jackets, with internal wiring that could be plugged into the aircraft's electrical system, for heating at high altitudes. They also possessed enviably sturdy boots and warm gloves. When they saw the tattered outfits we were wearing, the grateful young airmen began to distribute their clothing with largesse, reassuring us that once they got back to base, any missing items would be replaced free of charge. I gratefully accepted a leather jacket and a pair of gloves.

When the group was flown out to southern Italy a few days later, they were a sight to behold: practically in rags and in their bare feet, they looked like Partisans themselves; but they were ten very happy men.

Shortly after the group departed, a Partisan appeared at the animal hospital, bearing a rifle with a bayonet fixed to its muzzle. He presented me with a dispatch ordering me to accompany him at once to the regional command post. I became greatly alarmed; the commander of the Kordun area was the feared Captain Joco Eremić, who was notorious for his uncompromising and unreasonable severity. With no alternative but to obey, I marched with the Partisan to the command post, a cluster of huts on a hillside a few kilometres away. As soon as I arrived, I was ushered into Eremić's room. He was a short, skinny man with a permanent scowl.

Did I admit, Eremić confronted me immediately, that I had accepted money and items of clothing from the Americans?

I smelled danger. There was no standard Partisan practice for this type of situation. A military commander or political commissar could arbitrarily and retroactively apply his personal set of regulations according to whim, formulating them to suit his purposes. Whenever a commander or a commissar had it in for someone, this was the way to get rid of them.

I was able to deny, truthfully, that I had accepted any money, but I had to admit that some American items were in my possession. Eremić now pronounced the law, freshly concocted for the occasion: in view of the fact that I was in charge of the platoon that had picked up the Americans, accepting anything from them was a grave breach of Partisan morality. It would have been pointless to say that I had never heard of such a rule, that in fact there was no such rule, or that it was unfair to hold me to rules that were known only to him. I was convinced that he could have me shot on the spot if he so desired. He could certainly have applied the more usual means of elimination, transferring me to the 13th Battalion, the unit supposedly used for carrying out suicide assaults on enemy positions, in which no one survived for any length of time. I am not certain that this battalion actually existed, although it was often referred to in Partisan discourse. Most probably it did not, as such, but it represented the Partisan way of thinking. As in any war, the army had to carry out a certain number of frontal attacks and other high-risk missions that would, necessarily, result in a high death toll. It seemed quite logical—and was certainly the practice—to employ soldiers for this purpose who were politically not entirely reliable or who had committed some real or imagined disciplinary infraction. If human lives had to be expended for final victory, it made sense to use up less reliable and desirable human material, preserving the more trustworthy, less problematic elements for a trouble-free Communist future.

Now that I had admitted the facts of my purported infraction, I feared for my life. I racked my brains for a plausible excuse. The only one I could come up with was that I had never intended to keep any of the items of clothing for myself and had always planned to distribute them to other members of my platoon.

Eremić, naturally, suspected that I was lying. Confident that he was setting a clever trap for me, he replied, with obvious relish, that if this was so I had most certainly informed my political commissar of my intentions. I had no choice but to confirm that this was correct. At that instant, both he and I knew the trap had been sprung.

I will never forget the sadistic smirk on Eremić's face as he said that he would soon uncover the truth by questioning my commissar. Normally, he would have detained me at his headquarters until the commissar could be summoned, but he seemed to derive a perverse pleasure from this game of wits. He was like a cat circling a trapped mouse, allowing it to scamper to and fro, relishing the moments before striking, confident all the while that the mouse could not get away. He ordered me to return to my unit and to tell my commissar to report to him at once. By obliging me to arrange for my commissar's testimony, thus setting the stage for my own unmasking and eventual conviction, he was obviously deriving further sadistic pleasure. He ordered the Partisan with the bayonet to escort me back to my unit and to return with the commissar.

I was desperate, quite like a trapped animal. No escape was possible. We were surrounded by Germans, there was no chance of hiding within the Partisan-held area, and I certainly could not hope for a change of mind or for mercy from Eremić. My only hope was to persuade my commissar to lie for me.

When the guard and I reached the animal hospital, I suggested that he wait in the courtyard while I located the commissar. I guessed that he would probably be tired and appreciate a rest before marching all the way back up to the command post. The guard agreed.

My political commissar was still Milić Hajdin, whose repeated offers that I join the Communist Party I had always politely rejected. Nonetheless, we liked and respected each other. I found him and quickly explained the danger I was in. He, of course, knew perfectly well that I had intended to keep the items of clothing in question for myself; it was useless to try and persuade him otherwise. I told him that I honestly believed my life was now in his hands. I put it to him starkly that if he was going to tell the truth to Captain Eremić, I was already a dead man; if he lied and confirmed that I had asked him to distribute everything to the others, I might be saved.

Without hesitation, Hajdin agreed to lie. He said that he thought I had done nothing wrong—adding that he instinctively disliked and mistrusted Eremić, an instinct that was soon to be proved right. With the guard still resting in the courtyard, I was able to give Hajdin the American jacket and gloves, which he quickly distributed to other Partisans in the platoon. He then reported to the guard and hiked back with him to the regional command post. Try as he might, Eremić could not shake Hajdin's testimony confirming my story. My commissar had saved my life, asking for nothing in return.

This was the end of the story for me, but unfortunately, Eremić's malice claimed other victims. One of them was the truck mechanic who, a few months earlier, had offered me the opportunity (which I had declined) to execute a German prisoner. He was a tough old fighter, loyal to the Partisans beyond question. One day, he had exchanged pistols with an American airman, trading his small-calibre Italian Beretta for the American's more powerful Colt 45. Nobody imagined that this might be in violation of some rule, but Captain Eremić found out about it and was merciless. From one day to the next, the mechanic was gone, dispatched to the "13th Battalion"—or executed.

It always struck me as ironic—and almost incomprehensible—that in an environment in which people stood to lose their very lives for reasons

▲ *Milić Hajdin is on the far right. Next to him is his girlfriend, our*
platoon cook. The little girl is Dragica, daughter of our landlady, who
also appears in the photographs on page 133. I am third from the left.

connected with clothing, there should be a widespread Partisan custom
called "swapping." On the spur of the moment, one Partisan would
challenge another to an immediate and complete exchange of clothes.
The clothes on a Partisan's back were usually all he possessed, but it
was considered cowardly to refuse. The swap invariably included not
only clothing and shoes (if there were any), but also the entire contents
of pockets, including wallets, photographs, and everything else they
happened to hold. After the swap, tough negotiations would commence
and deals would be struck, with each Partisan trying to retrieve some
of his prized possessions, such as family photographs or other personal
items. It was a form of gambling, an emotional release from the grueling
realities of daily life.

As it turned out, not long after my run-in with Captain Eremić, my
commissar's instinctive mistrust of him proved well founded: Eremić
defected to the rival resistance movement, the Chetniks. Apparently he
was one of the many moles planted by the Chetniks not only to spy on the
Partisans but also to weaken them by eliminating as many as possible.

▲ *When I revisited the Kordun area of Yugoslavia in 1981, I was told by local Communist Party officials that Eremić had survived the collapse of the Chetniks, fled Yugoslavia, and immigrated to Canada after the war. Eremić's obituary (he died in Canada in 2002), which I discovered online, mentioned that he was a Chetnik but not that he had also been a Partisan—an omission that would seem to corroborate the allegation that he was a mole.*

If I remember correctly, these are the Party officials who informed me about Eremić. The picture was taken in the summer of 1981. Tito had been dead for over a year, but his portraits were still everywhere and devotion to him was as ardent as ever. While welcoming me as a former comrade, his hand on my shoulder, the official on the left was phoning regional Party headquarters for confirmation that it was acceptable to talk to me.

It had been easy for him to infiltrate their ranks and become an officer because, as a Serb, he was by origin, language, and religion no different from most other Partisans in our area. The Partisans, similarly, had moles among the Chetniks.

Before defecting to the Chetniks, Captain Eremić may have had a hand in the disappearance of my commander at the animal hospital—and dear personal friend—Vlado Horvatić.

19 VLADO

WHEN I FIRST MET VLADO HORVATIĆ, in the summer of 1942 in Novi Vinodolski, he was married. His wife was a lovely young woman from Zagreb. Vlado, as he once reluctantly admitted to me, was half Jewish, while his wife was Catholic. By the time I encountered Vlado again, in the Partisans in early 1944, he had separated from his wife. She had returned to Zagreb, where she was living with her mother. Concerned about his wife's economic circumstances, Vlado had accepted some dollars from one of the US airmen in the ten-man crew that we had picked up. Just as I didn't think there was anything illegal in accepting tokens of gratitude from people we had rescued, particularly in view of the chronically inadequate conditions under which we were operating, neither did he. There were certainly no known regulations prohibiting it.

The only way to send the money to his wife was to use the services of an elderly woman who often crossed the Partisan and German–Ustashe lines, smuggling personal, non-military items from one area to the other. She also carried private messages between members of families who had been separated by the occupation and civil war. The Partisans—and probably the other side as well—knew about her crossings and undoubtedly used her services whenever convenient. But one day, as she was about to cross into the German–Ustashe-controlled area, the Partisans arrested her. They found the US currency on her, probably with a note from Vlado.

In late autumn 1944, Vlado was suddenly arrested, and disappeared forever. Whether this was due to the habitual merciless Partisan "justice" directed against fickle bourgeois intellectuals whom they never fully trusted, or to betrayal by a personal enemy, or to a mole, has never been clarified. In view of what happened to me, I think it likely that Captain Eremić, who was still our area commander, was behind it.

I never succeeded in finding out exactly what happened to Vlado; what is certain is that he was never heard from again.

His signature on my Partisan pass is the only trace I have of this extraordinary man, who found it easier to talk to animals than to people, and to whom the Partisans owed so much for his incomparable service at the 8th Division animal hospital.

Overnight, I found myself in charge at the animal hospital. The chronic shortage of professionals of any kind in the Partisans, let alone veterinarians, meant that it was going to be very difficult to find a replacement. Meanwhile, although I was not yet twenty, I had to pretend that I was up to the job. I knew considerably less about treating animals than anyone around me realized, particularly in view of the tall tales that Vlado had mischievously spun about my supposed expertise. But it would have been very risky for me to reveal now that all of this had been invented, or at least grossly exaggerated. It took far less than that to be accused of sabotaging the Partisan war effort, the penalty for which was grimly familiar. I had to carry on as best I could, attempting to convey the impression that I knew what I was doing, while a great deal of the time I did not.

With the precious help of my peasant assistants, most of them full-grown men with years of hands-on experience with farm animals, I somehow managed to carry on with our regular routine. I sometimes wonder whether they ever realized how much I relied on their practical as well as instinctive knowledge. There were many close scrapes during the period that I was in charge, but fortunately, no major disasters; I only hope I did not cause too much suffering to those patient and trusting animals. All in all, I do feel at peace with myself on this subject; I think that my presence, on balance, did more good than harm.

Thankfully, after a few weeks, a new head arrived: Dr. Armando Gambetti, from Trieste, a former Italian army veterinarian who had somehow ended up in the Partisans. I was very relieved to see him. Like me, and probably for similar reasons (except that he was not Jewish), he had temporarily modified his name to the more Slav-sounding

"Gambetić." He was a cultured man and an excellent vet, and although I knew him for only a brief period, he became one of my few good friends.

Vlado's disappearance was to have another, unexpected consequence. He had a girlfriend, a Jewish refugee who was also in the Partisans. A few weeks after he was arrested, she came to see me, in a desperate state. She had been very much in love with Vlado and was heartbroken by his disappearance. Her distress was now compounded by the discovery that she was pregnant by him. She had decided not to have the child and told me that she would rather kill herself. Her attempts to provoke an abortion by trying a variety of "home remedies" had all failed. She was frantic and pleaded with me for help.

Obviously, I could not even think of attempting anything myself. No one was more aware than I of my medical (and veterinary) incompetence. At a loss, I decided to approach Dr. Franz, an almost mythical figure in the Partisans, whom I had never met before. It was widely known that one of the few medical doctors for miles around was a Dr. Franz, working for the Partisans in a makeshift hospital hidden in the nearby Petrova Gora mountains. All kinds of rumours swirled around him. I had heard that he was a German *Wehrmacht* doctor who had been kidnapped by the Partisans. With many seriously injured combatants on their hands, some of them requiring amputations, and no qualified surgeon available, the Partisans had allegedly given Dr. Franz a choice: if he performed these operations conscientiously and to the best of his ability, they would subsequently release him and permit him to rejoin his German army hospital post. If he refused, they would kill him. It was said that Dr. Franz agreed to perform the operations and that he carried them out to the Partisans' satisfaction. They were about to release him when he made them a surprising offer: as the Partisans obviously needed his services more urgently than the Germans, he would stay on with them—on condition that they also "kidnap" his wife and daughter, who were living in the German-occupied zone, and enable them to join him. This was done, and Dr. Franz continued practising as a surgeon for the Partisans.

This is what I knew, as I set out for the Petrova Gora mountains, a few hours' walk eastwards from the village of Kordunsko Zagorje, where I was stationed. I found the hospital, which was hidden in the heart of a very thick forest to protect it from detection from the air. There were also

▲ *Standing over the entrance to the underground installations of
the Petrova Gora hospital in 1981. The memorial on the left is to
Dr. Marija Schlesinger, a Jewish doctor who served at the Partisan
hospital until her death in 1943. She apparently asked to be buried
over its entrance in order to conceal it from the Germans.*

underground installations to which the wounded could be transferred
during periods of air attack and ground offensives.

Dr. Franz received me very courteously, surprising me by treating
me as a medical "colleague." He became even more friendly when he
realized that, like him, I was from Austria. We conversed amiably in
our native German for a time, until I screwed up the courage to tell him
the real reason for my visit. His initial reaction was to refuse outright:
performing an abortion was entirely out of the question, he replied. But
then I began to describe the girl's desperate state of mind, telling him
that I was sincerely concerned (which indeed I was) that she might
carry out her suicide threat. At first, I think he suspected that I was the
real father of the child, but as our conversation proceeded, he gradually
accepted the truthfulness of my story. He eventually agreed to carry out
the abortion. He set a date on which she should begin to simulate an
acute attack of appendicitis, which even I, as a vet, could diagnose. I was
then to have her evacuated to the Petrova Gora hospital, where Dr. Franz
would perform an emergency "appendectomy."

Everything went according to plan.

I learned after the war that the Austrian surgeon's full name was Dr. Franz Kleinhappel. He had studied medicine in Salzburg, married a girl from Montenegro, and settled in the Yugoslav town of Banja Luka in 1929. In a phone conversation in 2002, his daughter told me that her father had indeed been kidnapped by the Partisans in January 1942. A young woman, who had been Dr. Kleinhappel's patient, appeared at his practice and asked him to accompany her urgently to the bedside of her grandmother, who was gravely ill. The doctor followed her, but when he reached the supposed home of the ailing grandmother, he was kidnapped and taken into Partisan-occupied territory. He was asked to perform emergency surgeries, which he did. But there was never any question of the Partisans allowing him to return to his home; on the contrary, he made three unsuccessful attempts to escape. When the Partisans briefly managed to occupy Banja Luka in the autumn of 1944, his wife and daughter were also kidnapped and the family was reunited. After the war, Dr. Kleinhappel opted to remain in Yugoslavia, eventually becoming Director General of the Yugoslav Ministry of Health. He died at the age of ninety-five.

In the mid-1950s, I saw a German-language film titled Die Letzte Brücke (The Last Bridge). *I was struck by the similarities in the plot to Dr. Kleinhappel's story. In the film, a German doctor serving with the Wehrmacht in Yugoslavia is lured into an ambush by a woman claiming that an injured child needs attention, but is then kidnapped by the Partisans and ordered to perform emergency operations. The doctor tries three times to escape but develops an empathy for the suffering of the local people, eventually dying while seeking medical supplies for the Partisans. Curiously, the "Dr. Franz" character in the film is a woman doctor, played by the well-known Viennese actress Maria Schell; this permits the development of a romantic subplot involving a German soldier.*

In my 2002 conversation with Dr. Kleinhappel's daughter, I was surprised to learn that she had never heard of the film, let alone that it might be based on her father's story. I recently saw it again; the premise seems quite obviously based on Dr. Franz, although his name is not mentioned anywhere in the credits.

▲ *An Austro-Yugoslav co-production, Die Letzte Brücke was awarded an International Prize at the 1954 Cannes festival, with a special mention for Maria Schell's performance.*

20 DEPARTURE

I CELEBRATED MY TWENTIETH BIRTHDAY on 23 January 1945—a
day that turned out to be one of the most dramatic in my life.

I was in particularly high spirits, having recently heard that the
Allies were finally going to evacuate about one hundred non-Yugoslav
Jewish refugees from my area to liberated southern Italy, and that my
uncles and I were going to be included in the group.

Walking through the countryside on a dirt road a few kilometres from
the animal hospital, elated at the prospect of soon taking one step closer
to the free world, I became aware of the approaching buzz of a low-flying
aircraft. Glancing over my shoulder, I saw that a small plane was bearing
down upon me. I quickly recognized it as a German *Fieseler Storch* or
"Stork," so named because of its fixed landing gear, which jutted out like
the legs of a stork about to land.

The plane's ability to fly so low that it could practically skim the
ground made it particularly appropriate for attacks on infantry, which
the pilot could strafe with the craft's powerful machine gun. The *Storch*
was already so near that I could discern the pilot's silhouette outlined
in the cockpit. Instinctively, I dived under a thick clump of bushes. The
plane flew over me, its machine gun blazing. As soon as I heard the engine
receding into the distance, I peered cautiously out of the bushes, only to
see that the plane was banking sharply and coming back. I looked around
and noticed that on both sides of the dirt road there were steep embank-
ments, forming deep ditches filled with dense vegetation. The plane was
now coming at me from the side, at 90 degrees to the road. I gathered my
energy, raced across the road as fast as I could, and rolled down into the
ditch. In a hail of machine gun bullets, the plane passed over my head,
no more than 10 metres above ground. I hoped that perhaps now the pilot

◂ *A German* Fieseler Storch, *the type of aircraft that attacked me on my 20th birthday*

would move on, seeking more promising targets, but instead he veered around and came roaring back, firing continuously from the machine gun. As he approached, I raced across the road again, rolled to the bottom of the ditch on the other side and hugged the ground as closely as possible. Bullets whistled through the air around me—all missing me, fortunately. Evidently, the pilot had it in for me because he refused to give up. He came back repeatedly, trying to surprise me by approaching at different speeds and at a variety of angles, his machine gun never ceasing to spit out a hail of deadly bullets. Incredibly, he missed me every time, wasting an enormous quantity of ammunition in the process. The last of the seven or eight swoops was particularly low and the firing particularly intense, after which he simply disappeared over the horizon, believing, perhaps, that he had finished me off. But I was unharmed, apart from a few scratches from the thorny bushes. My twentieth birthday party came to an end, and I was very happy to have survived it.

When I saw Alfred Hitchcock's film North by Northwest *in 1959, I could scarcely believe my eyes. The scene in which Cary Grant is chased by a crop-duster through an Iowa cornfield bore an uncanny and frightening similarity to what I had experienced in Yugoslavia less than fifteen years earlier. To this day, whenever*

that film is shown on television, I remain riveted to the screen,
still unnerved by the fact that Hitchcock could have indepen-
dently conceived a scene that so resembles what happened to
me—although in my case, the episode did not end with the plane
crashing in flames.

The negotiations to obtain permission for us to leave Yugoslavia had been long and arduous. Ever since the Italian capitulation in September 1943, several hundred Jewish former inmates of the camp on Rab had been stranded with the Partisans. Representatives of the refugees had tried repeatedly to organize an evacuation to liberated southern Italy, but although the Partisans were willing, the Allies were not interested, replying that the empty space in the aircraft returning to their Italian bases after delivering supplies was reserved for the evacuation of stranded Allied soldiers and injured Partisans. This would have been a convincing explanation had the planes indeed been returning full, but the truth was that they often returned empty; it became obvious that the Allies were reluctant to involve themselves in the thorny question of evacuating Jews.

Within the larger group of some seven hundred refugees, there was a smaller subgroup to which my uncles and I belonged: the approximately one hundred non-Yugoslav Jews, refugees from Austria, Hungary, Romania, and elsewhere. Our group was mostly made up of women and children, and of men who were no longer of fighting age, such as my uncles Robert and Julius. Only three of us were active Partisans: Franz Schulbaum, from Vienna (with whom I had manufactured "yellow stars" in Derventa four years earlier); another young Viennese man by the name of Kurt Pollak; and myself. The self-appointed leader of this hundred-strong group of foreign Jews was a Romanian refugee named Schechter. He had repeatedly approached the Allied liaison officers to the Partisan Command, beseeching them to recommend our evacuation, but had always been turned down—that is, until Major Randolph Churchill, son of the British prime minister, appeared on the scene. If our group was eventually evacuated from Yugoslavia, it is primarily thanks to the personal efforts of Major Churchill. In the summer of 1944 he was stationed with the Partisans as head of the British Military Mission to Croatia; within a few months he would overcome the opposition—or at least the indifference—of his superiors and secure Allied consent for our evacuation.

Understandably, the name Churchill was magic, even to the dour and suspicious Partisans. My only encounter with Major Churchill, however, had not been very reassuring. I caught sight of him by chance—I believe it was in the town of Glina, the headquarters of the 4th Corps, to which I belonged and to which he had been attached. He drove up in a battered, absurd-looking vehicle, from which he emerged in a visibly drunken state. The vehicle, I subsequently learned, was called a jeep. I had never seen or heard of one before, and my spirits sank when I first saw it: I could not imagine how the Allies hoped to win the war if they were unable to provide the son of Winston Churchill with a more dignified means of transportation. As for his drunkenness, I was told by one of the Partisans who had gathered excitedly around him that this was more or less a constant; it came to be generally accepted and even expected.

> *The episode of the evacuation of our group of "one hundred and eight" Jewish refugees appears, in fictionalized form, in the novel* Unconditional Surrender *by Evelyn Waugh. Waugh was stationed with the Partisans together with Randolph Churchill, but the interventions on behalf of the Jews, attributed in his book to Waugh's alter ego Guy Crouchback, were in fact overwhelmingly attributable to Churchill. The AFHQ (Allied Forces Headquarters) document on the next page indicates that Randolph Churchill was personally pressing for the evacuation of seven hundred Jewish refugees from my area, and that he was requesting that aircraft be dispatched specifically for this purpose. His appeal was turned down, in agreement with his superior, Brigadier Fitzroy Maclean. The handwritten note at the bottom reads:*

> > *Brig (Maclean) discussed with AOC (Air Officer Commanding)*
> > *No special effort to be*
> > *made to get them out but*
> > *to come out as opportunity*
> > *offers in returning supply aircraft.*

LABE V LFFK MR XSC/D6S/25 TJJJJ CXR JJCM 21   1415

A.F.H.Q. MESSAGE CENTER

(ENCIPHERED FORCE 399)

INCOMING MESSAGE

Time of Origin 25 MIL

From   XBAR-BAOMIS DAF

Time Received 25 B300

To   FREEDOM
CHARLIE OBOE/399
Ref. No.   Precedence   O P   Classification SECRET

FOR MA TO SAC PLEASE PASS TO BRIGADIER MACLEAN FROM STIGET.
RANDOLPH CHURCHILL RECENTLY RAISED THE QUESTION OF
EVACUATING APPROX 700 AGED JEWS FROM CROATIA AND ASKED
THAT SPECIAL SORTIES SHOULD BE DESPATCHED FOR THIS PURPOSE.
HE FEELS VERY STRONGLY THAT EVERY EFFORT SHOULD BE MADE.
I MENTIONED THIS TO AOC WHO STATED HE CONSIDERED IT WAS NOT
(NOT) POSSIBLE AT PRESENT TO ALLOT AIRCRAFT FOR THIS SPECIAL
PURPOSE.
PLEASE CONFIRM YOU AGREE WITH AOC'S DECISION AND DO NOT
WISH TO PRESS THE MATTER FURTHER

X 594/25

Bng discussed with AOC.
No special effort to be
made to get them out but
to come out as opportunity
than injecting supply aircraft

THIS MESSAGE WILL NOT BE DISTRIBUTED OUTSIDE BRITISH OR
U.S.A. GOVERNMENT DEPARTMENTS OR HEADQUARTERS OR RE-
TRANSMITTED EVEN IN CIPHER WITHOUT BEING PARAPHRASED.
(MESSAGES MARKED O.T.P. NEED NOT BE PARAPHRASED).

26/10

PSS/NS/E 44/60,000—AFHQ Press 1854

Fifty years after the end of the war, I fulfilled my long-held desire to meet Churchill's as well as Waugh's commander, the legendary figure who had headed the Allied Mission to Yugoslavia, Brigadier Fitzroy Maclean. As evidenced in the document above, he had taken no special interest in the plight of the Jewish refugees, but his presence with the Partisans had been a source of great encouragement—and of vital material assistance—in the war against the Germans. The Partisans, including myself, greatly admired and even revered him. I wrote to Sir Fitzroy in 1995, mentioning that I was writing my memoirs and asking whether he might receive my son Joseph and me for an interview about the war years. He graciously agreed, and in late November 1995, he and his

*With Sir Fitzroy
Maclean in Strachur,
29 November 1995* ▸

*wife Lady Veronica Maclean invited us to their castle in Strachur,
Scotland. Unfortunately, Sir Fitzroy died only six months later.
Lady Veronica passed away in 2005.*

*The following excerpt from our conversation begins with a
reference to Maclean's personal popularity among the Partisans
and to the fact that they invariably received him warmly.*

FITZROY MACLEAN: I would never have had a bad reception anywhere,
and never did have a bad reception. It was the obvious thing to
do—they wanted you there and knew I was a source of supplies.
Anyhow, the party line given out by Tito was to treat me well—
in an interesting situation, because what started by being, as it
were, a diplomatic friendship became a genuine friendship by the
end of the war. And when the split came with Moscow they were
prepared ... They made feelers of one kind or another.

VERONICA MACLEAN: Well, I think you had a lot to do with it. People
will say I'm blowing my husband's trumpet—but I do think, in a
funny way, that his personality had a lot to do with making it a

popular mission. And the officers you chose had a lot to do with it; you had very, very good officers, didn't you?

FM: [chuckling] Including Randolph Churchill and Evelyn Waugh ...

VM: Well, they were the funny ones ...

FM: We had a lot of funny ones.

IMRE ROCHLITZ: In your book *Eastern Approaches*, you're not very complimentary about Randolph, although you don't say very much...

FM: Randolph was a great personal friend of mine but he could be a headache. He was a pain in the neck in many ways, but he was very brave.

IR: Don't you think he drank too much, even then?

FM: Oh, he always drank much too much, he was intolerable in ordinary, private life. [to Veronica] You saw him trying to win a seat in Parliament, contesting an election, didn't you, when he was intolerable, well before the war.

VM: He always fell out ... He was very argumentative, very egocentric—

FM: But he had courage, you see ...

VM: He was brave and he had charm—

FM: And a good brain and he was a loyal friend ...

VM: But he had every other fault. [chuckles]

IR: Did you actually choose him?

FM: I chose him—well, I'll tell you exactly what happened ... [VM and IR laugh] Because I'm going to write a book of memoirs and put in all the things that I didn't put in *Eastern Approaches*. What happened was that when I went to report to Winston in Cairo in the winter of 1943, I found Randolph, who was as usual getting drunk, leaping on blondes, insulting generals, and making a real nuisance of himself. He had a terrible job, which was conducting distinguished newspaper people up to the front and explaining to them what was going on and telling the generals how to win the war, and all that. And he came to me and said, "I've got this awful job, which I hate because I want to do a real job, and I'm doing more harm than good ..."

I said, "Well, I can see that ..."

"Will you give me a chance to come to join you?"

I thought to myself, well, it would...contain Randolph [chuckles], it would help the British war, it would get him out of trouble, I would have him under military discipline and command, and I would be in touch with his father ... So I said, "All right—but I wonder how easy it will be to arrange."

Winston quite liked the idea—he was fascinated by Tito, he liked the "cowboy and Indian" side of it—

VM: He had a romantic imagination ...

FM: But the generals all said to him, "Prime Minister, we can't agree to this because he will be taken prisoner and the Germans will then cut off his toes and send them to you in matchboxes ... It will put you off your, you know ... we don't advise it."

Randolph was very keen to come and I quite liked the idea of having him—because, you know, there was never a dull moment with Randolph. I thought it would be quite fun and I also thought the Partisans would be quite amused by it. So in the end we prevailed, he was allowed to come.

He was awful in Bari, when we were waiting to be dropped in. Then he was dropped in and I thought, "Well he can't do any harm now." He suffered a bit of a bump but it didn't do him any harm. Then we got on these horses and rode up to a place in the Potoci, somewhere up in the hills. I had a marvellous sergeant called Sergeant Duncan, who looked after me. He came to me and said, "You know what those Partisans have done, they've put that Major Churchill in the same hut as you and I know you won't have that." So I said, "We'll make other arrangements." I said to the Partisans, "You know, I don't have other officers ... I have my own hut." And they said, "Well, we thought you would make an exception for the prime minister."

So I said, "What do you mean, the prime minister?"

"Well, Mr. Churchill, he's dropped in."

They thought Randolph was the prime minister himself. They said, "Well, you know, we're the only people who are fighting the Germans and he's naturally come to see how we're getting on."

So then we had Randolph move. There was an enormous pig that lived in a little hut with lace curtains. I said, "You can move that pig out and put Major Churchill in." The pig was furious and Randolph wasn't very happy, so there was a lot of grunting.

Anyhow, there he was. But he was very brave. And the Partisans were bewildered by him, they didn't know what to make of him at all. But it was quite a good thing from the point of view of the mission.

We'd always been on Christian name terms—we'd been at school together—but he used to make a point of coming in and saluting, saying, "Permission to speak, Brigadier," and so on ...

After a bit, he came to me and said, "Permission to speak," and all that. "This is all very fine, you know, I enjoy being here but unfortunately my brother officers, the other members of your mission, are neither my social nor my intellectual equals." This was a moment when the German First Alpine Division, those horrible ski troops, were attacking us. We were under snow, we couldn't move, they had skis and we didn't. I said, "Randolph, I'm sorry, I'm rather too busy ... but I will bear your problem in mind. Now you can go away."

That was why I got Evelyn Waugh—because I thought they could argue amongst themselves—and sent them both five hundred miles away, where you were, in Croatia; they could spend the rest of the war arguing who is whose intellectual and social equal.

IR: Did he stay till the end of the war?

FM: Randolph lasted till we got to Belgrade, because he certainly caused me great embarrassment in Belgrade. And Evelyn Waugh stayed on after I'd gone and caused awful trouble by getting into touch with a lot of Ustashe sympathizers, who were keen Catholics. He made a lot of reports—this was after I'd left—to the Foreign Office. He was a nuisance.

VM: He was very anti-Communist ...

FM: Yes. Well, so was I, but I thought I saw something else going on. Winston's directive to me was quite clear: "Your job is to find out who is killing the most Germans and how we can help them kill more." That being so, there was no doubt whatever that it was the Partisans. And I said to Churchill: "On the other hand you must retain that they are one hundred percent Communist and they will bring in a Communist regime—what sort of a Communist regime, one doesn't know." That's when he said to me: "Are you going to live in Yugoslavia after the war?" I said, "No plans." [laughter]

IR: Well, you have a house in Korčula ...

FM: And now I have a house in Korčula, everybody reminds me of that ... I'm an honorary citizen.

In late 1944 or early 1945, Randolph Churchill obtained final approval for the evacuation of our group of about one hundred non-Yugoslav Jews to southern Italy. But even with official Allied and Partisan consent for the evacuation of the group as a whole, the three of us who were members of the Partisan army first had to obtain military discharges. I had never been sworn in as a Partisan, nor had I signed any document volunteering or promising to serve with them for a specific length of time. I had no military induction number or identity card (to my knowledge, such a thing did not even exist)—but such technicalities were irrelevant—I was de facto a Partisan and required a discharge. I was very worried. How was I going to obtain one without incurring the wrath of my commanders, who had unfettered powers over life and death?

The officer on whom my discharge depended was Colonel Miloš Šumonja, former commander of the 8th Assault Division (to which I belonged), recently promoted to commander of the entire 4th Corps. Šumonja knew me well. We had developed an amicable, even cordial relationship during his frequent inspections of the animal hospital. He was originally from Montenegro, a southern province of Yugoslavia, and had been a schoolteacher before the war. He was only twenty-six years old, had joined the Partisans early, and was a brilliant officer. His rise through the ranks had been meteoric. His promising future (he eventually became Chief of Staff of the Yugoslav army, and later Ambassador to the Netherlands) was also attributable to his personal toughness and ruthlessness; he expected absolute, unquestioning loyalty to the Partisan cause.

One day in early 1945, shortly after I had heard that Mr. Schechter's appeals to Major Churchill were beginning to bear fruit, Col. Šumonja rode up to the animal hospital. He was accompanied, as usual, by his political commissar, Col. Dušan Hrstić. The two colonels dismounted, ordered that their horses be fed and groomed, and proceeded to carry out a routine inspection of the hospital. I had always enjoyed accompanying Šumonja on these inspections; he was obviously pleased with my work, and it was reassuring to know that my commanding officer thought well of me. This time, however, I was gripped with fear. What would I say if Šumonja brought up the subject of my desire to leave the Partisans? As we strolled through the hospital grounds, I racked my brains desperately but could not think of a reply that might satisfy him. But if he did raise the subject, I knew I had to be ready to respond in accordance with his mood (he was, in fact, quite moody and short-tempered).

The inspection came to an end, and the two colonels mounted their horses. They seemed about to ride off when Šumonja unexpectedly reined in his horse, looked down at me, and almost as an afterthought, said, "I have received orders from the General Staff for Croatia to give you a discharge, if you apply for one, so that you can go to southern Italy. But I am sure you do not want to leave. Correct?"

I was stunned. I had not been expecting him to raise the subject in this manner, at the very last moment. I was speechless. Šumonja continued, "As soon as the war is over, you will go to Leningrad as an army officer, at army expense, to study medicine. After you complete your studies, you will return to serve as a doctor in the Yugoslav army."

In one of our previous conversations, I had indeed mentioned that I planned to study medicine after the war, but never before had Šumonja suggested that I study in Leningrad as a Yugoslav officer. I was acutely aware that, to his way of thinking, this was an offer so fabulous that I could hardly refuse. In reality, the idea filled me with horror, but I knew I could not refuse outright. By making this offer, Šumonja was letting me know that he was taking me under his wing. Declining to go to Leningrad would be considered not only an act of treason against the cause but also a grave personal betrayal. I knew I was skating on very thin ice. I did some quick thinking and, as sincerely and guilelessly as I could, stammered my reply: of course I did not want to leave Yugoslavia; however, as a result of the war I had lost touch with my mother and brother—my only close family— and I fervently hoped that they had somehow made it to southern Italy (this was a convenient lie—I knew that my mother had been deported to Poland and was almost certainly dead, and that my brother had enlisted in the British navy). I only wanted to go to southern Italy in the hope of finding them, I explained, attempting to be as affirmative as I dared in confirming that I wanted to leave while doing my best to avoid provoking his immediate wrath. Had he taken offence at my answer, my fate could have been sealed there and then.

Šumonja spoke slowly, emphasizing every word: "You do not want to leave the Partisans." With that, he turned his horse and rode off with his commissar.

For the next few days I was in despair. The message was clear: if I knew what was good for me, I had better not apply for a discharge. I tried to reassure myself that there was still hope, that as the days went by Šumonja's opposition to my departure might soften, or perhaps some other circumstance might arise, enabling me to obtain a discharge without having to clash with him personally. But I was very worried.

A few days later, orders arrived at the animal hospital stating that "Second Lieutenant Rohlić" was to be relieved of his duties and dispatched to Corps Headquarters in the town of Glina, where he could apply for a discharge. This is when I discovered that I was a Partisan *potporučnik* or second lieutenant; no one had ever notified me that I held the rank. The new head of the animal hospital, and my immediate commander, was Dr. Milovan Adamović, a fully qualified veterinarian who had only recently joined the Partisans. He duly issued me with a travel pass, and I set out on foot for the town of Glina, some 50 kilometres away.

> *I learned after the war that shortly after my departure, Dr. Adamović (see photograph on page 137) was arrested and shot by the Partisans as an alleged spy for the Ustashe. Although I never felt comfortable with him during our short acquaintance, and instinctively distrusted him, I have no way of knowing whether there were any grounds for this charge. People were executed in the Partisans for so many reasons, as well as for no reason at all.*

I arrived in Glina. Major Churchill had originally planned for our group to be evacuated in the Dakota aircraft that were landing regularly at the makeshift airfield in nearby Topusko, but Allied Headquarters in Italy had again rejected the idea. Churchill then drew up an alternative plan, by which four trucks were to transfer us from Glina to the town of Split, on the Adriatic coast (where I had first entered what was then the Italian zone of occupation, less than three years earlier). A British vessel was then to transport us from Split across the Adriatic Sea to liberated southern Italy.

The hundred refugees—including my uncles Robert and Julius—had already gathered in Glina, and the trucks designated to take us to Split were expected at any moment. I could no longer wait; I had to decide whether to apply to Šumonja for my discharge. And I could not avoid Šumonja, who was at his headquarters in Glina.

By pure chance, I learned that Šumonja's administrative assistant was a Jewish girl by the name of Irena Gaon, who had been interned with me in 1943 in the Italian camp on Rab. I decided to consult her. As there was no possibility of reaching her by telephone (there were limited field phone connections, and only between important Partisan commands), I simply hid behind a tree near Šumonja's headquarters and waited until Irena walked out in the evening. She confirmed my worst fears: Šumonja was livid with rage and talked about me all the time. He had treated me with special favour, he said, and had bestowed all manner of privileges on me; now I was about to betray him personally, as he expected me to appear any day and apply for a discharge. Irena summed up matters in these words: "If you show your face to Šumonja and ask him for a discharge, this means your end. You are not going to get out alive."

I was desperate. I consulted with my uncles Robert and Julius, and together we went to see Mr. Schechter, the leader of our group. Schechter immediately understood my predicament and courageously offered to try to smuggle me out. Needless to say, if the Partisans were to discover me hiding among the refugees—without having obtained a discharge—there were likely to be dire consequences for everyone, not only for me personally. Although it was clear that my clandestine presence would endanger the entire operation, Schechter agreed that I could join them.

The trucks arrived the very next day. There were four of them, flatbeds with canvas awnings, paid for—I believe—by the American Joint Distribution Committee, a Jewish welfare organization. The trucks were to become Partisan property after they had transported us to Split. As the hundred refugees congregated around the vehicles with their bags and bundles, I was reunited with my friend Franz Schulbaum. He had served in front-line units, had been injured in combat, and had suffered from severely frostbitten toes; Šumonja had granted him a discharge without a problem. Kurt Pollak's parents, who were also among the refugees, were distraught, however. Kurt had reported to Šumonja's office a few days earlier, had applied for a discharge—and had not been seen since. The trucks were about to leave, and after much hesitation, Kurt's parents opted to leave Yugoslavia together with the rest of the group, hoping that their son would be able to join them later in Italy.

> *For years, the Yugoslav authorities would deny any knowledge of Kurt's whereabouts or fate. Finally, after many inquiries and official appeals, they informed his parents merely that he had died in prison. To my mind, this is a perversion of the truth: I believe it was Col. Miloš Šumonja who ordered the execution of Kurt Pollak for daring to ask for a discharge, just as he would have eliminated me had I set foot in his office.*

The refugees began to board the trucks; in the general hubbub and confusion, I managed to hop into the back of one of them without being noticed and to take cover under a blanket. Uncle Robert climbed in behind me and immediately sat on top of me as though I were a large bundle.

After a short time, the trucks left Glina. When I was certain that we were well into open countryside, I came out from under the blanket to stretch my limbs. To my surprise, none of the other passengers asked any awkward questions. All of them, naturally, knew me, and although they may have been intrigued by my sudden appearance, it did not seem to unduly perturb them: formalities, they must have thought, were Mr. Schechter's concern, not theirs. Also, they may have presumed that I did not want to be seen by my Partisan comrades for a variety of personal reasons—none of which were any of their business. For the next few hours, I remained on the lookout, diving back under the blanket every time we drove through villages or whenever Partisans came into view.

The trip to Split took nearly all day; we made our way slowly down to the coast, passing by the burned-out carcasses of several German and Italian tanks, too many of which had rattled over those roads before us, leaving them in a state of complete disrepair.

We made one stop for refuelling, in the town of Zadar. By now I had come out from under the blanket more or less permanently, confident that we were sufficiently distant from the Partisan area where I might be recognized. I had last seen Zadar in the summer of 1942, on my way to Italian "free confinement" farther north, in Novi Vinodolski, and I remembered it as a lovely old town on a small peninsula. I looked out of the truck and was stunned by what I saw: the town lay completely in ruins. Zadar was not an important military target in itself, but it was a harbour town, and after the Italian capitulation, a German garrison of several hundred had been stationed there. Allied aircraft returning from their bombing runs in southern Germany or central Europe were sometimes prevented from emptying their entire loads by bad weather or heavy anti-aircraft fire; to avoid the risks of landing at their bases with bombs on board, they had often dropped them on Zadar. It was a convenient target, lying along their return flight path, protruding clearly from the coastline and easily discernible from high altitudes.

During our short stop in Zadar, I struck up a conversation with a local Partisan. He told me, with utmost earnestness, that only one major building in the entire town had not been damaged in the bombings. This was because it belonged to General Eisenhower in person, he confided, who had issued orders to his air crews to spare his property. I was anxious to get on my way and refrained from voicing any doubts regarding his assertion.

The sun was already setting when our four trucks pulled into Split. I became very uneasy, having no idea what would happen next. No one knew when and how we were to board the boat for southern Italy, and what further controls we might undergo beforehand. Our reception, by a group of local Partisans, did not bode well. They were suspicious, refusing at first to let us off the trucks. After some wrangling and a great deal of bureaucratic confusion, they finally decided that we would be put up for the night in two classrooms in a school building. They added, with typical arbitrariness, that no one would be permitted to leave the school building until the following morning, when we would be escorted directly to the boat. Armed guards would be posted at the school to enforce this directive.

The situation seemed dangerous to me: I was the only one in the group wearing a Partisan "uniform" (leather boots, a mixture of items of clothing from different sources, and an American Colt 45 strapped to my belt). This would undoubtedly attract attention, and I would certainly be questioned if I attempted to spend the night in the school with the rest of the refugees. Therefore, as we climbed down from the trucks, I suddenly resumed the role of Partisan officer. I stood to one side, barking the occasional instruction and pretending to supervise the evacuees as they unloaded their luggage. The other Partisans standing about did not notice my abrupt transformation.

I accompanied the group to the school, where everyone settled in for the night as best they could, and then, with as much nonchalance as I could muster, made for the exit. Just as I was walking out, a Partisan guard made a half-hearted attempt to ask me for identification. I pulled rank on him, gave him a disdainful look, and confidently strode out. Fortunately, he did not react.

Since I had no documents to justify my presence in Split, I could not ask the local Partisan authorities for accommodation. I decided instead to try to locate Carmen, my good friend from the summer of 1942, with whom I had spent many a pleasant afternoon, to the accompaniment of the shrill *vocalises* of her elder sister. I found her easily; she had indeed married her poet fiancé, and they were both glad to see me and to put me up for the night. I revealed to them only that I was leaving for southern Italy—without, of course, troubling them with the secret that I was being forced to "desert" from the Partisans. I felt I could have told them the truth (although I knew little about Carmen's husband), but there was no sense in burdening their consciences.

Early the next morning I went back to the school building. The guard at the entrance—I believe he was the same one as the night before—let me through without a challenge. After a short wait, word arrived that the group was to load all its luggage onto one truck and prepare to be escorted on foot to the harbour.

Now was the time for me to metamorphose from Partisan officer into civilian refugee. This was not particularly difficult, as not all of my items of clothing were of army-type. Several members of our group were themselves wearing the odd piece of military clothing (whether US, British, Italian, or Partisan), and I was able to make my appearance blend in with theirs with only a few changes. When I was certain no one was looking, I got rid of my pistol, hiding it under a pile of rubble. Most important, I changed my bearing and demeanour from that of a cocky Partisan, which I had purposefully assumed when walking in and out of the school building, to that of a passive, exhausted refugee. My transformation passed completely unnoticed by the guards accompanying us.

We were led on foot and under armed escort to the nearby port, where a large British landing craft was waiting for us, its front end lowered. I can hardly describe the excitement and happiness that overcame me as I set my eyes for the first time on an Allied warship. Controlling my emotions with great difficulty, I walked into the vessel, together with my hundred and seven companions. Only three members of my family were making it alive out of Yugoslavia: Robert, Julius, and I. My dear mother, her husband, his mother, my uncles Ferdinand and Oskar, and my aunt Camilla had all been murdered by the Germans or the Ustashe in the two and a half years that had passed since I arrived in Split in the summer of 1942.

We sat in the landing craft for what seemed an eternity, waiting for the truck carrying the luggage to arrive. I was afraid that the Partisans might seize this opportunity to make an individual check of our identities, but they seemed to have lost all interest in us. The truck eventually drove up, the luggage was loaded on board, and the landing craft set off across the Adriatic Sea in the direction of Bari.

I could no longer contain my elation. As the craft was pulling out of the harbour and heading into international waters, I felt I had to express my gratitude to someone. I stood up, and with a clumsiness that still embarrasses me, shouted over the roar of the engines at a startled British sailor: "It's good to be on His Majesty's Ship!"

The formulation was awkward, but the sentiment was sincere. I was at the beginning of a new life.

EPILOGUE

THE FIRST THING I DID when I reached Italy was to try and locate my brother Max, who was in England. I knew that if my mother was still alive, she would also contact him. I filled in the forms at the Red Cross bureau in Bari and waited. To my relief, I soon received word from him—although there was no trace of my mother. Max hitched a ride on a military transport plane and flew to see us.

▲ *Bari, southern Italy, 1945: (l. to r.) my brother Max,*
Uncle Julius, Uncle Robert, and me.

Max had survived by escaping from Vienna to England in 1939, as part of a Zionist agricultural training program. He later volunteered for the British navy and become an intelligence officer. His duties included listening in on German radio communications and translating them into English. When he had enlisted, he had been told to change his Germanic-sounding name, in order to avoid execution as a traitor in the event of capture. He had changed it from Maximilian Rochlitz to John Michael George Rock, a name he kept for the rest of his life. It had been a wise precaution, as two of the ships he served on during the war were torpedoed. The sinking of one of them, a Canadian destroyer, became the subject of a book and of a documentary film, Unlucky Lady: The Life and Death of HMCS Athabaskan (2001). *Of the 261 sailors on board, 128 lost their lives. Some of the men who abandoned ship were captured by the Germans, but Max, fortunately, was rescued. He emigrated to the United States in 1949 and lived for the rest of his life in Seattle, where he died in 2004 at the age of eighty-two.*

My aim was to get to the United States as soon as possible. While I waited for a visa, I obtained a job with the UN Relief and Rehabilitation Agency in Bari. I was delighted, because it permitted me, finally, to wear a US army uniform. Later, I moved to Rome, where I worked as a welfare officer for the American Joint Distribution Committee (the Jewish relief organization that, apparently, had supplied the trucks for our evacuation from Yugoslavia).

My main responsibilities were to organize the supply of food, clothing, and personal necessities to several hundred Holocaust survivors who were housed in displaced persons camps on the outskirts of Rome. The British were then the mandatory power in Palestine, and they severely restricted Jewish immigration. The Allies had permitted the Joint Distribution Committee to run these camps, on the understanding that British restrictions would be respected. My unofficial task, however, was to facilitate the illegal immigration of these refugees to Palestine. *Aliya Bet*, the underground Jewish immigration network, would alert me every time they were about to evacuate refugees to a ship standing ready off the Italian coast. I would make sure not to visit the camps on that day; *Aliya Bet* operatives would evacuate the inmates to the ship (often with the complicity of the Italian authorities, who delighted in infuriating the British) and replenish the camps with an identical number of newly arrived refugees. When I resumed my visits, I would duly report that the number of camp inmates had remained unchanged, pointedly ignoring the fact that they were all fresh faces. This went on for many months and involved several hundred refugees.

In 1947, I received my long-awaited immigration visa and set sail for the United States. Thanks to a scholarship from a Jewish charity, the Hillel Foundation, I was able to attend the University of Washington, in Seattle. Later, I graduated from New York University Law School, got married, and had four children.

But I'll tell you about that another time.

ACKNOWLEDGEMENTS

WE WOULD LIKE PARTICULARLY to thank Irene Rochlitz, who has been present at every stage of the long journey to publication, always providing invaluable insight, critical comment, and affectionate support; this volume is also her achievement. We are deeply grateful to Angela Debnath, Alejandro Rodriguez-Giovo, Robert Ashworth, Eugene Rizzo, and David Gouldstone for their careful reading of the manuscript and constructive suggestions; to Nina Goslar for her helpful research; to Falguni Debnath and Marlene Kadar for their precious support, and to Carole Luby for her extraordinary friendship.

The illustrations included in this volume are drawn from the personal collection of Imre Rochlitz and from the archives of Parstel Ltd. Films, producers of *The Righteous Enemy*, with the following exceptions:

p. 14   Courtesy of Dr. Alfred Rosenfeld

p. 22   Bundesarchiv, Bild 102-13276

p. 40   *Abwege* (G. W. Pabst, 1928), Erda-Film GmbH

p. 65   United States Holocaust Memorial Museum Photo Archive, #64309

p. 77   Croatian State Archives, Ustashe Police Headquarters—Jewish Department (Ravnateljstvo ustaškog redarstva—Židovski odsjek), no. 2147/1942. Published online by the Jasenovac Memorial Site: www.jusp-jasenovac.hr/Default.aspx?sid=7241

p. 93   Italian Ministry of Foreign Affairs, Archivio Storico Diplomatico (ASD) Gab AP 35. "Croazia"

p. 103   Italian Ministry of Foreign Affairs, Archivio Storico Diplomatico (ASD) Gab AP - 42 AG Croazia 35

p. 122   Courtesy of Charles J. McCann

p. 158   Bob Williams/The Commercial Appeal

p. 165   Courtesy of Dale E. Martz

p. 182   National Archives (UK), WO 202/293

APPENDIX

BELOW ARE THE NAMES and addresses of Allied airmen, escaped POWS, and other servicemen recorded on pages 33—43 of my expired Hungarian passport, the only paper available to me while I was in the Partisans in 1944. I actively took part in the rescue of many of them, while assisting those rescued elsewhere before their evacuation back to Allied bases. A few of the airmen added dates beside their names, which may refer to the date they were downed, to the date they were evacuated, or to the date of the inscription. The four servicemen with RAMC after their names belonged to the Royal Army Medical Corps.

Where the type of aircraft and date of downing appear in capitals, the information has been added by me, based on data retrieved from MACR (Missing Air Crew Report) files available online.

S/Sgt. James R. Mund   18 NOVEMBER 1944, B-24
1002 Homer Avenue
Toledo, Ohio

Sgt. S. R. Apter
133 Old Montague Street
Stepney, London

Arthur R. Johnson   7 OCTOBER 1944, B-24
113 North 7th Street
Sterling, Colorado

Arnold Dupree   7 OCTOBER 1944, B-24
503 Masonite Drive
Laurel, Mississippi

Lt. R. E. Reed   18 NOVEMBER 1944, B-24
R.D. #2
Williamsburg, Pennsylvania

Leland M. Brown   18 NOVEMBER 1944, B-24
113 Wade Street
Montgomery, Alabama

Edward Watson
Flimby, Maryport
Cumberland, England

Lt. Henry Flesh   13 OCTOBER 1944, B-24
100 Orchard Lane
Piqua, Ohio

Lt. Warren Mugler   13 OCTOBER 1944, B-24
Baia, Kansas

Sgt. R. A. Kemmerle   13 OCTOBER 1944, B-24
1326 Euclid Avenue
Dallas, Texas

Fernando O'Dell   13 OCTOBER 1944, B-24
3326 Rivera Street
El Paso, Texas

Sgt. Wesley Roberds   13 OCTOBER 1944, B-24
211 S. Wood
Caney, Kansas

Lt. Dale Davidson   13 OCTOBER 1944, B-24
912 Noyes Street
Evanston, Illinois

S/Sgt. James H. Melanson   13 OCTOBER 1944, B-24
3118 Washington Street
Roxbury, Boston, Massachusetts

Lt. Dale Martz   13 OCTOBER 1944, B-24
1189 Elm Avenue
San Diego, California

S/Sgt. Carl Thorberg   13 OCTOBER 1944, B-24
3428–33 Avenue South
Minneapolis, Minnesota

Lt. John Hassan   13 JUNE 1944, B-24
313 Beech Street
East Pittsburgh, Pennsylvania

John Szablinski   9 JUNE 1944, B-24
R.F.D–No. 9
Norwich Town, Connecticut

Lt. Barney R. McLaughlin   10 MAY 1944, B-17
2301 Mistletoe Avenue
Fort Worth, Texas

Lt. W. E. Chapman   13 JUNE 1944, B-24
Louisville, Kentucky

Capt. D. Eric Davies, RAMC
1A The Arcade
Merthyr Tydfil, Wales

S/Sgt. D. W. Foster, RAMC
6 Tierney Road
Streatham Hill
London S.W. 2, England

S/Sgt. W. R. Jackson   14 JUNE 1944, B-17
317 West 7 Street
Flint, Michigan

Sgt. Royce F. Austin   8 JULY 1944, B-24
R.F.D. Underhill, Vermont

Lt. John H. Nutter   8 JULY 1944, B-24
Rupert, West Virginia

John R. Thompson   8 JULY 1944, B-24
Starkville, Mississippi

Ernest H. Jensen   8 JULY 1944, B-24
San Francisco, California

Wm. R. Sutton   8 JULY 1944, B-24
Muskegon, Mich.

Chas. E. Johnson   10 MAY 1944, B-24
375 10th Street N.E.
Atlanta, Georgia

G. A. Zonghetti   10 MAY 1944, B-24
Bronx, New York
980 Morris Park Avenue

Allan Berry   ESCAPED POW
Cr. McDonald Street
West Australia

Lt. Jos. Konieczny   10 MAY 1944, B-17
324 Avenue East
Bayonne, New Jersey

Mjr. A. F. McCoubrey, RAMC
28 Church Street
Coatbridge, Great Britain

S/Sgt. W. D. H. Kear, RAMC
10 Fairfield Road
Lydney, Gloucester, UK

Lt. J. A. Foster   10 MAY 1944, B-24
8222 Evans Avenue
Chicago, Illinois

Ernest J. Brough   ESCAPED POW
Myrtleford
Victoria, Australia

Elton W. Ankney   24 AUGUST 1944, B-24; ESCAPED POW
Sweetwater, Idaho

Helmer M. Leiran   10 MAY 1944, B-24
Waukon, Iowa

2nd Lt. Samuel Garber   10 MAY 1944, B-24
223 East Fillmore Avenue
St. Paul, Minnesota

Lt. H. W. Roberts   10 MAY 1944, B-24
Sioux City, Iowa

S/Sgt. Melvin H. Briner   10 MAY 1944, B-17
205 Fairmont Street
Latrobe, Pennsylvania

S/Sgt. Philip Barber   23 APRIL 1944, B-17
Bethelridge, Kentucky

Lt. W. M. Girardeau   24 AUGUST 1944, B-24
404 S. Capen Avenue
Winter Park, Florida

Sgt. Kenneth Moore   24 AUGUST 1944, B-24
7811 Cler Place
St. Louis County, Missouri

Sgt. Tommy Monacelli   24 AUGUST 1944, B-24
General Delivery
Easton, Washington

Sgt. Benard W. Atkinson   24 AUGUST 1944, B-24
Tioga, Louisiana

Eric Baty   ESCAPED POW
Waipui R.
Kaiti, Gisborne, New Zealand

Lt. James S. Thomas   23 APRIL 1944, B-24
606 North "F" Street
Muskogee, Oklahoma

B. F. Erwin   23 APRIL 1944, B-24
2215–36 Avenue North
Birmingham, Alabama

Paul Miller   23 APRIL 1944, B-17
R.R. 17, Box 658
Indianapolis, Indiana

Ralph Taylor   23 APRIL 1944, B-17
Genoa, Nebraska

Lt. James E. Lackey   10 MAY 1944, B-17
116 Oxford Avenue
Buffalo, New York

Lt. M. E. Clark   10 MAY 1944, B-24
Groton, South Dakota

Lt. Edward F. Smithwick   10 MAY 1944, B-17
120 Vermilyea Avenue
New York, New York

Lt. John L. Lewis   10 MAY 1944, B-17
139 West Wayne Avenue
Wayne, Pennsylvania

Robert Bicher, Jr.   23 APRIL 1944, B-24
140 Berdy Street
Hackensack, New Jersey

Joseph O. Alley   23 APRIL 1944, B-24
4305 West 22nd Street
Little Rock, Arkansas

Albert G. Willing, Jr.   23 APRIL 1944, B-17
542 Woodbine Avenue
Oak Park, Illinois

Lt. M. S. Rouse   23 APRIL 1944, B-24
107 Hickory Street , Box 65
Springhill, Louisiana

R. M. Miller   23 APRIL 1944, B-24
Main Street
Montgomery, Pennsylvania

J. F. Beaulieu   23 APRIL 1944, B-24
P.O. Box 84
Shawmut, Maine

GLOSSARY OF NAMES AND PLACES

A pronunciation guide appears in parentheses with some terms.

ANSCHLUSS Nazi incorporation of Austria into the German Reich, 12 March 1938

CHETNIKS Yugoslav resistance movement loyal to the Serbian monarchy; fought against the Germans and Italians and, later, with them against the Partisans

CHURCHILL, RANDOLPH, MAJOR Son of British prime minister, Fitzroy Maclean's representative as Allied Mission liaison officer to Partisans in Croatia; instrumental in ensuring evacuation to liberated Italy of over 100 Jewish refugees (including me)

CONFINO LIBERO Literally, "free confinement"; a form of administrative limitation of movement applied by the Italians

DÉNES, FERDINAND My uncle, awarded the highest Austro-Hungarian medal for bravery in the First World War; used his decoration to obtain my release from the Jasenovac death camp; murdered by the Germans in 1944

EREMIĆ, JOCO (*Eremitch, Yotso*) Partisan commander in the Kordun known for his unreasonable harshness; probably a mole for the rival Chetniks, which he later rejoined

GLAISE-HORSTENAU, EDMUND VON (*Glaiz-Horstenow*) Leading Austrian Nazi, who served as German plenipotentiary general in Zagreb, 1941–1944; protested against Ustashe barbarity and was instrumental in my release from Jasenovac

GOLDENE TAPFERKEITSMEDAILLE Highest First World War decoration for bravery in the Austro-Hungarian army, awarded to my uncle Ferdinand Dénes

HAJDIN, MILIĆ (*High-din, Militsh*) Communist political commissar of my Partisan unit; saved my life by lying for me

HANES, HORACE A. Downed American fighter pilot I encountered in 1944; later set a world record for supersonic flight and became a US Air Force major general

HERZER, IVO My close friend in the Italian internment camps and after the war; one of the first to promote public recognition of the humane Italian attitude towards Jews in Croatia

HORVATIĆ, VLADO (*Horvatitch*) Chief veterinarian of the 8th Partisan Assault Division, my direct commander and close friend; disappeared mysteriously in late 1944

INDEPENDENT STATE OF CROATIA Fascist and genocidal state ruled by the Ustashe, 1941–1945

JASENOVAC (*Yasenovats*) Ustashe death camp 100 kilometres southeast of the Croatian capital, Zagreb, where I was a grave-digger in 1942; an estimated 100,000 Serbs, Jews, Gypsies, and political opponents were killed there.

KLEINHAPPEL, FRANZ Austrian doctor kidnapped by the Partisans and forced to perform emergency operations; stayed in Yugoslavia after the war and became director general of the ministry of health

KONFESSIONSLOS Bureaucratic term signifying "without religion," often used during the 1930s by Jews in Vienna to conceal their faith

KORDUN Region in central Croatia where I served with the Partisans in a veterinary unit

KRALJEVICA (*Kralyevitsa*) Italian concentration camp on the Adriatic coast of Croatia where 1200 Jewish refugees, including me, were interned in 1942 and treated very humanely

LIKA Mountainous region in central Croatia, adjacent to Kordun

MACLEAN, FITZROY, BRIGADIER (LATER SIR) Named by British Prime Minister Winston Churchill to head Allied mission to Yugoslavia, 1943

MIHAILOVIĆ, DRAŽA (*Mihailovitch, Draja*) Commander of the royalist Chetniks, executed by the Yugoslav regime after the war

PARTISANS Communist resistance movement in Yugoslavia during the Second World War, led by Tito; victorious in 1945

PAVELIĆ, ANTE (*Pavelitch, Anteh*) Leader of the Ustashe, ruled as dictator of the Independent State of Croatia, 1941–1945

PIETROMARCHI, LUCA (*Pietromarki*) High-ranking Italian foreign-ministry official; played central role in preventing deportation of Jews from Italian-occupied territories

PROPUSNICE (*propusnitseh*) Croatian travel permits, often acquired illegally

RAB Known in Italian as Arbe, an island off the Croatian Adriatic coast where 3,500 Jews were interned in July 1943 and well treated by the Italian army; in a nearby camp, thousands of Slovenian men, women, and children died of maltreatment by the Italians

ROATTA, MARIO, GENERAL Commander of the Italian army in Croatia; favoured humane treatment of Jewish refugees while brutally repressing resistance to Italian rule

SCALES, JUNIUS I. American Communist activist, my close friend in liberated southern Italy, 1945; only person in the United States ever imprisoned solely for Party membership

SEVENTH OFFENSIVE Also known as *Rösselsprung*, or "Knight's Move," a German military offensive in May 1944 that attempted to capture Tito and wipe out Partisan resistance

ŠIK, LAVOSLAV (*Shik*) Prominent Croatian lawyer and historian of Yugoslav Jewry; a distant relation, he provided me with shelter and support; murdered at Jasenovac in 1942

ŠUMONJA, MILOŠ (*Shumonya, Milosh*) Partisan officer, my commander in the 8th Assault Division of the 4th Corps, later Chief of Staff of Yugoslav Army

TITO, JOSIP BROZ (*Yossip Broz*) Commander of the Partisans, became president of Yugoslavia at war's end; remained in power until his death, in 1980

USTASHE Fascist nationalist movement, ruled the Independent State of Croatia, 1941–1945; brought to power by the Germans and Italians, they carried out genocidal policies against Serbs, Jews, and Gypsies, killing hundreds of thousands

SELECTED BIBLIOGRAPHY

Carpi, Daniel. "The Rescue of Jews in the Italian Zone of Occupied Croatia." In Yisrael Gutman and Efraim Zuroff, eds., *Rescue Attempts during the Holocaust*, Proceedings of the Second Yad Vashem International Historical Conference, April 1974, pp. 465-525. Jerusalem: Yad Vashem, 1977. http://www1.yadvashem.org/odot_pdf?Microsoft%20Word@20-%204803.pdf.

Churchill, Winston S. *His Father's Son: Life of Randolph Churchill*. London: Weidenfeld & Nicolson, 1996.

Gottlieb, Hinko. *The Key to the Great Gate*. Trans. Fred Bolman and Ruth Morris. New York: Simon & Schuster, 1947.

Herzer, Ivo. *The Italian Refuge: Rescue of Jews during the Holocaust*. Washington: Catholic University of America Press, 1989.

Hilberg, Raul. *The Destruction of the European Jews*. Rev. ed. New York: Harper and Row, 1985.

Klarsfeld, Serge. *Vichy-Auschwitz : le rôle de Vichy dans la Solution finale de la Question juive en France 1943-1944*. Tome II. Paris: Fayard, 1985.

Maclean, Fitzroy. *Eastern Approaches*. London: Jonathan Cape, 1949.

Pavlowitch, Stevan K. *Hitler's New Disorder: The Second World War in Yugoslavia*. New York: Columbia University Press; London: Hurst, 2008.

Rochlitz, Imre. *Testimony No. 32300*. Videotaped interview, 23 July 1997. USC Shoah Foundation Institute. http://college.usc.edu/vhi.

Rochlitz Joseph. *The Righteous Enemy*. Documentary film. Italy/UK, 1987/1994. www.josephrochlitz.com.

Rochlitz, Joseph. *The Righteous Enemy: Document Collection*. Rome: Author, 1988.

Rodogno, Davide. *Fascism's European Empire: Italian Occupation during the Second World War*. Trans. Adrian Belton. Cambridge: Cambridge University Press, 2006.

Scales, Junius Irving, and Richard Nickson. *Cause at Heart: A Former Communist Remembers*. Athens, GA: University of Georgia Press, 1987.

Sebald, W. G. "Against the Irreversible: On Jean Améry." In *On the Natural History of Destruction*. Trans. Anthea Bell, London: Penguin, 2003.

Shelah, Menachem. *Blood Account: The Rescue of Croatian Jews by the Italians 1941-1943*. Tel Aviv: Sifriat Hapoalim, 1986. [Hebrew: *Heshbon Damim*]

Shelah, Menachem, ed. *History of the Holocaust: Yugoslavia*. Jerusalem: Yad Vashem, 1990. [Hebrew].

Steinberg, Jonathan. *All or Nothing—The Axis and the Holocaust 1941-1943*. London: Routledge, 1990.

Walston, James. "History and Memory of the Italian Concentration Camps." *The Historical Journal* 40.1 (1997): 169-83.

Waugh, Evelyn. *Unconditional Surrender*. London: Chapman & Hall, 1961.

Zuccotti, Susan. *The Italians and the Holocaust: Persecution, Rescue and Survival*. New York: Basic Books, 1987.

INDEX

THE RIGHTEOUS ENEMY

A documentary film by **Joseph Rochlitz**
based on *Accident of Fate* by Imre Rochlitz

Italian officials (circled) who obstructed the deportation of Jews from Italian-occupied territories

At the height of World War II, while the Nazis and most of their allies were deporting and exterminating the Jews of Europe, some 40,000 found protection in the most unlikely of places: territories occupied by the army of Fascist Italy.

In areas under their occupation in Croatia, France, and Greece, Italian soldiers and diplomats refused to collaborate in the "Final Solution," despite orders from Mussolini himself to comply with the German requests.

This documentary film takes the form of a personal investigation by the director, Joseph Rochlitz, whose father, Imre Rochlitz, was saved by the Italians in occupied Croatia. The film widens out to describe the Italian rescue efforts in France and Greece between 1941 and 1943, and seeks to understand the motives behind this extraordinary Italian attitude.

Produced in 1987 and re-edited in 1994, *The Righteous Enemy* includes rare interviews with some of the protagonists of the Italian rescue efforts, as well as the testimony of Jews saved by their actions.

Historical consultants appearing in the film are Menachem Shelah (Yad Vashem) and Serge Klarsfeld, the French lawyer and historian.

The National Center for Jewish Film
Brandeis University
Lown 102, MS 053
Waltham, MA 02454
Phone (781) 736-8600
www.jewishfilm.org

BOOKS IN THE LIFE WRITING SERIES
PUBLISHED BY WILFRID LAURIER UNIVERSITY PRESS

Haven't Any News: Ruby's Letters from the Fifties edited by Edna Staebler with an Afterword by Marlene Kadar / 1995 / x + 165 pp. / ISBN 0-88920-248-6

"I Want to Join Your Club": Letters from Rural Children, 1900–1920 edited by Norah L. Lewis with a Preface by Neil Sutherland / 1996 / xii + 250 pp. (30 b&w photos) / ISBN 0-88920-260-5

And Peace Never Came by Elisabeth M. Raab with Historical Notes by Marlene Kadar / 1996 / x + 196 pp. (12 b&w photos, map) / ISBN 0-88920-281-8

Dear Editor and Friends: Letters from Rural Women of the North-West, 1900–1920 edited by Norah L. Lewis / 1998 / xvi + 166 pp. (20 b&w photos) / ISBN 0-88920-287-7

The Surprise of My Life: An Autobiography by Claire Drainie Taylor with a Foreword by Marlene Kadar / 1998 / xii + 268 pp. (8 colour photos and 92 b&w photos) / ISBN 0-88920-302-4

Memoirs from Away: A New Found Land Girlhood by Helen M. Buss / Margaret Clarke / 1998 / xvi + 153 pp. / ISBN 0-88920-350-4

The Life and Letters of Annie Leake Tuttle: Working for the Best by Marilyn Färdig Whiteley / 1999 / xviii + 150 pp. / ISBN 0-88920-330-X

Marian Engel's Notebooks: "Ah, mon cahier, écoute" edited by Christl Verduyn / 1999 / viii + 576 pp. / ISBN 0-88920-333-4 cloth / ISBN 0-88920-349-0 paper

Be Good Sweet Maid: The Trials of Dorothy Joudrie by Audrey Andrews / 1999 / vi + 276 pp. / ISBN 0-88920-334-2

Working in Women's Archives: Researching Women's Private Literature and Archival Documents edited by Helen M. Buss and Marlene Kadar / 2001 / vi + 120 pp. / ISBN 0-88920-341-5

Repossessing the World: Reading Memoirs by Contemporary Women by Helen M. Buss / 2002 / xxvi + 206 pp. / ISBN 0-88920-408-X cloth / ISBN 0-88920-410-1 paper

Chasing the Comet: A Scottish-Canadian Life by Patricia Koretchuk / 2002 / xx + 244 pp. / ISBN 0-88920-407-1

The Queen of Peace Room by Magie Dominic / 2002 / xii + 115 pp. / ISBN 0-88920-417-9

China Diary: The Life of Mary Austin Endicott by Shirley Jane Endicott / 2002 / xvi + 251 pp. / ISBN 0-88920-412-8

The Curtain: Witness and Memory in Wartime Holland by Henry G. Schogt / 2003 / xii + 132 pp. / ISBN 0-88920-396-2

Teaching Places by Audrey J. Whitson / 2003 / xiii + 178 pp. / ISBN 0-88920-425-X

Through the Hitler Line by Laurence F. Wilmot, M.C. / 2003 / xvi + 152 pp. / ISBN 0-88920-448-9

Where I Come From by Vijay Agnew / 2003 / xiv + 298 pp. / ISBN 0-88920-414-4

The Water Lily Pond by Han Z. Li / 2004 / x + 254 pp. / ISBN 0-88920-431-4

The Life Writings of Mary Baker McQuesten: Victorian Matriarch edited by Mary J. Anderson / 2004 / xxii + 338 pp. / ISBN 0-88920-437-3

Seven Eggs Today: The Diaries of Mary Armstrong, 1859 and 1869 edited by Jackson W. Armstrong / 2004 / xvi + 228 pp. / ISBN 0-88920-440-3

Love and War in London: A Woman's Diary 1939–1942 by Olivia Cockett; edited by Robert W. Malcolmson / 2005 / xvi + 208 pp. / ISBN 0-88920-458-6

Incorrigible by Velma Demerson / 2004 / vi + 178 pp. / ISBN 0-88920-444-6

Auto / biography in Canada: Critical Directions edited by Julie Rak / 2005 / viii + 264 pp. / ISBN 0-88920-478-0

Tracing the Autobiographical edited by Marlene Kadar, Linda Warley, Jeanne Perreault, and Susanna Egan / 2005 / viii + 280 pp. / ISBN 0-88920-476-4

Must Write: Edna Staebler's Diaries edited by Christl Verduyn / 2005 / viii + 304 pp. / ISBN 0-88920-481-0

Food That Really Schmecks by Edna Staebler / 2007 / xxiv + 334 pp. / ISBN 978-0-88920-521-5

163256: A Memoir of Resistance by Michael Englishman / 2007 / xvi + 112 pp. (14 b&w photos) / ISBN 978-1-55458-009-5

The Wartime Letters of Leslie and Cecil Frost, 1915–1919 edited by R.B. Fleming / 2007 / xxxvi + 384 pp. (49 b&w photos, 5 maps) / ISBN 978-1-55458-000-2

Johanna Krause Twice Persecuted: Surviving in Nazi Germany and Communist East Germany by Carolyn Gammon and Christiane Hemker / 2007 / x + 170 pp. (58 b&w photos, 2 maps) / ISBN 978-1-55458-006-4

Watermelon Syrup: A Novel by Annie Jacobsen with Jane Finlay-Young and Di Brandt / 2007 / x + 268 pp. / ISBN 978-1-55458-005-7

Broad Is the Way: Stories from Mayerthorpe by Margaret Norquay / 2008 / x + 106 pp. (6 b&w photos) / ISBN 978-1-55458-020-0

Becoming My Mother's Daughter: A Story of Survival and Renewal by Erika Gottlieb 2008 / x + 178 pp. (36 b&w illus., 17 colour) / ISBN 978-1-55458-030-9

Leaving Fundamentalism: Personal Stories edited by G. Elijah Dann / 2008 / xii + 234 pp. / ISBN 978-1-55458-026-2

Bearing Witness: Living with Ovarian Cancer edited by Kathryn Carter and Lauri Elit / 2009 / viii + 94 pp. / ISBN 978-1-55458-055-2

Dead Woman Pickney: A Memoir of Childhood in Jamaica by Yvonne Shorter Brown / 2010 / viii + 202 pp. / ISBN 978-1-55458-189-4

I Have a Story to Tell You by Seemah C. Berson / 2010 / 318 pp. (b&w photos) / ISBN 978-1-55458-219-8

We All Giggled: A Bourgeois Family Memoir by Thomas O. Hueglin / 2010 / 246 pp. (illustrations) / ISBN 978-1-55458-262-4

Accident of Fate: A Personal Account, 1938–1945 by Imre Rochlitz with Joseph Rochlitz / 2011 / 240 pp. (colour and b&w photos) / ISBN 978-1-55458-267-9